D1144837

MAPPING THE SHIFT IN BUSINESS DEVELOPMENT SERVICES
Making Markets Work for the Poor

Edited by Malcolm Harper and Jim Tanburn

PUBLISHING

SAMSKRITI

Published by:
ITDG Publishing
Schumacher Centre for Technology and Development
Bourton Hall, Bourton-on-Dunsmore, Warwickshire CV23 9QZ, UK
www.itdgpublishing.org.uk

Published in India, Nepal and Bangladesh by:
SAṀSKṚITI
C-9020 Vasant Kunj, New Dehli 110070, India

First published in 2005 by ITDG Publishing

ISBN 1-85339-590-0 hb
ISBN 1-85339-591-9 pb
ISBN 81-87374-40-3 pb (SAṀSKṚITI)

© ITDG Publishing 2005

All rights reserved. No part of this publication may be reprinted or reproduced or
utilized in any form or by any electronic, mechanical, or other means, now known or
hereafter invented, including photocopying and recording, or in any information
storage or retrieval system, without the written permission of the publishers.

A catalogue record for this book is available from the British Library.

ITDG Publishing is the publishing arm of the Intermediate Technology Development Group.
Our mission is to build the skills and capacity of people in developing countries through
the dissemination of information in all forms, enabling them to improve the quality of
their lives and that of future generations.

Printed in India

Contents

Contents

Preface

The chapters in this book cover 14 years of the evolution of assistance to small businesses. During this period, the whole approach to the provision of such services has radically changed; these chapters reflect and illustrate the important transformation that has taken place.

The chapters have been chosen from the four hundred or more papers that have appeared in the 56 issues of the international journal *Small Enterprise Development*, since it was launched in March 1990. It has been difficult to make the choice but the task has been made easier by the fact that perhaps half the content of the journal has focused on one particular aspect of small enterprise development, namely financial services, or microfinance. Much of the material on microfinance has indeed not been about enterprise development at all, or only peripherally. It has covered topics such as regulation and supervision, insurance or management information systems, which relate to microfinancial services in general, and not particularly to those designed to serve small or micro-enterprises.

Even before the journal was started, the field had been bedeviled by acronyms, such as SSE, SSI, MSE and SME, the 'M' standing either for 'medium' or for 'micro'. These applied to the types of enterprises that were served, however, and not to the services themselves. During the past 10 years, however, a new acronym has appeared: 'BDS', or 'business development services'. This term has more or less replaced its predecessor, 'NFS', or 'non-financial services'. 'BDS' has the advantage of being positive, describing what the services are rather than what they are not (unlike the still widely used term 'NGO', or 'non-government organizations'), but it has one disadvantage; it includes all the vast number of different types of service that businesses use. A term that describes so much variety has its shortcomings; some of the more recent chapters in this collection propose solutions to this excessive breadth of meaning.

'Business development services' covers everything a business might want, except financial services. This omission is a supply-oriented one. The term was taken up, in response to the success of microfinance, by agencies and consultants who provided non-financial services. Microfinance seemed to offer a sustainable and even profitable way of helping poor people to escape from poverty. The great pressure on microfinance institutions (MFIs) to achieve sustainability, combined with bad experiences in linking financial services and BDS, led to a clear separation between the disciplines. Because of the ease with which new MFIs could be opened and 'grown', donor funds were increasingly diverted into support for them. Donors and others involved in BDS were therefore challenged to rethink their approach, triggering a healthy crisis in the 'industry'.

The content of *Small Enterprise Development* has also to some extent been driven or even distorted by this artificial distinction between financial services and BDS. Although financial services often have to be closely integrated with other services, such as working capital for increased sales or fixed capital for new technologies, most issues of the journal have focused on microfinance or on BDS, as if the two types of service were not connected. The services must of course be totally integrated at the level of the enterprise, but our readers are not business people; they are generally advisers, facilitators or suppliers of financial or other services, whose work is mainly paid for by donors or governments.

Meanwhile, businesses of all sizes need many services apart from finance, and the lack of such services is often as important a constraint to the development of businesses as their need for finance. Donors, and governments, can usefully facilitate their provision, and have achieved a great deal by doing so in many different circumstances. But readers must be aware that few if any of the papers are written by the owners of small-scale businesses themselves. And, unlike many of the papers about microfinance, most of the later papers at any rate are not written by people who themselves have first hand experience of providing the services. This is because one defining feature of the new approach to BDS is that it is not about direct provision of services – it is about promoting, facilitating, subsidizing or otherwise assisting businesses to provide services to other businesses.

The providers are themselves usually small businesses, so that BDS can be seen as a subset of small enterprise development, which is concerned with those enterprises that provide services to other small enterprises. In so doing, they help themselves and they help their clients; the aim of BDS promotion agencies is to enable them to do this, sustainably, for as long as the services are needed. It is hoped that this collection of papers will help them to do this more efficiently and effectively.

INTRODUCTION
MALCOLM HARPER

In the past 20 years there has been a revolution in the provision of credit and other financial services for small enterprises and the poor. Microfinance, pioneered by the Grameen Bank in Bangladesh and other institutions in Latin America and elsewhere, has made it possible for poor people for the first time to access reasonably priced financial services from regulated formal institutions. More recently, another closely related revolution has started, which may have the potential to be equally dramatic.

Small enterprises need credit but they also need many other services. They need skills, information, individual advice, marketing channels, raw material supplies, premises, record keeping and accountancy, equipment and technology, repairs and maintenance. In addition to all these services, the smallest businesses in particular also need representation through effective forms of association, to protect them from official harassment and to ensure that their interests are taken into account in local planning and other decision-making processes. Without these other services, credit alone may do no more than add the burden of debt to all the other problems entrepreneurs have to face.

Governments and foreign donors have until recently responded to these needs by trying themselves to provide the services; they have provided industrial estates, training and extension services, raw material supplies, common facility workshops, new business incubators and a whole host of other services. Government bodies and non-government organizations have also attempted to promote associations to represent the interests of small and micro-businesses. Despite, or perhaps because of, heavy subsidies, these services have generally been inadequate in quantity and of poor quality. They have often been hijacked by the most powerful and least needy businesses, and their main effect may have been simply to crowd out potentially more effective private suppliers and initiatives.

Policy makers in donor organizations and governments have now come to believe that small and micro-scale entrepreneurs are willing and able to pay the market price for good-quality services, and that small businesses, in the private sector, are usually the best source of services for other small businesses. The main role of governments is to ensure that there is a 'level playing field' for private businesses, not to try to replace them.

Research shows that the private sector is already providing a range of services in parallel with publicly funded provision; it is able to cater to specific market segments without problem. Nonetheless, in other areas, modest subsidies may be needed at first, to 'prime the pump' for private providers, and there may also be a need to vacate the institutional space that has hitherto been occupied by redundant government sponsored service institutions. This can be facilitated through the restructuring and privatization of ineffective and redundant official service providers. It may initially be necessary to subsidize the provision of information to potential and actual suppliers of services about the business service opportunities that exist, and to help them develop and market these services to entrepreneurs, but the goal is to make markets work in business services as well as in other products.

This change is of course consistent with the neo-liberal market-led approach to development, and the chapters in this collection demonstrate how this approach has influenced all kinds of donor and government support for small business service provision since 1990. They also show how the small business development sections of donors, and of the non-government organizations and other agencies that work for them, have responded to this challenge.

The services covered by the phrase 'business development services' have existed as long as business itself, and the majority of them are of course supplied by small businesses. 'New paradigm' microfinance emerged during the 1980s and it appeared at last to make it possible for small and micro-enterprises to solve what had always been one of their main problems – the shortage of credit. Most remarkably, the suppliers of credit could be sustainable or even profitable enterprises themselves. During the mid-1990s the providers, consultants, trainers and others who supported, and often themselves provided, non-financial services realized that they needed a new term to embrace their offering.

The new approach to financial services, pioneered by the Grameen Bank in Bangladesh and other institutions in the 1970s, is indeed a major innovation. It may not have the potential totally to eliminate poverty, as some of its over-enthusiastic proponents claim, but tens of millions of poor people have already been able significantly to improve their well-being because of their new-found access to reliable and reasonably priced financial services. The new approach to other business services, characterized by the new term, is of much more recent origin, but it is instructive to compare this approach with what went before, and with the transformation that microfinance has wrought in the provision of financial services. Can BDS achieve similarly dramatic results?

The table opposite briefly summarizes some of the defining characteristics of the traditional and of the 'new paradigm' approaches to the provision of financial and business services.

The shift to 'new paradigm' microfinance has been taking place for almost 30 years, whereas the new approach to BDS is little more than five years old; many of the replacements shown in the table for business services are thus expected but not yet achieved on a large scale.

Clearly the two types of services, and the transformation processes that are affecting their provision, are not strictly comparable. Two particular differences are especially striking, however.

The services that are provided:

○ Microfinance consists mainly of loans and, more recently, savings services. Insurance, money transfers and other services are beginning to be provided by some institutions, but all the services are strictly related to finance; the general view is that microfinance institutions, like banks, should focus only on the provision of financial services.
○ Business development services include everything that businesses buy, except finance. This includes almost every imaginable service.

Table   Comparison between approaches to the provision of microfinance and business development services

Aspect	'Old' development finance to 'new paradigm' microfinance	Old style business assistance to 'new paradigm' BDS
Sustainability of provision	Permanent government or donor subsidy *replaced* by temporary start-up subsidy leading to 'sustainability'.	Permanently subsidized official provision *replaced* by enhancing pre-existing indigenous provision or, where necessary, pump priming subsidy, eliminated as service markets develop.
Cost of service	Grants, cheap 'soft' loans and other free services replaced by market-priced credit and savings products.	Narrow range of high-quality, high-cost services with subsidized delivery replaced by larger range of market-driven and market-priced services, delivered at quality/price mix determined by end-users.
Clients	Large and often ill-targeted poverty elimination schemes replaced by direct tailor-made provision to the poor, through small groups or individually.	Official public sector providers reaching a few businesses, badly, replaced by facilitation of private sector providers to reach businesses that need their services (or which they need in their supply chain).
Poverty impact	Short-term benefits, often hijacked by intermediaries, replaced by long-term vulnerability reduction and income increases for large numbers.	Few benefits to a minority of businesses, replaced by long-term benefits to providers and clients, indirectly benefiting the poor through job creation.
Gender impact	Overwhelming majority of male beneficiaries replaced by 90% + female beneficiaries.	Mainly male clientele replaced by general SME owner population, with no specific gender target.
Services provided	'Integrated development programmes' including standardized grants, cheap loans, training, etc. replaced by tailor-made loans and savings products, usually on a minimalist basis without non-financial services.	Limited range of business services replaced by facilitation of providers of every service that businesses need and that can be delivered on a commercial basis.

The institutions that provide them:

○ Microfinance services are in most countries mainly provided by a fairly small number of specialized institutions, many of which have actually been established by donors; most are still subsidized in some way or another.
○ Business development services are provided by other businesses, mainly quite small ones, and one major objective of the development process is to encourage the emergence of far larger numbers of such businesses.

'New paradigm' microfinance is actually little more than the long overdue and fairly simple application of the 'fours Ps' of common sense marketing to financial services.

For poorer consumers, the *products* have to be designed to suit their needs, the *places* where the services have to be provided must be accessible, and the *promotion* has to suit low levels of literacy; fortunately, the *price* of micro-loans is less important than access, so the whole system can be financially sustainable.

The promotion of 'new paradigm' BDS is much more complex. The range of services is vast, and, more importantly, it is of the essence of the new approach that the promoters of BDS should not themselves deliver the services. Their task is to facilitate, to encourage, to develop, to assist, on occasion to subsidize, but not to provide. The range and imprecision of the words illustrates the difficulty of the process; it is always much harder to facilitate others to do things than to do them yourself. In this respect, BDS has leap-frogged microfinance, where the assumption was generally that it would be quite acceptable to displace existing private sector provision, since that was exploitative and generally undesirable. The establishment of totally new institutions was therefore the initial focus, although there is a growing realization that existing banks are often the best suppliers of micro-financial services. BDS has from the outset been about building wherever possible on pre-existing commercial provision.

Mapping the shift in business development services: overview of the chapters

JIM TANBURN

THE CHAPTERS IN THIS COLLECTION demonstrate how the thinking about business development services (BDS) has evolved since the early 1990s. Some describe specific experiences; others are more abstract, taking stock and pointing the way towards better approaches. This chapter, and indeed the book as a whole, is not concerned so much with specific solutions to particular problems: 'BDS' covers a very wide range of contexts, target groups and services, and there are no universal solutions. But there are underlying approaches and implicit assumptions that are common to most BDS activities, and the opportunity here is to work out which are the right questions to ask.

To some extent, therefore, the book is not really about BDS *per se*, or even about markets; many of the questions and reflections in this book can readily be applied to development practice in any discipline, and indeed we are increasingly seeing convergence with other disciplines, such as agricultural extension. For example, suppliers of agricultural inputs are increasingly being seen as valid – and sustainable – sources of information about modern farming practices; similarly, traders in agricultural produce are being seen as important sources of market information for farmers, in areas such as food standards and packaging.

The 'shift in business development services' has essentially resulted from the willingness of many individuals in many agencies to share their experiences in an open and frank way. Going beyond the usual window dressing, they have 'gone public' with what worked, and what did not. This was partly the result of a community of practitioners experiencing a crisis of self-confidence; nonetheless, the willingness to share information has made rapid learning possible, and has led to a Community of Practice around the common theme. The contributors to this book clearly are members of this community, and their inputs have been very important. The references to their chapters are illustrative of how the thinking about BDS has changed over the years.

The traditional approach

This compilation includes two examples of interventions that adopted a traditional approach to the promotion of small enterprises; both are among the best of this type, and seem very likely to have delivered real benefits to significant numbers of poor people. Kashyap writes in Chapter 1 about experiences in India in 1991: expert diagnosis apparently showed that rural producers suffered from a lack of access to urban markets. The solution identified was for a parastatal organization to fund all the costs for selected rural producers to participate in exhibitions, to display and ultimately sell their products.

This chapter contains a number of implicit assumptions; for example, it assumes that it would be good to make a 'serious effort to…eliminate the ubiquitous "middleman"'. Presumably, these middlemen were, at the time, the main channel through which rural producers could, in practice, access urban markets; elimination therefore seems to be rather a radical solution. It implies that the current trading networks were beyond redemption, and that complete substitution was the most desirable solution. The establishment of District Supply and Marketing Societies was proposed, presumably becoming themselves middlemen in due course.

The parastatal also paid the costs for rural producers to participate in the exhibitions, on the assumption that they would be willing to pay the full costs themselves within three years. This seems reasonable, on the basis that sales rapidly increased to be four times the costs. Nonetheless, one wonders about the mixed messages being received by these rural artisans, whose first impression was of a free service.

Training in marketing skills was also provided, although it is not clear whether this was also free of charge. Needs for quality control and innovation had not been addressed by the time of writing, although it was acknowledged that there were a variety of needs that the parastatal could not address on its own, within a short time-frame.

While the work described clearly delivered important and impressive benefits to a select group of fortunate rural artisans, it probably did not change the underlying situation in ways that could reach millions of potential beneficiaries. While some artisans may have observed what happened, and worked to copy it for themselves, others may have concluded that such benefits were possible only when the government stepped in. It is hard to tell from the chapter whether close attention was paid to an analysis of the trading network, to understand the margins, the costs and the power relationships, and therefore to see whether it might be built on in any way.

In Chapter 2, written in 1991, Walsh, Kane and Nelson also illustrate the traditional approach. The authors describe the development of a business training course for rural women by a Kenyan NGO. It was recognized that rural women operate under many constraints, and this context was taken into account during the design process. So the need for a systemic approach was recognized, but the chapter still leaves many questions unanswered; for example, it is not very clear what the training actually consisted of, nor whether it could be offered on any basis that might become sustainable.

A further issue that this chapter raises is how to assess the impacts of the activities. It notes that 'revenues increased by 60 per cent, profits doubled' and that therefore 'the new business training programme had a positive effect overall on the financial performance of the groups trained'. But there was apparently no control group, so the reader is left to wonder if indeed all of these benefits could be attributed to the intervention.

This chapter does, meanwhile, start to point to the more general problem; 'despite strong support from the government and private agencies, the record of business promotional efforts with the groups shows that many have failed to generate significant income for programme participants.' Writing in 1992, Marsden takes up this theme in Chapter 3; 'a reappraisal of development strategies has been taking place over the past five years, spurred by evidence of public sector inefficiency and of market distortions caused by excessive government intervention.'

Glimpses of alternatives

Marsden also begins to point to solutions, for example by highlighting the importance of what has come to be known as embedded services. 'In many cases, modern African entrepreneurs are able to obtain relevant information and advice through market networks for no additional charge. Transfer of know-how is a normal feature of commercial relationships, included in the price of physical products or services being exchanged and dissemination of reliable information is seen as a means of reinforcing commercial linkages and is motivated by mutual self-interest.'

He also suggests that this might be an interesting avenue to explore, as an alternative to the typical arrangements prevailing at the time. 'The interviews [which he had conducted with African entrepreneurs] suggest that market networks are more effective mechanisms for the transfer of know-how than technical assistance networks composed of public institutions, NGOs, and government departments.'

The chapter is probably based on Marsden's extensive experience, but cites interviews with only 36 African entrepreneurs, 75 per cent of whom had been assisted by the IFC's African Project Development Facility to prepare proposals for financing. No details of this assistance are given. The recommendation, that development support should focus on 'modern' enterprises, probably therefore needs further evidence to support it.

Pressures for change

Six years later, the debate was beginning to focus on specific problems, as Schmitz makes clear in Chapter 4. 'Most attempts to provide non-financial assistance suffer from three deficiencies:

○ they are too supply-oriented: that is, overly focused on inputs for production (skills, technology, raw materials) and not sufficiently concerned with who would buy the outputs
○ they are rarely sustainable: the cost of reaching out to a multitude of small firms is high, and cost recovery for support services tends to be poor
○ they tend to have a one-off effect on the performance of the assisted enterprise, rarely leading to a better capacity for self-help and continuous improvement.'

This last deficiency, in particular, highlights the need to move to a more systemic approach. Schmitz goes on to propose an approach whereby 'public intervention merely facilitates… and works as a catalyst'. This is a powerful idea, but it is less clear how it might look in practice. Inspirational examples are given from Brazil, Denmark and New Zealand, using government subsidies particularly to build trust between enterprises. But it is not very clear from the chapter how these interventions will upgrade the system as a whole, although it is hoped, in the New Zealand case, that the private sector will increasingly take responsibility for organization and funding.

One solution proposed is for donors to pay part of the costs for small enterprises to participate in exhibitions; 'the advantage of this kind of subsidy is that it is easy to administer'. Another, more systemic, approach proposed is to target, or work with, business associations and other forms of enterprise groupings. This clearly has a number of potential advantages, including some economies of scale, and empowerment of the target group. Schmitz goes on to suggest that 'where they do not already exist, it means linking support to the formation of such groups'.

In general terms, the suggestion seems to be that, where the system does not already exist for delivering support, the project should establish it. While in principle this is clearly an option, it does raise questions about how durable such groups would be, if they were formed within the usual project timescale in order to access project support. So, while giving some clear pointers to the nature of the problem, and to the fundamentals of a possible alternative, the specifics were still proving elusive, at the time this chapter was written.

In Chapter 5, Dichter intensifies the debate, starting with the title: 'Compromise and cheating in small enterprise development'. 'We have to question the entire direction the Small Enterprise Development field is taking. I believe that direct action to assist microenterprises and small businesses will show itself increasingly to be a dead end.' He explores the motivations of all those directly involved (including donors) to continue the prevailing system, whereby inputs are provided free of charge. He concludes, though, by pointing to the need to work more in arms-length, indirect ways. Again, much of his analysis and argument could be applied to development work in general, although the specific illustrations from SED work are of course telling.

Writing in 1996, Tanburn argues in Chapter 6 for building on private sector dynamics, as an alternative to more traditional approaches. 'The response by development practitioners [to the predicament of MSEs] has often been to provide support services which are to some extent scaled-down versions of services designed originally for larger companies. While helpful to the MSEs that benefit, such services will probably always require some external subsidy, and their outreach is therefore limited by the size of the subsidy available.

'Meanwhile, the private sector is already providing almost all of the services that MSEs need, such as the provision of raw materials, commercial information and distribution channels, in self-sustaining ways; could these ways be enhanced and made more effective, possibly without the long-term involvement of any of the traditional MSE support institutions?'

The answer to this question is not immediately clear from that chapter, however, since the work described in it is essentially through NGOs rather than through commercial partners. Nonetheless, it does describe serious efforts to design services that people in small enterprises feel they want, and that they are therefore willing to pay for. The idea is also introduced that development practitioners should be aware of the possibility that their work might damage local service systems, albeit unintentionally.

Similarly, Choy and Goh describe experiences in Singapore by parastatals to promote franchising, in Chapter 7, as a means to have the commercial sector play a greater role in service provision. Apparently, the assistance took the form of grants, for training, consultancy and marketing, and it is not clear what impacts the successful examples actually had. Nonetheless, it describes a serious effort to enhance commercial, and therefore sustainable, systems in various creative ways.

Sustainable organizations versus pro-poor systems

Clearly, one dilemma running through all of the chapters is whether the focus should be on organizations that are expected to become sustainable, or on entire systems. In Gibson and Harper, Chapter 8, the organizations under discussion are the BDS providers, while the systems are primarily markets. Historically, the development focus has often been on building capacity, and this has taken the form of creating and supporting organizations. For example, the initial focus in micro-finance was indeed on micro-finance institutions: how to run them and how they can become self-sustaining.

So this exchange highlights a 'fault line' running through the development community up to the present time; after all, development has to be delivered, presumably through local partners, and it is natural to focus on those partners. But considerable criticism has been directed at various agencies about how little seems to remain of many projects, immediately after they have ended. This has become a sensitive point, and the initial response to this was indeed to put great pressure on all projects to make their operations self-sustaining within the lifetime of the project; there was, however, generally little thought given at the time to which functions could, or should, become sustainable, and which functions should realistically be expected to pass away.

Many project proposals were therefore written, which talked of the project facility becoming self-sustaining on one page, and of 50 per cent cost recovery on another. In reality, very few projects have achieved more than 50 per cent cost recovery, and virtually none has become truly sustainable, with income generated from commercial sources (rather than just migrating to a different donor).

There are many valid reasons for this, partly to do with the fact that service provision does not lend itself to economies of scale and standardization in the way that micro-finance does. Furthermore, many donor-funded BDS providers are clearly linked, in the minds of their target group, with public subsidy, so there is great resistance to paying the full costs of service provision. Besides, the operating costs of these providers tend to be too high for small enterprises ever to be able to afford; finally, they are generally staffed by people who signed up to do development work, rather than to operate a business.

Whatever the reason, it was becoming clear by the mid-1990s that there was an urgent need for change, and that the more traditional remedies and solutions were probably not going to address that need. The scene was set, therefore, for a radical review of approaches to BDS.

The change process starts

In 1995, the Committee of Donor Agencies for Small Enterprise Development formed a working group to consider the theme of Non-Financial Services, and one of its first actions was to adopt the term 'Business Development Services'. It also began a process of knowledge gathering, whereby member agencies contributed case studies on BDS; these studies were synthesised into the *Preliminary Guidelines* (Committee of Donor Agencies, 1998, also referred to by Bear, Gibson and Hitchins).

Known as the 'yellow book', these guidelines went through various drafts, with inputs from many people; finally, they were published in 1998 and, looking back on them, it is clear that the thinking was beginning to change – but it was far from clear exactly where it was going, at that time. There are repeated references to the need to be 'business-like'; headings such as 'Creating business-like (non-profit) BDS organizations' illustrate the dilemmas that were being struggled with at the time.

A section intriguingly called 'Building on BDS already being provided by the private sector' refers mainly to traditional apprenticeships, sub-contracting exchanges and sister industry programmes – not necessarily the most promising examples. Another section talked of 'developing commercial entities', which was a veiled reference to the enthusiasm at that time for establishing new marketing NGOs, primarily in Latin America, in order to link rural producers to Fair Trade and other markets.

But there were also some clear pointers to the future. 'It may be that "indigenous" approaches to BDS should be given much more consideration.' Again, 'commercial organizations are the most successful providers of services to SMEs and extending the range of commercial BDS provision is an important current trend.'

Discovering parallel provision

Until this point, 'indigenous' providers of BDS had not really been researched or, if they had, the findings (and implications) had not been fully taken on board by the majority of those working in the field. Many interventions were still based on an apparent assumption that indigenous service providers within the private sector were not worthy of support; they were, by implication, either so inadequate or of such questionable integrity as to be beyond redemption.

Alternatively, this ignoring of local provision might have been the result of difficulties for consultants on design missions, under tight time constraints. Indigenous providers would, by definition, be operating outside the development mainstream, at a financial scale similar to their target group. They would look different, speak a different language, and possibly not have the usual facilities, like telephones, which development experts would normally need, in order to achieve a timely consultation. To quote from one report, private training providers 'are not always easy to find, as they are generally unknown by the practitioners working in government ministries, donor projects and NGOs ... private for-profit providers of training for the informal sector tend to adopt informal sector characteristics themselves. They are difficult to define, to find and to interview' (Haan, 2002).

Nonetheless, there has now been a significant body of research into the characteristics of commercial BDS providers. Suzuki, writing in Chapter 9, gives a summary of current knowledge – scattered as it is – about the sorts of training being provided on a commercial basis to small enterprises in many developing countries, without any external or public support. She confirms some assumptions, for example by noting that commercially delivered training is more an urban than a rural phenomenon. But she challenges other assumptions, arguing for example that commercially delivered training actually reaches women in small enterprises very effectively.

She also gives a number of examples of 'embedded' training – provided at little or no up-front cost to people living in poverty, by entrepreneurs looking for specific products. In effect, therefore, she challenges the assertion that commercially delivered training can benefit only the relatively wealthy, who can afford to pay full fees up-front.

Based on this kind of research, and on papers presented at five Conferences hosted by the Committee of Donor Agencies for SED between 1998 and 2000, *Guiding Principles* were drafted, and given wide circulation. Extensive consultation and dialogue with many groups led to the publication of the current version (Committee of Donor Agencies for SED, 2001); this document encouraged donors to think more systemically. It argued for building wherever possible on existing and indigenous provision of services within the commercial private sector, rather than establishing parallel and potentially competing provision.

Which services do people really want?

In order to consider how systems for service provision could be upgraded, it is clearly important to understand what services people actually want, now. Arguably, the traditional development tool of participatory consultations only works when something is going to be directly given or subsidized, and the question is around the best way to give it. Where the aim is to upgrade an entire system, participation works less well, since most people will ask for a subsidy if they think one might be available.

Miehlbradt reports in Chapter 10, therefore, on the application of commercial market research techniques to demand for business services. The chapter summarizes the findings of 13 BDS market assessments, which immediately challenge the idea that, because a service package has been 'proven' or successful in one country, it can be replicated elsewhere. 'The studies show few predictable similarities among markets' for the various services considered.

Indeed, she goes further, concluding that the market assessments show that the services supported by development agencies are often not the same services as the ones most in demand. Similarly, 'price is rarely the key criterion in an SE's choice of service providers. Rather, BDS markets tend to be driven by quality characteristics such as providers' reputation, recommendations from others and the types of services available.' Importantly, the chapter concludes by proposing a methodology for translating the market research findings into practical next steps – a challenge to this day for many involved in BDS projects around the world.

This application of market research, to identify current demand for services, represents a shift away from supply-led solutions; some would argue, though, that this should be carried further, to put the final choice of services completely in the hands of the end-user. In this logic, one challenge is to encourage people in small enterprises to try new services for the first time. Once they have tried it once, hopefully with beneficial results, they will be more likely to purchase services on their own, after the project has finished. The key, then, is to find ways to reduce the cost of that initial purchase, to make it more likely, and development banks in particular have worked with various mechanisms, such as vouchers and matching grants, to achieve this reduction in initial cost of the service.

The debate is not a simple one, however. In principle, such interventions should stimulate market development; in practice, however, subsidizing the actual purchase of services in a market where supply is rather limited could drive up the price of the service. Also, some argue that these instruments were not originally designed to develop entire service markets, but rather as an efficient way to deliver subsidies to recipient businesses. Chapter 11 by Phillips is particularly interesting in this respect, since it presents matching grants as a tool for service market development – underlining how quickly and thoroughly the idea of developing BDS markets has apparently moved into mainstream thinking.

But that speed of change into a new 'paradigm' has left some possible inconsistencies, and there is probably potential to think through the implications in more detail. For example, Phillips notes that, in order to fulfil its facilitating, or market development, function, 'support could be in the form simply of a matchmaking information service'; in other words, it might not be necessary to have any cash grants at all. The information service could, on its own, be sufficient to develop a service market. Elsewhere, however, it is asserted that 'operating cost as a percentage of grants disbursed gives an indicator of cost-effectiveness' – even though this indicator, taken alone as an indicator of performance, would pressure project staff to reduce non-grant facilitating functions (like information services) to a bare minimum.

Phillips also builds a case for transaction subsidies, as delivering possibly greater benefits than non-transactional subsidies; this is in contrast to the BDS *Guiding Principles*, which encourage donors to think of using subsidies either pre- or posttransaction. At the time of writing, this debate is far from being resolved, and further empirical data are needed. For example, Phillips has published a more recent article (Phillips and Steel, 2003), which looks specifically at the Kenya Voucher Programme. While not included in this compilation, that article suggests that there have been market development impacts, although it also suggests that they might have been greater if the proportion of the training paid for by the vouchers had been lower.

The debate continues

At the time of writing, BDS remains a fertile field for discussion and exchange; in Chapter 12, Bear, Gibson and Hitchins highlight some of the issues where they feel that a clear position is called for. One in particular is a call for more wide-ranging consideration of systems in designing BDS interventions. 'Commonly absent from market assessments have been any wider examination of the institutional environment for BDS and of market-supporting functions. ... "Institutions" here refers both to the formal and informal frameworks within which markets operate that determine critical features of markets, such as information, incentives, values, standards and so on, and consequently govern transaction costs and access. The institutional environment pertaining to a specific market is therefore influenced by wider social and cultural norms, as well as through the actions of formal organisations, for example, governments or associations.'

Philip agrees: interventions to address distortions in BDS markets must take into account 'the social and political dimensions underpinning them'. Since this is one of the few aspects on which both articles agree, it must be worth thinking about. But it is not comforting for those responsible for BDS projects who have already noticed that taking a more systemic approach involves more work than the replication of methodologies 'proven' elsewhere, or one-off hits with a small but fortunate target group. The scope of their examination seems to be expanding without limits, but presumably the lesson is that, the more you can understand about the situation, the better your intervention design will be.

Otherwise, Philip questions the value of enhancing commercial delivery of services, which makes an interesting contrast with her earlier paper for *SED* (Philip, 2002, not in this compilation) on the case of the Mineworkers' Development Agency. In that article, she is enthusiastic about future plans to work with commercial traders, to franchise support packages and to pioneer processes for later take-over by local entrepreneurs.

In Chapter 13, she also would like to remove basic 'business-to-business' services from the discussion, even though those are probably most important to her preferred target group of microenterprises. By way of contrast, Bear et al argue for adoption of the term 'Business Services', partly on the basis that the term 'BDS' is an exclusively development term. A quick search on the internet reveals, though, that the term 'business development services' is in widespread use in the private sector.

Current issues

In addition, there are many in the development community who would tend to agree with Philip, that the 'D for Development' in BDS is a necessary and central part of the field; one of the features of BDS has been that it has been quite a 'broad church', acting as a forum for people with quite diverse perspectives and approaches. This is best illustrated in McKee's synthesis of outcomes from the 2003 BDS Seminar, in Chapter 14, which gives a rather thorough overview of the key issues at the time of writing.

Bateman takes a different tack, arguing in Chapter 15 that there are some circumstances when donor support to government agencies would be highly effective; while the article contrasts this with the establishment of Business Support Centres in Eastern Europe (hardly a systemic approach itself), it does make an interesting case for support to government agencies where there have been historical episodes involving 'a major historical and system discontinuity, corrupt bureaucracies, huge cultural shift and the need for reconstruction and development from a very low base of economic activity'.

Another issue relates to the quest for methodologies, while building on local conditions and initiative – in other words, how to do it? Tomecko addresses this question in Chapter 16; he divides BDS partners into private service providers, membership organizations and government agencies. Drawing on very specific experiences from Nepal, he gives many pointers about how it can be done in practice.

A major concern for many is how to apply a systemic approach in order to reach women in particular with BDS on a sustainable basis; Tanburn provides a few pointers in Chapter 6, but these are typical of the current anecdotal and patchy understanding in the field. Nonetheless, many feel that women entrepreneurs should not be relegated to the status of 'needing permanent subsidy'; rather, the development community should be working harder to find practical ways to empower women to play their part within normal market settings.

Looking at the big picture, Downing points out in Chapter 17 that women-owned enterprises are more likely to diversify horizontally, rather than growing vertically, as women tend to find it more difficult to travel, to access capital, to put a lot of time into one enterprise, and to reinvest profits in one enterprise. One implication is that impact assessments should look for diversification as much as for business growth, although this is clearly going to be difficult.

Another implication is that women may be trapped in a cycle that prevents real long-term growth. 'On the other hand, women's greater diversification than men's may represent the most efficient adaptation to an environment of shallow markets, limited access to financing, and an undeveloped legal system.' Clearly, it is important to know which is the case when designing and evaluating interventions, particularly when those interventions have a sub-sector focus.

Kobb takes up the theme of assessing impacts in a rigorous way, in Chapter 18, and notes several factors that militate against accuracy:

○ personal bias among the interviewers was very significant; some interviewers reported three times higher incomes, on average, than other interviewers
○ in practice, it was very hard to define a proper control group
○ other challenges included attribution, seasonality, lack of records, under-declaration of income, sampling, corruption, and self-selection of the treatment group.

Based on all of these hurdles, Kobb concludes that 'willingness to pay' would be the best indicator, supporting Tomecko's observation that the proportion of the total activity cost paid by the partner is a good indicator of success. But apparently the project which Kobb was looking at was not working in a commercial way; he therefore proposes 'willingness to forgo a cash payment' in return for free training, as the best indicator.

In other words, the entrepreneur has to choose the free training rather than a cash payment, for the activity to be considered successful. This seems to suggest that, for project interventions where the service is provided on a commercial basis, sustainability is probably the best proxy for ultimate impacts. The link between sustainability and impact seems to have been accepted, at least implicitly, in the microfinance field, and it might be expected to be at least as valid in the BDS field too. But there remains great potential for rigorous studies to validate it as a hypothesis.

Conclusion

The idea of developing markets for business services has attracted great interest – probably because it is a concrete and visible illustration of the concept of 'Making Markets Work for the Poor' (e.g. Sida 2003; DFID 2000). Markets represent a system, in this thinking, which can be supported in various ways to be more pro-poor; by considering the system as a whole, the prospects for sustainability are greatly enhanced.

By implication, donor-funded initiatives to 'make markets work' involve a bridging of systems or cultures, in ways that work for both sides; this is a core issue for development work in general. Practitioners must understand fully the systems of donor agencies and of small enterprises, since the 'cultures' of each are quite different. Partly, these differences are a function of the size of the relative organizations; the table below gives some illustrations of the different qualities of organizations of different sizes.

The challenges and opportunities inherent in bridging these systems deserve our serious consideration, based on an honest review of the empirical evidence available; thankfully, the BDS community continues to share experience and information to a remarkable degree (see for example www.ilo.org/dyn/bds). BDS projects, as they move increasingly to systemic solutions, are providing us with this evidence, and the implications will be important for the development community as a whole.

Table Qualities indicating the possible differences in culture between development agencies and the small enterprises they are aiming to support

Large-scale organizations	Small-scale enterprises
Predictable	Calculated risk
Visible, influential	Profitable
Powerful	Creative
Paperwork-based	Verbal/personal
Established	Flexible
Formal	Informal
Stable	Fulfilling
Balance of interests	Depending on one person
Demarcated	Multi-tasking

References

Committee of Donor Agencies for Small Enterprise Development (1998) 'Business Development Services for SMEs: Preliminary Guidelines for Donor-Funded Interventions'.

Committee of Donor Agencies for Small Enterprise Development (2001) 'Business Development Services for Small Enterprises: Guiding Principles for Donor Intervention' www.ilo.org/dyn/bds/bdssearch.globalDCDocs?p_doc_type=DCGUIDES&p_lang=en or http://www.sedonors.org/html/bds_guidelines.html

Department for International Development (DFID) (2000) 'Making Markets Work Better for the Poor: A Framework Paper'. Economic Policy and Research Department and Business Partnerships Department, London.

Haan, Hans Christiaan (2002). 'Training for Work in the Informal Sector: New evidence from Kenya, Tanzania and Uganda', InFocus Programme on Skills, Knowledge and Employability, ILO Geneva.

Philip, Kate (2002) 'The quest for rural enterprise support strategies that work – the case of Mineworkers' Development Agency'. *Small Enterprise Development* Vol. 13, No. 1, March 2002.

Phillips, David, and William Steel (2003) 'Evaluating the Kenya Voucher Programme'. *Small Enterprise Development* Vol. 14 No. 4, December.

Sida (2003) 'Making Markets Work for the Poor: Framework for Sida's Support to Private Sector Development'.

1 Marketing rural products in India

PRADEEP KASHYAP

This paper was first published in June 1991.

Small-scale rural producers in India are often limited by the markets within their reach. In the past they have been unable to sell directly to urban consumers, and instead their products have been bought up by middlemen. This article describes the 'Gram Shree' or 'wealth of villages' exhibitions which have provided an urban market-place for rural artisans to sell their products, at the same time as receiving practical advice on marketing from experts. The organizers of the exhibition, the Council for the Advancement of People's Action and Rural Technology (CAPART), have also helped producers to negotiate contracts with large customers directly without going through wholesalers.

ECONOMIC GROWTH HAS BEEN the overriding aim of government policy for decades and unemployment has continued to rise, particularly in the case of the Third World, to ever more dramatic levels. Various ILO studies have stressed that there is not the remotest hope that Western technology with its capital-intensive bias can create the basis for ensuring employment for the nearly 100 million additional job seekers in India from now to the end of the twentieth century. A World Bank report echoes ILO's observations: no imaginable rate of increase in industrial and service output can absorb the expected supply of workers. Progress towards full employment is clearly impossible without a substantial expansion of employment in rural areas (World Bank, 1972).

Rural Development, as a concept for growth, social justice and poverty alleviation, is one of the principal areas of emphasis of India's seventh Five-Year Plan. The Ministry of Agriculture, Department of Rural Development works towards improving the quality of life in rural areas through several anti-poverty programmes. The Integrated Rural Development Programme (IRDP) is a centrally sponsored scheme to assist selected families of target groups to cross the poverty line (annual family income below Rs6400; US$1 = Rs17) by taking up some economic activity. In addition the Development of Women and Children in Rural Areas (DWCRA), a UNICEF-supported scheme, seeks to provide income-generation activities to women. In the financial year ended March 1989 the government had disbursed Rs20 billion in grants and loans under these two schemes. The products of these programmes are wide-ranging: textiles, handicrafts, processed foods, leather goods, stone and wood carvings, pottery, cane furniture and other village industry items.

India has had an ancient tradition of village industries and crafts. In the past, production, markets and employment were concentrated in self-sufficient village economies. Rural artisans marketed their products through local shops, fairs held periodically throughout the year, mobile sales at which goods are carried from village to village, and direct sales from their homes. In the eighteenth century the British shifted the production and marketing base from villages to towns and cities, but even today the basic raw materials for the urban organized sector come primarily from the rural unorganized sector. As a legacy of the British rule, however, the value addition takes place in urban production centres, thereby depriving rural producers of this legitimate economic component.

Marketing for rural producers

Rural marketing has not really developed in independent India. The concept has been restricted to the sale of urban corporate sector products such as soap and tea in rural markets. The establishment of effective marketing channels going the other way – from rural areas to urban markets – has not been seriously attempted. To start off, such a marketing division was established in February 1989 at the Council for the Advancement of People's Action and Rural Technology (CAPART), an autonomous body engaged in rural development through NGOs under the aegis of the Department of Rural Development. This division planned new initiatives in tackling the marketing problems of rural producers through the sponsorship of short-duration sales exhibitions, the creation of permanent sales outlets, establishing links with shops and providing consultancy services.

Six exhibitions were planned during 1989 over the months of September, October and November at Bhopal, Calcutta, Bombay, Udaipur, Bangalore and New Delhi to provide an opportunity for IRDP and DWCRA beneficiary groups to sell their products in urban markets. It became clear from the outset that although such exhibitions allowed the producer to interact directly with the buyer so as to understand the latter's tastes, preferences and choices, they served only a limited objective owing to their extremely short duration (five days in each case). It was decided, therefore, to expand the role of these exhibitions to include buyer–seller meetings at which long-term bulk contracts might be achieved by the participating groups. Several potential clients representing the railways, defence, police, hotels and others were to be invited. Seminars and workshops were also planned to upgrade the marketing skills of the producer groups.

A total of 300 groups (an average of 50 groups per exhibition) from all parts of India participated in the six exhibitions. Against an overall expenditure of Rs600 000, sales of Rs3 million were registered. As most of the participants belonged to the below-poverty-line stratum of society, return travel, modest accommodation and food expenses for two participants per group, as well as the exhibition-site rent, publicity expenses and other costs were borne by CAPART. These subsidies are to be reduced gradually in future and are to be withdrawn completely within three years, by which time groups are expected to make adequate profits to cover their expenses. At the exhibitions each group was provided with a 10 square metre stall to display and sell their products. Publicity was arranged centrally by CAPART through attractive posters and banners displayed at prominent locations; brochures were direct-mailed to shop owners, bulk buyers, exporters and selected individuals. Press conferences were organized to ensure wide media coverage, and television stations were contacted to give exposure to this national effort. The turnout of visitors was very high, and at several exhibitions many groups exhausted their stocks by the fourth day.

As a small division located in Delhi alone, CAPART was unable to take over the marketing function for groups spread over the length and breadth of India. It was therefore decided to upgrade the groups' marketing skills gradually, so that over a period of time they would be well equipped with modern marketing tools and techniques to counter urban competition effectively. Towards this end CAPART organized workshops for the participating groups during the exhibitions. Experts specializing in design, marketing, packaging and market research came from the National Institute of Design, Indian Institute of Management, Indian Institute of Packaging, and also included practising corporate managers.

Marketing advice

This was perhaps the first time that a direct, informal, on-the-ground interaction between professionals and rural artisans had taken place. Before the workshop, the experts went around the stalls inspecting products, understanding the production processes, listening to producers' problems, suggesting design and packaging improvements and examining costing and pricing approaches. The workshops turned out to be lively. Though most producers were uneducated rural people, this did not inhibit them in the least from expressing their problems before the sophistication of highly educated professionals. The workshops were full of illustrations. In Bombay, a talk about the latest packaging materials was interrupted by a middle-aged woman. 'Your talk is irrelevant to us. My group makes biscuits at a village bakery and our problem is that they break in transit. Can you offer me practical suggestions for improving the packaging of these biscuits?' At once the atmosphere was transformed from a lecture to a purposeful business meeting. This accent on discussing real-life problems related to product design, costing and pricing, quality and standardization, distribution and packaging became a hallmark of the workshops. One participant summed it up: 'Experts were not allowed to protect themselves behind words.'

Several marketing lessons were learnt from the experiences of participants. At the crowded exhibition in Bombay, a stall owner was selling good-quality cotton cloth at the relatively cheap rate of Rs15 a metre. During his rounds, an expert suggested to him that a price tag, prominently displayed, would help in attracting customer attention. Since the owner remained unaffected by this suggestion, the expert brought a boldly painted price tag the next morning and persuaded the owner to display it prominently. The following day the stall owner reported that his sales had risen to Rs5400 from the previous day's Rs1400. As this story gained currency at the exhibition, so did support for the mysteries of modern marketing.

Direct buying contracts

A serious effort was also made to bring producer and consumer into direct contact, thereby eliminating the ubiquitous 'middleman'. The prevailing marketing system can be typified by the case of the Indian Railways, the world's largest rail system and consumer of millions of brooms annually. These are bought from city wholesale suppliers who procure them through middlemen from rural producers. The same distribution channel works for hundreds of city institutions, offices and hotels. The rural producer gets a fraction of the final price, the wholesaler capturing a disproportionately large slice of the profit. To begin the process of direct buying, CAPART invited several large institutions and helped them identify suitable products for bulk buying, negotiating terms and conditions of sale on behalf of the rural producer. At the

Bangalore exhibition one group procured a Rs200 000 order from a city department store for supplying dried grapes in the store's brand packaging. A similar commercial success was claimed at Udaipur when a local hotel placed an order for metal inlay furniture worth Rs250 000 with a local master craftsman.

Besides receiving substantial advances, producers expressed satisfaction with the contract prices. The buyers also felt that they had struck a bargain: both buyers and producers were happy to do business without the middleman. Since the exhibitions, the railway headquarters at New Delhi has circulated the list of the 300 participating groups with their product details to its 59 divisions with a request to encourage buying from them. To assist producers in meeting this emerging demand, District Supply and Marketing Societies (DSMS) are being set up. The DSMS will buy raw materials in bulk for distribution to local producers, and will undertake the marketing of the finished products. Thirty DSMSs are already operational, but 400 more are needed to cover all of India's districts.

The consumer and producer surveys carried out at the exhibitions have yielded a wealth of information which could help in formulating an effective national marketing strategy. The findings reveal a demand on the part of consumers for rural products resulting from a feeling that their purchase serves a good cause. In addition, the quality and workmanship was largely found to be acceptable and the prices reasonable. The surveys confirmed the fact that production groups lack adequate working capital and suffer from insufficient knowledge of markets. Most sell goods in their own or nearby villages, lacking viable mechanisms for sale in bigger towns and cities. Product decisions were found to be based not on market needs but on the availability of local skills and raw materials. As a result, the production of non-traditional items like voltage stabilizers, transistors or other electronic items, was generally unpopular and, wherever attempted, lacked quality and finish.

Gram Shree

To give their work a distinct identity the exhibitions were named 'Gram Shree' or the 'wealth of villages', and the name is now well known. Producers made no claims about either the quality or sophistication of their products, and as many garish decorations, crudely finished dolls or leaking pickle jars could be seen as high-quality silks, finely embroidered cushion covers and exquisite cane furniture. It is intended to bring all IRDP and DWCRA products under the banner of one brand – Gram Shree – and simultaneously to set up standards and controls for ensuring the quality to make rural products competitive in urban markets.

The Industrial Revolution was accomplished largely through small-scale industries with modest capital, under one hundred workers at most, owned and managed by a single individual or family. Larger firms were slow to emerge. As late as 1900, the hundred largest British industrial firms accounted for no more than 10 to 15 per cent of manufacturing value added, and the same held in the rest of Western Europe and North America (World Bank, 1978). The real business of India continues to be in the villages where over 70 per cent of the population struggles for a livelihood in a host of small business and microenterprises. CAPART's exhibitions and workshops have been a marketing attempt to boost rural incomes through enhancing employment opportunities. By 1991 the 16 exhibitions held had registered sales of Rs10 million against an overall expenditure of Rs2.2 million; and the sales target for 1991–2 is RS12 million with a reduced expense budget of Rs1.6 million. In addition, CAPART has received several requests from NGOs for organizing smaller satellite Gram Shrees in their own regions, for which modest funds are being provided by CAPART. Thus the total number of exhibitions may exceed 20 this year, benefiting almost 20 000 rural producers.

References

World Bank (1972) *Development Review*, Washington DC.
World Bank (1978) *Employment and Development of Small Enterprises*, policy paper, Washington DC.

About the author

Pradeep Kashyap is Chief Executive Officer of MART, a leading livelihoods promotion agency in India.

2 A case for business training with women's groups

MARTIN WALSH, KEVIN KANE and CANDACE NELSON

This paper was first published in March 1991.

In Kenya there are an estimated 20 000 organized women's groups whose combined membership accounts for more than 10 per cent of the country's adult female population. Not surprisingly, both governmental and private agencies view these women's groups as excellent agents through which to implement a wide range of development goals. Of these, income generation for women has been among the most popular and the most problematic. Despite strong support from the government and private agencies, the record of business promotional efforts with the groups shows that many have failed to generate significant income for programme participants. Success has proved elusive because of marginal economic climates, inadequate designs, persistent beliefs about appropriate activities for women, and insufficient skills in business management among both would-be entrepreneurs and those who set out to assist them.

In contrast to the poor performance of small enterprise promotional efforts with women, minimalist credit methodologies (credit without other assistance such as training and technical assistance) are fast gaining recognition as the key to success for programmes in this sector. While the record for minimalist credit is impressive so far, Tototo Home Industries, a Kenyan NGO working to support the development of rural women's group enterprises, found that credit was not always the critical factor for this population. They learned that poor business performance is often rooted in rural women's immediate social and economic environment – in other words, in the informal sector itself. Women are first and foremost members of households and this experience is not often conducive to the operation of an independent business. To confront the poor performance of rural women's businesses, Tototo developed a new approach to business training based on a unique combination of anthropological research, elements from a standard business skills curriculum and nonformal education. While the Tototo programme was developed specifically to address problems identified with women's groups in coastal Kenya, similar problems are common to nascent groups elsewhere in Africa. Consequently, the training has proved adaptable to other situations in East and Southern Africa.

TOTOTO HOME INDUSTRIES was founded in Mombasa in 1963 as a project of the National Christian Council of Kenya (NCCK). Its rural development programme evolved in response to requests by existing women's groups that have proliferated in Kenya since independence. While Tototo did not itself organize the groups, it did face the challenge of helping women pursue self-help activities to meet needs they regarded as priorities.

To carry out this mission, Tototo sought the help of World Education, an American NGO. In 1978 the two organizations set up a programme of technical assistance and training for rural women's groups in Coast Province. World Education introduced Tototo to nonformal education, and together they conducted participatory training with women's groups focusing on collective problem solving, decision making and action planning. The success of the pilot programme spurred expansion, and by 1985 Tototo was working with 45 women's groups. Although the programme was not designed to promote small businesses specifically, most of these groups chose to start income generation projects, including bakeries, tea shops, animal husbandry, and maize mills.

The popularity, rapid growth and apparent success of the programme led its sponsors to pose a series of questions about the impact of women's participation in income generation projects on their family and community life. In 1985, an anthropologist from World Education conducted an intensive study of selected women's groups and their businesses, which identified the multiple constraints operating upon women's group enterprises (Walsh 1985; McCormack et al. 1986).

Research results indicate that the greatest constraints on women's group businesses are those which are part of the socio-economic fabric of their immediate environment. Women run their group businesses as they would their household enterprises, employing forms of social and economic calculation different from those required for a business to make a profit and provide regular returns to its members. Resources are invested in and withdrawn from household enterprises whenever the need arises; the requirements of consumption and diverse social obligations take precedence over the seemingly intangible questions of profitability and reinvestment that should govern a business.

Because women owe primary allegiance to their households, their group businesses often compete poorly with the demands that households and household enterprises make upon their resources and time. The fact that groups model their businesses on members' experience and skills from domestic enterprises often creates a situation of competition between the group and the individual members' economic pursuits when the two overlap. Novel forms of compensation for members' time invested in group business in some cases exacerbate this conflict of interest. For example, a group bakery allowed members to bake for themselves as well as for the group. Soon, members were giving priority to 'private' baking and competing directly with their group business in a limited village market.

Other related factors interfere with the profitability of rural women's groups and their enterprises. As a visible asset in the community, the women's groups are under considerable pressure to contribute time, labour and financial resources to other community development efforts (pressure that targets women more explicitly and to a greater degree than men). In fact, group members themselves often regard group resources as available to meet personal needs, leading to indiscriminate withdrawals. Unexplained losses or accidents have sometimes been attributed to witchcraft, affecting members' commitment to continue working in their businesses.

A participatory business training

Hampered by such conditions, most of Tototo's groups were struggling to operate the businesses they had initiated. Clearly, the nonformal training with which Tototo had started was not meeting the needs of the women's groups as these evolved over time. As originally designed, the training did not address either the business skills the women needed or the contextual constraints they would have to overcome if they were to free themselves of dependency on the advice and assistance of Tototo. This ensured their continuing dependence upon external assistance and financial interventions that treated the symptoms of the problem rather than its cause.

To help address these problems, World Education provided Tototo with a business specialist to train Tototo's field staff in skills they would need to pursue solutions with the women's groups. Sceptical of the highly technical nature of traditional business education, however, the two organizations decided that they must develop a participatory business training programme. The research findings were then used to help develop this training, resulting in an unusual and innovative collaboration between an anthropologist, an MBA programme specialist and nonformal trainers (Nelson and Walsh 1990).

Tototo selected eight groups to serve as pilot sites for the study of business concepts and problems as well as for the testing of interventions and training exercises. The business specialist worked intensively with Tototo's staff both in the Mombasa office and at these sites. Once confident of the new skills they were learning, the field staff played a key role in developing the business training to be used with rural women. Experienced trainers and communicators, the field staff helped the business specialist translate the formal principles and lessons into imaginative exercises that could be understood by their rural clients. Thus, the nonformal education methodology which had formed the original basis for World Education's collaboration with Tototo eventually made a double contribution to the business training. It moulded the composition and invaluable skills of Tototo's field staff and it provided the essential methods and guidelines for the new training exercises which they played such a large part in devising.

In consultation with the anthropologist, the business specialist recommended bringing about a change in group business practice away from the household and towards a more formal company model. To effect this transformation, he needed to determine which formal business principles were essential.

Where other methods are designed to impart the formal knowledge that trainees are assumed to lack, this training aimed to build upon the existing entrepreneurial knowledge and talents of women's group members. Rural women have considerable experience running enterprises (e.g. petty trading, the sale of firewood, the production and sale of cooked food, handicrafts, and the production of palm-thatch roofing materials), but they rarely recognize these activities as forms of business, and usually deny that they have any business experience. One reason for this is that small-scale commodity production and trading are generally directed towards securing basic household subsistence and thus appear conceptually inseparable from other economic activities, such as direct production for use in the home or casual wage labour, which are undertaken towards the same end. Tototo and World Education developed training exercises that were designed to draw out the existing components of women's experience which are essential to good business practice, and to distinguish and discourage those practices which are not. This was the foundation of the general approach to the training, and governed the presentation of the themes described below.

The central importance of profits

A primary objective of the business training programme was to ensure the profitability of the group businesses involved. Many of the groups in Tototo's programme were struggling to break even, partly because groups were in the habit of removing money from their businesses on an irregular basis. They did so for a variety of purposes: sometimes to satisfy their members' demand for monetary return, to meet diverse non-business expenses including contributions to other community self-help efforts, or to invest in other projects and enterprises. Withdrawals were usually made without regard to their effects on business profits or to the need to accumulate and reinvest in further expansion of the business. Group members rarely made basic economic calculations of this kind.

The practice of groups in this respect mirrors the situation in their members' households. The products of domestic enterprises are typically consumed, pooled, distributed among kin, or shifted from one enterprise to another at will. The combined contribution of seasonal or intermittent enterprises to the subsistence of the household and its wider social obligations is more important than the specific performance and notional profitability of any one venture. Accumulation can and does take place in this context, but not in a form that is enterprise specific.

Against this background the training team judged it necessary to start at the very beginning – by emphasizing the importance of profits as the main business goal. They reinforced the women's existing understanding of profit as revenues minus expenses. This simplified definition of profits as net cash flow proved perfectly adequate for the purposes of women's group enterprises. In these small-scale informal sector businesses the value of fixed assets – hence the role of depreciation – is insignificant and can be safely excluded from a profit analysis. Specific exercises were designed to help the women identify practices conflicting with the bottom line such as irregular withdrawals of cash and goods from the business and high non-business expenses. The remaining training exercises stressed the profit motive while simultaneously teaching skills in marketing, assessing business opportunities, and record-keeping.

The concept and calculation of profits was further refined with the introduction of different kinds of expenses and guidelines on how these could be minimized. Simple economizing measures, such as bulk purchasing and investment in money-saving equipment, were introduced. The trainers particularly emphasized cutting down on unnecessary non-business expenses. Finally, the training team designed specific exercises to promote good cash control practices, which were necessary both to minimize the possibility of unauthorized cash withdrawals and to provide the basis for proper accounting. These interventions enabled groups to retain earnings to reinvest in their business.

The provision of regular returns

Another major objective of the business training programme was to ensure that group members benefited directly from their businesses by receiving regular returns on their labour and other investments. Previously, few of the groups provided monetary returns to their members and they almost never did so regularly on the basis of profits. Some businesses barely broke even; others banked their profits in the absence of a system for

dividing them. When women did benefit materially from their collective enterprises it was usually through limited distributions of the product, price rebates and favourable terms of credit, or free access to the facilities of the business or service.

In the absence of regular compensation, group members' commitment to their businesses invariably dropped off and, instead, they concentrated their efforts on individual and household enterprises offering the promise of more immediate returns. Another reaction was for group members to make unwise or unauthorized withdrawals from their businesses: unwise in that they were based on need rather than profit, and unauthorized in the sense that cash or goods were stolen or taken without the full knowledge and consent of the group. In either case, the businesses themselves suffered as their productivity and profitability were undermined.

The business training encouraged the regular provision of returns in two different forms: dividends and wages. Trainers stressed the need for groups to provide dividends on the basis of profits (net cash flow) as an incentive to their members. Higher profits should yield higher dividends to members. Groups determine for themselves the precise proportion of their profits to be divided and retained: in practice, dividends now vary between 25 per cent and 33 per cent of net cash flow. Monthly distributions are the norm, though for businesses with a clearly defined cycle of production and sales, the frequency of distribution can be adapted.

Like dividends, wages were paid only sporadically to group members. In most cases, women provided labour to the group business on a part-time basis. While this type of labour is appropriate for many village women whose household responsibilities and multiple economic pursuits preclude full-time employment, its voluntary nature undermined their commitment to the business. The business specialist helped the Tototo field staff to see that remuneration was critical to the health of the group business and included this message in the training they designed. The final decision about the form and amount of payment lay with the women's groups. Some chose to pay wages to members on a daily basis as a proportion of receipts; others opted to pay a fixed sum.

Financial records

The determination of profits, the calculation of dividends, and the need for groups to analyse business performance and make appropriate plans all require some form of financial record. Record-keeping is also essential to ensure the financial integrity of a collectively owned business: in its absence there is a potential for the misappropriation of funds, or the suspicion of it.

While Tototo had introduced a simple bookkeeping system to all groups, many members could not read or understand the records. Even literate members had difficulty understanding the accounts, a reflection of their background in households that have little need for record-keeping or experience in bank transactions.

The business training adopted a novel solution to this problem. Group bookkeepers and other members were shown how to prepare monthly financial statements for each of the businesses they ran. They drew these on large sheets of newsprint for presentation to a meeting of the whole group. Most importantly, the statements were drawn using two sets of visual symbols as well as written words and numbers. The first was a set of financial symbols, pictorial representations of the main categories of a typical financial statement: income, cost of goods sold, operating expenses, non-business expenses, profits (net cash flow), the total sum of dividends distributed, dividends per individual group member and retained earnings. The sums appropriate to each of these categories were then filled in using a set of money symbols drawn in distinctive shapes and colours to match the different denominations of Kenyan currency. Field tests demonstrated that these could be readily understood and counted by both non-literate and literate group members, all of whom were familiar with the different currency note denominations.

Using this method of pictorial statements group members have ready access to the basic information they need on the financial performance of their businesses. These statements are also of considerable help to Tototo field staff in the course of their regular follow-up visits.

With respect to marketing, households engaged in production for direct consumption have little need to satisfy any customers but themselves. It was common for groups to initiate enterprises on the basis of members' domestic experience without giving much thought to the wider market for the goods they produce or the services they provide. In response to this problem, exercises were developed using the standard business class formula of the 'Six Ps' or 'Marketing Mix': products, places, people, price, promotion, and the business plan. Tototo's field staff illustrated these marketing elements with stories and role plays drawn from the women's groups' actual situations.

Analysis of the overall performance

The new business training programme had a positive effect overall on the financial performance of the groups trained in 1986 and 1987. The revenues and profits accruing to groups from their businesses increased in the wake of the training, in some cases dramatically. In the process, a significant number of businesses incurring losses were made profitable. The sum of dividends distributed by groups also increased and therefore, presumably, so did the direct benefit of group businesses to their members. It might be added that the figures as presented do not specify wage payments made to group members: if these were included then the return to members' labour and other investments would be shown as even further improved.

The overall improvement in business performance and practice can be seen at a glance from Table 2.1. These figures are averages per business as opposed to per group.

On average, then, business revenues increased by some 60 per cent, profits doubled, and dividend distributions increased by an order of magnitude and more between January 1986 and June 1988. This covers the period immediately prior to the introduction of the business training as well as that following its implementation among 16 groups and a total of 30 businesses they conducted.

Table 2.1   Average performance of business (in Kenyan shillings)

Six-month period	1–6/86	7–12/86	1–6/87	7–12/87	1–6/88
Number of businesses	27	30	30	28	28
Revenue (KSh)	11 343	12 821	15 901	16 777	19 750
Net cash flow (KSh)	1 717	2 052	2 921	3 297	3 431
Dividends (KSh)	48	361	1 196	1 092	1 262

Examination of the results by individual group produces a more chequered picture with considerable variation between groups and their levels of business activity and performance. These differences are attributable to the widely varying resources and opportunities available to each group. For those groups with few opportunities, the training could not create a business success. Similarly, it was not designed to address problems of relations or group dynamics that often hinder business performance.

Conclusion

The analysis presented above indicates the potential effectiveness of an approach to business training developed at Tototo Home Industries in Kenya. With some additions and modifications, Tototo has continued to use this approach to train women's groups on the Kenyan coast as well as in training consultancies it carried out in a number of other countries, both in collaboration with World Education and independently (Walsh 1989; 1990). This experience has shown that the business training can be readily adapted to a variety of training situations and purposes.

The process by which the approach was developed should act as an object lesson for development planners. One way of looking at this is in terms of the interaction between different parties, each bringing their own skills and knowledge to bear upon the process. The long-term collaboration between two NGOs, one from the USA and one from Kenya, initiated this process; while at another level the interaction between an MBA and well-trained local field staff completed it. Equally important in this process was the role played by applied research, more intensive and conducted over a longer period than is usually the case in development projects.

The result was an innovative approach to business training for women's groups based on a detailed understanding of the social and economic context in which women's groups and their businesses operate. This sensitivity to context is reflected in its methodology and principal themes, and distinguishes it sharply from approaches that are based on knowledge of the formal sector alone. Moreover, it promises a degree of success which has hitherto remained elusive to women's groups and to related microenterprise development programmes.

References

McCormack, J., M. Walsh and C. Nelson (1986) *Women's Group Enterprises: A Study of the Structure of Opportunity on the Kenya Coast*, World Education Inc., Boston, MA.

Nelson, C. and M. Walsh (eds) (1990) *Faidika! Business Training for Women's Groups the Tototo Way, developed by Kevin Kane and the staff of Tototo Home Industries*, World Education Inc. and Tototo Home Industries, Boston, MA and Mombasa, Kenya.

Walsh, M. (1990) 'Tototo Home Industries: Assistance Strategies for the Future. Teaching Note', in Mann, C.K., M.S. Grindle and A. Sanders (eds) *Seeking Solutions: Case Leaders Guide*, Kumarian Press, West Hartford, CT.

Walsh, M. (1989) 'Tototo Home Industries: Assistance Strategies for the Future', in Mann, C.K., M.S. Grindle and P. Shipton (eds) *Seeking Solutions: Framework and Cases for Small Enterprise Development Programs*, Kumarian Press, West Hartford, CT.

Walsh, M. (1985) 'Interim Report for a Study of Income Generation and its Effects among Women's Groups in Kenya's Coast Province', report to World Education Inc., Boston, MA.

About the authors

Martin Walsh is now a Research Associate in the Department of Social Anthropology, University of Cambridge, UK. Kevin Kane is a Director of the BEES Consulting Group, Johannesburg, South Africa. Candace Nelson manages the Africa Grants Program on behalf of the McKnight Foundation and continues to research, write and train in microenterprise development as an independent consultant. She resides in Concord, MA. This paper was abridged from an unpublished monograph prepared for World Education in 1990 by Martin Walsh and Kevin Kane, 'Business Training for Women's Groups: Development and Innovation on the Kenyan Coast'.

3 African entrepreneurs: pioneers of development

KEITH MARSDEN

This paper was first published in June 1992.

This discussion presents the findings of a survey of modern indigenous African entre-preneurs. Far from being what has been described as 'the missing middle', these entrepreneurs can be seen as the true pioneers of development in sub-Saharan Africa. With the proper support, this productive sector can be expected to grow, and with that expansion, help alleviate poverty and stimulate social progress. The intended audience consists of policymakers, aid donors, and advisers concerned with African economic development, and this chapter addresses some key issues of strategy and policy as they are seen through the eyes of modern African entrepreneurs. It is hoped that this different perspective will be helpful in designing programmes to foster African entrepreneurship.

Promoting Africa's private sector: key issues

ENTREPRENEURSHIP HAS LONG BEEN RECOGNIZED as a key factor in the development process. Yet private entrepreneurship has been downplayed in many African coun-tries over the past 30 years. In part, that occurred because indigenous entrepreneurs were presumed to be scarce and foreign entrepreneurs were distrusted. But the belief was also widespread that entrepreneurial functions could be better performed by the state than by private individuals. Control had to be exercised through state ownership of the means of production or through licensing, regulations, and taxation. The argu-ments made for extensive government intervention in the economy were widely embraced in Africa, although the span of government control has varied from coun-try to country, and over time. Dissident views, such as those of Peter Bauer, were largely ignored or rejected.

A reappraisal of development strategies has been taking place over the past five years, however, spurred by evidence of public sector inefficiency and of market distortions caused by excessive government intervention. During the next three decades, the popu-lation of sub-Saharan Africa is expected to grow by at least 600 million persons – more than doubling the size of the labour force. Africa's indigenous entrepreneurs will play a central role in transforming African economies. A consensus, increasingly reflected in policy reforms and other initiatives, is forming around this vision of Africa's future.

A conflict over development strategy

While more and more policy makers and aid donors are coming to believe that future development in Africa rests with entrepreneurs and markets, there are different views on which entrepreneurs can most effectively lead this development – modern entre-preneurs that hire labour and are part of the formal economy, or the so-called informal sector.

Those who favour a development strategy based on the informal sector argue that this sector is dynamic and responsive to market forces and shifts in demand. It has close links with grassroots organizations, offers low start-up costs and easy exit, and uses domestic labour and raw materials intensively and efficiently. It provides opportunities for such disadvantaged groups as women and the poor, and low-cost, on-the-job training for apprentices in skills and occupations that are in demand. Many of those who believe that development efforts should rely on the informal sector see the modern sector as composed almost exclusively of inefficient and overprotected large firms under state or foreign ownership. In this modern sector, wage costs are said to be high, and political, rather than economic, criteria guide investment, location, and management choices. Imports are said to be 'reproduced' using 'transplanted' techniques and equipment without sufficiently adapting the technology and product designs to local conditions.

A recent World Bank report (1989) also draws a distinction between the informal and modern sectors, instead of the usual breakdown into sectors of economic activity. The informal sector is defined to cover the self-employed and microenterprises with unpaid family workers. The modern sector covers enterprises of all sizes that employ wage labour. All non-agricultural activities – manufacturing, mining, utilities, construction, transport, commerce, and other services – are encompassed within this dualistic structure. A similar distinction could be made between informal and modern enterprises in agriculture. Based on these definitions, the model projects that employment in the informal sector will rise by 6 per cent annually from 1990 to 2020. The informal sector's contribution to GDP is expected to rise by 7.5 per cent annually and its labour productivity to go up by 1.5 per cent annually. In contrast, employment growth in the modern sector is projected to just keep pace with the increase in employment in the economy as a whole. Labour productivity in the modern sector is expected to remain virtually stagnant, with a projected annual increase of 0.2 per cent. That means that by the year 2020, only one out of every 20 workers would be wage or salary earners, and that the modern sector's contribution to total GDP would decline from 47 per cent to 32 per cent.

The catalytic roles of modern African entrepreneurs
Some close observers of African economic development doubt that an informal sector -led strategy will work. They contend that there are many African entrepreneurs running modern businesses of all sizes and that many more Africans would join this modern entrepreneurial sector if appropriate opportunities were available. They also believe that the growth of the informal sector does not necessarily signify dynamism and efficiency. In fact, it is the entrepreneurial segment that uses appropriately-scaled resources, provides meaningful on-the-job training and, by offering improved products and techniques to those engaged in traditional agriculture and the informal sector, helps to alleviate poverty generally.

Action programme issues

These differences of opinion over the most effective development strategy are not merely a disagreement over semantics or an abstract model. To ensure concerted action among all partners in development, an action programme needs to be designed around the specific elements of the development strategy adopted. But an action programme may be ineffective or even counterproductive if the broad strategic goals are ill-advised.

The actions recommended by the advocates of an informal sector-led strategy emphasize social targeting and a combination of government paternalism, private philanthropy, and voluntary co-operation for the delivery of inputs. Specific steps include targeting assistance to economically and socially deprived groups such as redeployed workers, school drop-outs, women, and the poor; developing extension and information services based upon voluntary efforts of co-operatives, non-government organizations (NGOs), trade associations, and grassroots organizations; initiating government- and donor-funded programmes for basic research and dissemination of technology; launching public sector programmes to identify and develop prospective entrepreneurs; and channelling financial resources through microenterprise associations, using indigenous NGOs to define the needs of target groups, and pooling members' collateral to provide mutual guarantees for on-lent funds.

Those who want to promote entrepreneurship contend that whatever outside assistance entrepreneurs may need to run their businesses and overcome problems – information, advice, technology, services, or finance as well as physical inputs – can be obtained from other entrepreneurs through market networks. These networks exist and are more effective than the technical-assistance networks operated by government institutions and NGOs. But, these advocates say, these market networks could be strengthened and African entrepreneurship more effectively fostered, if tax and regulatory policies were more supportive of entrepreneurs, if foreign private investment and foreign–African partnerships were promoted, and if a higher proportion of foreign aid funding was channelled to the modern private sector.

Findings

Thirty-six entrepreneurs in six countries were interviewed. Three-quarters of them were selected from a list of people who have received assistance from the Africa Project Development Facility (APDF), an institution founded by the International Finance Corporation (IFC). The remainder were suggested by financial institutions and other contacts in the field. The criteria for selection of the entrepreneurs were African nationality, a track record of performance, and coverage of a representative range of activities in which African entrepreneurs are engaged. The majority were in farming and agricultural processing, and in services, while the others were engaged in a wide range of activities such as the manufacture of garments, furniture, rubber products, and pharmaceuticals. The countries selected by the IFC and APDF – Botswana, Côte d'Ivoire, Ghana, Kenya, Malawi, and Tanzania – cover almost the full spectrum of development strategies and philosophies applied in sub-Saharan Africa. Nevertheless, because the sample is small, the survey also examined evidence from a wider range of firms and countries to test the general validity of the findings. The major findings are presented below.

The middle is not missing

All the entrepreneurs interviewed are running modern enterprises with hired labour. A quarter of their enterprises are small (5–49 workers); half are medium-scale (50–299 workers), of which more than half employ over 100 workers; and a quarter are large enterprises with more than 300 employees each. Most said that they had numerous domestic competitors. In Botswana (1.1 million population), for example, there are 13 manufacturers of metal furniture and seven printing companies. In Tanzania, 5000 road transport companies are registered with the Central Transport Licensing Authority.

In three years the APDF has received over 2000 requests for assistance in preparing feasibility/market studies and project proposals to submit to financial institutions for funding and some 65 APDF-assisted projects in 18 African countries, and around 300 more, are in the pipeline. The average investment cost of the funded projects is US$1.5 million; thus covering the medium to large end of the spectrum of modern African enterprises. Many more entrepreneurs with smaller investment outlays expand their enterprises progressively, by adding or replacing a machine from time to time and by recruiting more labour. They do not need to carry out sophisticated studies. Others with strong links to foreign partners, financial institutions, and other sources of expertise, also do not require assistance. Chambers of Commerce and Industry visited during this survey reported growing memberships. In Malawi, for example, the Export Promotion Council has registered 108 private firms engaged in direct exporting in 32 product groups, more than half of which are owned and managed by Malawians.

The statistical authorities of most African countries have lacked the financial resources to carry out comprehensive establishment-level surveys and collection of micro-economic data. The Kenyan Central Bureau of Statistics, however, does undertake an annual survey, which showed that, excluding government and social services, the number of modern Kenyan entrepreneurs probably reaches several thousands. Fifty-one per cent of the establishments had one to nine paid employees; 31 per cent had 10–49 employees, and 18 per cent had more than 50 employees. A 1983 survey found 246 091 self-employed and unpaid family workers, compared with 1 093 278 wage and salary employees. In Ghana, the development of the modern private sector was held back by expropriations, heavy investment in parastatal enterprises, scarcity of foreign exchange, and declining per-capita incomes from 1965–84. Nevertheless, an official survey of larger manufacturing establishments (those with 30 or more employees) in 1984 recorded 206 wholly Ghanaian-owned private enterprises employing a total of 29 036 workers, with an average labour force of 140.

In sum, although the statistical coverage is far from complete, sufficient evidence is available to demonstrate a layer of modern African entrepreneurs lying between the informal sector on the one hand and large foreign-owned or state-owned enterprises on the other. But it would certainly be easier to formulate development strategies, and to chart the progress of African entrepreneurs, if the central statistical authorities of each country collected data on the structure of output, employment, and ownership on a regular basis.

Informal enterprises can be transformed into modern enterprises
Several APDF-assisted entrepreneurs began their businesses on an informal basis. A garment maker in Botswana began with US$100 in personal savings, a rented shed and

sewing machines, and two apprentices. She now employs 65 workers and her annual sales top US$300 000. A Malawian left school at 18 to work as a self-employed tobacco grader. He is now the owner and managing director of four companies engaged in tobacco growing and curing, commodity processing and exporting, property investment, and importation of machinery; annual turnover exceeds US$1 million. A family-owned conglomerate in Ghana, which manufactures clothing, spirits, furniture, textbooks, and other educational materials, and imports vehicles and equipment, grew out of a small dry-cleaning shop.

Broader statistical evidence is generally lacking. However, a recent World Bank study in Ghana reports that among a sample of very small firms established before 1975 average employment levels per enterprise declined from 4.3 workers at the start of operations to 3.4 workers in 1983. That was a period of increasing economic problems and income decline in Ghana. But from 1983 onwards, when policy reforms stimulated an economic recovery, the average employment level in these same firms almost doubled to 6.6 workers. This same study shows that a sample of somewhat larger firms established before 1975 grew even faster than did microenterprises. The average employment level among these larger firms moved from 20.5 workers in 1975 to 67.0 workers in 1989.

Correlation between the rates of growth of wage employment and of GDP

GDP grew fastest in countries with rapid increases in wage employment, such as Botswana, Côte d'Ivoire, Kenya and Malawi. In Ghana and Tanzania, however, low rates of growth of modern-sector employment coincided with slow GDP growth. The International Labour Organisation (ILO) and World Bank cross-sectional data also indicate a positive correlation worldwide. Historical trends reflect a tendency for incomes to rise as labour moves out of agriculture (where the proportion of self-employment and family labour is highest) into industry and services, and as the average size of enterprise increases to take advantage of economies of scale. A long-term strategy for Africa based on entrepreneurial growth would reinforce their historical trends.

The informal sector is not a source of economic dynamism

A cotton ginner in Malawi drew attention to the moribund state of village markets in a region that still depended on traditional subsistence crops. A charcoal manufacturer in Côte d'Ivoire pointed out the low efficiency of prevailing artisanal production methods. The owner of a tobacco estate in Malawi suffers from the low level of commitment of small-scale tenant farmers. A food manufacturer in Tanzania regretted the low level of skills in workshops and repairing transport vehicles. Modern entrepreneurs in Côte d'Ivoire complained of unfair competition from informal-sector enterprises that were less efficient but escaped the heavy burden of taxes and regulations imposed on the modern sector.

This anecdotal evidence is supported by a review in 1988 of studies of the informal sector in Africa carried out over several years. They found that working conditions in the sector are extremely poor, and that the traditional apprenticeship system used in the informal sector does not facilitate more efficient organization. Due to the heavy involvement of masters in production, time spent in specifically training apprentices is extremely low and whatever training that is provided does not involve any theoretical backup on the technologies of the machines in use and repair.

The ILO review goes on to report that the typical manager in the informal sector can not perform 'a correct cost-pricing exercise' and that only a third of informal enterprises keep records of any kind. One result of such weak management is the extremely low life expectancy of the enterprises – as low as five years on average. Furthermore, the lack of accumulation of experience in specific activities keeps the quality of the product at relatively low levels. These factors help to explain the declining share of the informal sector in the total urban labour force in African countries, which has declined from 60 per cent in the 1970s to 58 per cent in 1988. Projections show a further decline to 51 per cent in 2000. The ILO concludes that self-employment in the informal sector can only be a partial solution, if not marginal, to the current unemployment problem in African countries.

Modern African entrepreneurs help alleviate poverty and advance social progress

Illustrations of this include a Kenyan exporter of horticultural products who obtains 93 per cent of his samples from smallholders. He provides seeds and planting schedules, advises farmers on cultivation techniques and is instrumental in broadening access to markets, creating more regular employment, and diversifying rural incomes. In Côte d'Ivoire, a processor of frozen fish and crustaceans ensures a regular market outlet and income for 2000 artisan fishermen and their families. He provides them with fishing nets and iceblocks to increase their productivity and reduce spoilage. A Ghanaian producer of poultry and eggs helped to raise the protein intake of the urban poor during periods of severe import restrictions. His day-old chicks replenish the small flocks of rural households, thus maintaining consumption levels and a source of cash income for smaller farmers. Two female entrepreneurs in Botswana have recruited illiterate women (many, single mothers) for their garment and knitwear factories. These women have acquired skills and stable employment that would have been otherwise difficult to find. They can now support their families and ensure that their children get a better education.

In fact, all the entrepreneurs interviewed have created productive jobs for initially unskilled workers and devoted considerable time and resources to the development and upgrading of skills. These opportunities are often lacking within the informal sector, as noted above. The wages paid are usually higher than the statutory minimum wage or the prevailing agricultural wage rate, and the skills acquired are more marketable. Thus, social and labour market mobility is raised and other family members benefit in a variety of ways.

Modern African entrepreneurs appear to be efficient

Insufficient information was collected during the field interviews to make meaningful estimates of economic rates of return. However, the impressive growth records of the entrepreneurs interviewed in this survey do indicate an ability to meet local and foreign competition and satisfy market demand effectively. In most cases their market shares have risen significantly. Broader APDF data indicates that modern African entrepreneurs generally exhibit good judgment and sound business sense when making investments for expansion, modernization, or diversification projects. Assessment of 83 projects approved in 22 African countries showed an average projected internal rate of return of 29.5 per cent. Variation in profitability among different sectors, countries, and sizes of project was relatively small. These entrepreneurs were also prudent in taking on long-term debt obligations. The long-term debt/equity ratios of these projects averaged 62 per cent.

Further evidence of efficiency comes from a study (1987) of a sample of 106 modern manufacturing enterprises in Kenya conducted by the World Bank in 1986. The sample was classified into three groups: public enterprises, foreign private enterprises, and local private enterprises. The study found that locally owned private firms were the most efficient and profitable and the least protected (in terms of the effective rates of protection–ERP coefficients) of the three categories. The local private sector firms were efficient earners/savers of foreign exchange with low long-run domestic resource costs. Their financial rates of profit averaged 20 per cent, compared with 18 per cent for the foreign private firms and 15 per cent for the public enterprises.

The relative efficiency of modern African entrepreneurs can be influenced by many factors, including their personal characteristics. The profiles reveal a wide range of social and educational backgrounds and age groups. However, some generalizations can be made about their personal traits and attitudes that are relevant to their performance and which have been shown to be characteristic of entrepreneurs worldwide by authorities such as McClelland and Winter and a recent USAID-funded study by McBer et al.

Market networks already exist

Most of the entrepreneurs interviewed spoke about helpful relationships with other enterprises, in their capacities as suppliers of inputs, direct customers, or distribution links with final consumers. For example, the owner of a tobacco estate in Malawi values the technical information supplied by manufacturers of pesticides and insecticides. In his property investment and trading activities, he appreciates the high quality of work performed by companies that serve private business, such as accountants, auditors, architects and engineering services. In Côte d'Ivoire, a frozen-fish exporter received excellent co-operation from a local manufacturer of refrigeration equipment, who helped in the design and installation of his new factory. In Ghana, the owner of an advertising agency and a printing company gets a lot of new ideas from his major clients, and his banker helped him to introduce a new accounting system. A Tanzanian food manufacturer and sisal estate owner said that his wholesalers and retailers provide invaluable feedback on consumer reactions and preferences. A sisal broker had suggested a new packaging technique that had proved to be effective, and an auditing company had offered excellent accounting advice. The owner of cotton estates and a cotton ginnery in Malawi developed his investment and production plans in close collaboration with a large textile factory.

In many cases, however, modern African entrepreneurs are also able to obtain relevant information and advice through market networks for no additional charge. Transfer of know-how is a normal feature of commercial relationships, included in the price of the physical products or services being exchanged, and dissemination of reliable information is seen as a means of reinforcing commercial linkages and is motivated by mutual self-interest.

Tax reductions and deregulation are effective

Botswana's Financial Assistance Policy (FAP) contributed substantially to the development of Botswana enterprises and to the rapid expansion of private sector employment during the 1980s. Under the FAP, which was introduced in 1982, all agricultural and industrial enterprises, except the traditional activities of cattle ranching and large-scale mining, are eligible for assistance. 'Linking industries', that provide a marketing or collecting function in support of a large number of small-scale informal or formal sector producers, are also eligible, as are repair and maintenance facilities.

The first type of assistance is reimbursement of business (corporate) taxes on company income. Second, grants are paid to cover part of the cost of unskilled labour. These grants encourage employers to take on unqualified labour. Third, training of unskilled (and skilled) workers is fostered by training grants. These incentives are given automatically to eligible new investment projects. Expansion of existing enterprises also qualifies for assistance packages. These packages may include grants per job created; capital grants for the investment cost depending on location; sales augmentation grants; and unskilled labour and training grants.

On the other hand, there is evidence that an increase in the tax burden of the modern sector in Côte d'Ivoire has had negative effects. All forms of taxes on Ivorian manufacturing enterprises (including taxes on their inputs) recently increased from 41 per cent to 74 per cent, according to the sector. The growing tax burden was a major factor in the decline in competitiveness of Ivorian industry and has encouraged tax evasion, smuggling, and corruption. A delay in granting a 'convention' to a charcoal-manufacturing project in Côte d'Ivoire was a major reason why it did not get off the ground. This would have provided a corporate tax holiday and other fiscal incentives. In Kenya, high taxes on packaging materials are retarding the growth of packaged horticultural exports.

Punitive income taxes have restricted capital accumulation and discouraged entrepreneurs from entering the formal sector (where they would have to submit tax returns). Marginal income tax rates were as high as 85 per cent in Tanzania and 60 per cent in Ghana, equivalent to the 1980 US poverty line. An analysis of the links between taxes and economic growth in 20 countries found a negative relationship over a ten-year period (Marsden 1983).

Several cases illustrating the benefits of economic deregulation were revealed by the survey. For example, the liberalization of foreign exchange markets in Ghana has allowed a fishing company to maintain an overseas bank account, thus facilitating payment of foreign suppliers and encouraging commercial banks to extend credit to the company. In Tanzania, the introduction of foreign exchange retention accounts has made it easier for a transport business to acquire spare parts and expand without having to endure time-consuming approval procedures. A cumbersome bureaucracy and high personal and corporate taxes remained major constraints for a Tanzanian food manufacturer; and the expansion of furniture exports from Ghana is being held back by the difficulty in obtaining a forestry concession. In sum, although some progress in the tax and regulatory areas has occurred, there is still a long way to go before African enterprises can compete on an equal footing with countries in Asia and the Caribbean, which have provided low-tax, regulation-free regimes for their exporters (particularly those operating in export processing zones).

Foreign enterprises help to strengthen African enterprises

Promotion of African entrepreneurship is sometimes seen as a desirable alternative to foreign investment and as a means of increasing African self-reliance. The findings of this survey suggest that African entrepreneurs have much to gain from collaboration with foreign-owned enterprises, at home and abroad, and that African economies are also strengthened by this co-operation. Many APDF-assisted promoters have been keen to forge partnerships with foreign companies. These partnerships take various forms. A Kenyan horticultural exporter has acquired technological know-how and secure market outlets through links with a major French importer of horticultural products. An Ivorian pineapple producer has entered into technical and financial partnerships with an Italian entrepreneur with expertise in irrigation systems, and with a French company that has well-established distribution networks in Europe. A manufacturer of hair-care products in Botswana has obtained formulations and packaging know-how from a leading US producer of such products. A Kenyan hotel promoter has entered into a management contract with a leading US tourism company specializing in safari and golf holidays. In addition, foreign direct investment supplements domestic savings. The inflow of foreign private capital into Botswana's mining sector, in particular, has given a tremendous boost to the country's whole economy.

Entrepreneurs do not always welcome foreign investors as competitors in their own fields, but they appreciate the help received from those with whom complementary relationships have been established. When the point was put to them, they recognized that competition and complementarity are two facets of a market economy, and they are usually indivisible.

Insufficient financing is a major constraint

The scarcity of financing has been a significant impediment for most of the entrepreneurs. With APDF assistance, the preparation of well-conceived, fully-documented project proposals has meant that financing has been secured more readily than would otherwise have been the case. But the whole process has often been drawn out. Some apparently viable projects are still waiting for the approval of commercial banks and other financial institutions, where financial markets are short of funds and where government/public sector borrowing is given priority. Entrepreneurs felt generally the insufficiency of short-term credit to meet their working capital requirements. They feel that bankers apply conventional criteria concerning collateral, rather than assessing capacity to use funds productively. African entrepreneurs also face shortages of longer-term forms of financing. In part, the problem is the internal one of start-up businesses finding it difficult to accumulate funds from their own operations. Even more important, however, is the fact that most African countries simply lack the capital markets where funds might be raised. The type of venture resources familiar in other parts of the world do not exist in these countries. This inadequacy, in fact, has motivated IFC to make capital market development a central part of its future emphasis for the region.

The overall financial constraint on private enterprise is illustrated by Table 3.1 below.

With the exception of Kenya and possibly Côte d'Ivoire, the level of outstanding credit to the private sector is generally low in relation to GDP, especially for Ghana and Tanzania. Domestic savings have been depressed in these two countries, and the private sector has been crowded out of financial markets by government and public sector borrowing.

Private sector credit levels are particularly low when compared with the 1988 figures for the annual flow of foreign aid. No recent official estimates on the distribution of foreign aid between the public and private sectors are available. However, a World Bank analysis of outstanding medium- and long-term foreign debt to sub-Saharan Africa at the end of 1984 found that direct loans to private enterprises accounted for only 0.6 per cent. Foreign loans to development finance institutions, which finance private and public investment projects, represented just 0.8 per cent (Marsden and Belot, 1987). Foreign loans went mostly to government expenditures.

Aid flows that reach the private sector via domestic financial institutions would be included in the domestic credit data. The figures indicate that, at best, only a small proportion of foreign aid is being allocated to the private sector in Ghana, Malawi, and Tanzania. Yet evidence exists of a strong correlation between the growth of credit to the private sector and overall GNP growth. A study of 17 African and East Asian countries found that a 1 per cent increase in real credit to the private sector was associated with a 0.34 per cent rise in GNP per capita over the period 1962–82. There was a negative relationship between the share of domestic credit going to the public sector and GNP growth (Marsden 1986).

Foreign aid donors play a positive role in fostering African entrepreneurship

A wider range of modern African entrepreneurs could be helped if more official development assistance funds were made available as lines of credit to private financial institutions (commercial banks, development finance companies, merchant banks, and hire-purchase machinery leasing finance houses), for lending to African entrepreneurs. This would ease the financial constraints on entrepreneurs with smaller expansion or

Table 3.1   The level and distribution of foreign credit (1988)

Country	Credit outstanding to private sector as % of total domestic credit	as % of GDP	Foreign aid[‡] as % of GDP
Botswana	100.0*	9.8	7.8
Côte d'Ivoire	78.8[†]	40.6[†]	4.5
Kenya	53.4	18.4	9.4
Ghana	11.5	3.1	9.1
Malawi	36.8	7.4	30.6
Tanzania	6.6	2.6	31.2

* Government is a net lender in Botswana.
† Includes public enterprises; separate data not available.
‡ Net disbursements of official development assistance from all sources.

Sources: *IMF International Financial Statistics*, 1989, and the *World Development Report 1990*, IMF, Washington DC.

modernization projects and those who need additional working capital. Restricted access to credit is a more severe constraint than availability of technical assistance. Expanded credit facilities to private firms would strengthen those market networks which provide information and advice for the entrepreneur.

Conclusions

Some broad conclusions may be drawn from the findings above. Entrepreneurship is alive and well in Africa. It has flourished most under supportive policy regimes, but has managed to survive even in hostile environments. Second, there is no 'missing middle' in the African enterprise structure in these countries. Large numbers of African entrepreneurs employ wage labour and run enterprises on modern lines. Transition from informal to formal modes of organization does take place. Growth of individual enterprises from small- to medium- and large-scale operations, in terms of both production and employment, is quite feasible. Current pessimism about the scope for increasing wage employment in Africa is, therefore, unwarranted. Many countries that have encouraged private enterprise and competitive markets have witnessed a rapid expansion in wage employment and rising per capita incomes. On the other hand, countries that have emphasized central planning and state ownership often have experienced low rates of job creation and stagnant or declining incomes.

An alternative strategy, however, that would rely mainly on the informal sector as the engine for growth, looks less promising. An increase in the share of this sector in total employment has been associated in the past with poor overall performance on both the job and income fronts. Good economic performance has been linked with rapid expansion of the modern private sector and a decline in the contribution of the informal sector to the economy, initially in relative terms and eventually in absolute terms.

Foreign investment has not blocked African entrepreneurship. Many of the entrepreneurs acquired their basic technical or managerial skills working for foreign-owned companies. Foreign enterprises provide highly valued assistance to indigenous entrepreneurs, as suppliers, distributors and as partners in their businesses. The relationships between foreign and indigenous enterprises are often complementary, not just competitive.

The development of African private enterprise is being retarded by inadequate access to bank credit. There is also a general shortage of working capital because of low overdraft ceilings imposed by commercial banks, caused in part by the low levels of domestic savings. But private enterprises are also being crowded out of financial markets in some countries by heavy borrowing by governments and public enterprises, and a high percentage of foreign aid flows (grants and loans) is being used to boost public expenditure rather than private investment. In some countries the opportunity to accumulate investment funds within the firm is severely constrained by high rates of tax imposed on profits, dividends and personal income. Government controls and regulations also increase costs and squeeze profit margins.

Market networks composed of firms of varying sizes, and ownership structures engaged in complementary, mutually supportive activities, serve as vital mechanisms for the diffusion of information and expertise among the members of these networks.

In fact the interviews suggest that market networks are more effective mechanisms for the transfer of know-how than technical assistance networks composed of public institutions, NGOs, and government departments. Public and voluntary technical assistance networks often lack the specialized knowledge, human motivation, and competitive pressures to provide the inputs most needed by modern African entrepreneurs.

Modern African entrepreneurs are, therefore, no different from entrepreneurs elsewhere in the world. Their roles and characteristics correspond closely to those depicted by classical and mainstream economists. Entrepreneurs in Africa (both indigenous and foreign) do train labour. African countries that have encouraged private entrepreneurship have not been 'trapped in a low-level equilibrium'. Entrepreneurs have had ample 'effective inducements to invest' wherever governments have allowed relatively free, competitive markets. The success of current liberalization efforts in many African countries depends directly on developing a climate supportive of vigorous small businesses. Assisting entrepreneurs in taking advantage of new opportunities contributes substantively to the creation of that nurturing business environment and of the new jobs that are an important consequence.

References

ILO (1989) 'ILO African Employment Report', Addis Ababa, JASPA.

Marsden, K. (1983) 'Taxes and Growth', *Finance and Development*, September.

Marsden, K. (1986) 'Private Enterprise Boosts Growth', *Journal of Economic Growth*, First Quarter.

Marsden, K. and Belot, T. (1987) *Private Enterprise in Africa: Creating a Better Environment*, World Bank Discussion Paper No.17, July.

World Bank (1987) *Kenya: Industrial Sector Policies for Investment and Export Growth*, restricted distribution.

World Bank (1989) *Sub-Saharan Africa: From Crisis to Sustainable Growth*, Washington DC, World Bank.

About the author

Keith Marsden was a consultant to the IFC and is an adviser to several UN agencies including the FAO and Unctad (1988–to date). He is also a frequent contributor to the *Wall Street Journal Europe*. He has been an operations adviser in the World Bank (1979–88), senior economist in the International Labour Office (1965–78), UNDP expert in economic surveys in Egypt (1963–5), and economics adviser in the private sector (1954–63). This report was initiated by IFC's Economics Department in 1990 and the edited version printed with their permission.

4 Fostering collective efficiency

HUBERT SCHMITZ

This paper was first published in March 1998.

Industrial clusters of small enterprises can be found throughout the world. Clustering bestows certain advantages of collective efficiency on small enterprises, such as the external economies of proximity, (e.g. well-developed networks of suppliers and buyers) and the potential gains of consciously pursued joint action (e.g. several firms sharing an order). Many clusters arose without external intervention, but this article addresses what may be done to promote clustering in developing countries. Three essential elements of effective enterprise assistance are described: developing customer orientation, a collective approach, and building the cumulative capacity to upgrade. A number of cases are outlined, where clusters and networks have been promoted successfully, and several mechanisms are identified that build up customer orientation and competitiveness.

A LOT IS KNOWN about why small firms find it difficult to compete and grow. A lot less is known about how to help them overcome the obstacles. Effective lending schemes have helped to overcome financial constraints. Less progress has been made in non-financial assistance. This is the area for which this article suggests a way forward. It is addressed to the reader concerned with fostering economic development on the basis of small local industry.

Most attempts to provide non-financial assistance suffer from three deficiencies:

○ they are too supply oriented: that is, overly focused on inputs for production (skills, technology, raw materials) and not sufficiently concerned with who would buy the outputs
○ they are rarely sustainable: the cost of reaching out to a multitude of small firms is high, and cost recovery for support services tends to be poor
○ they tend to have a one-off effect on the performance of the assisted enterprise, rarely leading to a better capacity for self-help and continuous improvement.

The 'Triple C' approach

The approach set out below tries to overcome these deficiencies. It is customer oriented, collective and cumulative, hence dubbed the 'Triple C' approach. Its message is that policies and projects for small firms can be particularly effective when these three criteria are met.

Projects should be driven by the need to meet the demands of the customer. A customer orientation forces firms to tackle their key problems of competitiveness. Successful interventions are those which help SMEs to learn about the needs of their customers and obtain the technical assistance which enables them to meet these needs.

Second, intervention can be directed at groups of enterprises. This means targeting (or working with) business associations and other forms of enterprise groupings.

Where they do not already exist, it means linking support to the formation of such groups. This has two advantages: (1) the collective approach has lower transaction costs than assistance to individual enterprises; (2) it helps generate relationships between enterprises that improve their efficiency through the development of co-operation, and maximize the potential of the group through the development of mutual learning.

These two features establish the condition for the third 'C', the cumulative capacity to upgrade and become less dependent on support from outside. Being competitive is not a state, it is a process of remaining competitive through improvement. The object-ive of policy intervention at the micro level should be to develop the capability of groups of firms to generate processes of improvement deriving from inter-firm linkages and contact with the market. Thus, public support for a given purpose gradually becomes unnecessary and can shift to new challenges.

Exporting clusters in north and south

The Triple C is not a recipe dreamt up by researchers. It comes from observing how clustering and networking help small firms to compete in distant markets and to grow from small to medium and sometimes even large size. The most celebrated cases are the industrial districts of what has come to be called the 'Third Italy'. North-east and central Italy did particularly well during the 1970s and 1980s; exports, employment and income grew faster than in the rest of the country. Much of the prosperity was pro-duced by clusters of SMEs. Clustering here means the geographical and sectoral concentration of firms, for example, the tile cluster in Sassuolo, footwear in Brenta, knitwear in Carpi, packaging machinery in Bologna, farm machinery in Reggio Emilia, and many others. These clusters of SMEs competed by making highly differentiated products at short notice. By the 1990s, large enterprises had begun to fight back by restructuring internally and becoming more flexible. The clusters in turn had to reor-ganize and innovate. Not all have succeeded, and those which have look different from a decade or two earlier. Some now have large, home-grown enterprises in their midst.

Similar cases of small firm clusters becoming significant players in international markets are known from other European countries, but perhaps the most interesting come from less developed countries. For example, Brazil is today a major exporter of women's leather shoes, a position it owes to a cluster of local enterprises, most of which were small when they began to export in the 1970s. Until then, shoe manufac-turers of the Sinos Valley (in the state of Rio Grande do Sul) had produced only for the internal market; two decades later they were exporting 70 per cent of their output. Their growth and competitiveness cannot be understood by analysing enterprises individu-ally. The 500 shoe manufacturers draw on over 1000 suppliers of specialized inputs and services and on a range of self-help institutions. However, there is not just comple-mentarity and co-operation but also fierce local rivalry showing that the two do not exclude each other. The Sinos Valley is not the only shoe-producing cluster in Brazil but it is largely responsible for the country's export performance. Between 1970 and 1990, Brazil raised its share of world exports in leather shoes from 0.5 to 12.3 per cent.

Similarly, Pakistan is today one of the world's main exporters of surgical instru-ments, made by a cluster of manufacturers in and near the town of Sialkot in the

Punjab. As shown by Nadvi (1998), the instruments are made from stainless steel by over 300 manufacturers who farm out work to 1500 small enterprises specializing in particular stages of the production process. Alongside these manufacturers and their subcontractors, there are an estimated 200 suppliers of inputs and over 800 units providing various types of services. As in the Brazilian case, there is intense competition in all stages of the local value-added chain, but there is also co-operation both of the vertical and horizontal kind. Over 90 per cent of Sialkot's output is exported and around 90 per cent of these exports go to Europe and North America. This cluster is estimated to account for over 20 per cent of world exports, making Pakistan the second largest exporter of surgical instruments after Germany.

Other examples could be given of clustered small firms growing and becoming major international players: in Turkey (towels and bathrobes), India (cotton knitwear), Thailand (gems and jewellery), and Taiwan (computers). There are also examples of failure to grow, however, showing that economic gains do not necessarily result from clustering. A good deal of new research is underway to explain why.

While experiences vary, we can register the end of export pessimism in the small enterprise debate. Some recent case material shows fast industrial growth, based on local enterprises exporting most of their output. In the case of the Sinos Valley and Sialkot these enterprises were small a decade or two ago, since when some have grown into medium or large enterprises. These and other case studies have helped to shake off the previous pessimism on whether small firms can grow and compete in global markets. However, such cases do not give the impatient policy maker an immediate prescription. To draw policy lessons one needs to make a detour, which starts with an analysis of what explains their success.

The gains from clustering and networking

Successful enterprises in clusters have in common that they are demand driven and compete on the basis of their collective efficiency. Let us explain what this means. The concept of 'collective efficiency' helps capture the competitive advantage derived from:

○ local external economies
○ joint action.

The former are incidental benefits arising from proximity. Where firms cluster they are more likely to find suppliers of specialized inputs, buyers of their outputs, skilled workers, and information about new developments.

In contrast, the benefits from joint action are consciously pursued. Such joint action can be of two types: individual firms co-operating (for example, lending each other equipment) and groups of firms joining forces in business associations, producer consortia and the like. Joint action can be both horizontal (e.g. sharing a large order) or vertical (e.g. a supplier redesigning a component with the customer).

The combination of the incidental and consciously pursued effects can vary and helps to distinguish between clusters and networks.

○ *Clusters* refer to sectoral and geographic concentration of firms, where local external economies are likely, but joint action does not necessarily emerge. Where both occur, the notion of industrial districts is often used.
○ *Networks* refer to cases of inter-firm co-operation irrespective of whether firms are geographically close. The emphasis is on benefits from joint action, and local external economies are often small.

Some of the most celebrated cases in advanced and developing countries owe their success to this collective efficiency, often achieved without significant outside help from government or donors. But there are some new experiences in advanced and developing countries in which public intervention has been critical and which draw – in some cases knowingly, in others not – on the principles which underlie those successful clusters. Some of these experiences are highlighted in the next section.

Box 4.1   Triple C in Practice

A case study from the Brazilian State of Ceará shows the potential gains from an approach to SME promotion that is both collective and customer oriented. In a scheme jointly organized by SEBRAE, the Brazilian SME promotion agency, and the state government, demand for school furniture was channelled to a group of small firms in the town of São João do Aruaru. By putting their association at the heart of the bidding for and co-ordination of contracts, the scheme ensured that participating firms had an incentive to learn from each other and monitor each other's performance. It also facilitated learning from SEBRAE; association members began to meet prior to dealing with technical support staff, in order to discuss the issues which were of most concern to them. Small producers also faced the challenge of having to win the confidence of a sceptical buyer, as many in the state government had to be convinced that small local producers could deliver on time and to the required quality standards. This type of customer orientation provided pressure for improvement, and for mutual learning among the participating firms.

The impact of the programme on the town was startling. Before it started, there were four sawmills with 12 employees in the town. Five years later, there were 42 sawmills with about 350 workers, and a further 1000 people directly or indirectly employed in the woodworking industry. Importantly, the customer base has been diversified over time, so that now over 70 per cent of output goes to the private sector.

In sum, the case study shows that:
○ a collective approach to SME support is not limited to situations where large clusters of firms already exist
○ a collective approach facilitates group learning among producers, and learning from state support services
○ the need to satisfy the customer drives mutual learning and provides pressure for improvement
○ the combination of a customer-oriented and collective approach can lead to cumulative improvements in the competitiveness of SMEs.

Source: Tendler and Amorim (1996)

Promoting inter-firm co-operation

The main policy challenge in developing countries lies in fostering collective efficiency where clusters exist merely in embryonic form. Box 4.1 shows an example where this succeeded. In other cases, the practitioner finds that enterprises are not clustered together but operate in related fields. Can this be the starting point for a new initiative? The answer is yes. There are cases in which public policy helped foster collective efficiency where initial linkages were few or did not exist at all. These render useful lessons for developing countries.

One example is the Danish Network Programme, a government-subsidized initiative which ran from 1988 to 1993. The idea was to promote networking between firms to help them face increasing international competition. The key figure in the programme design was the 'network broker' who helped to identify opportunities, brought participants together and assisted in implementing new ideas or projects. The main challenge of the programme was overcoming firms' resistance to co-operation, not traditionally a part of the country's industrial culture, and convincing groups to take ownership of their network.

The programme was successful on a number of counts. It achieved a high uptake among SMEs. During the five years of its existence, over 5000 enterprises became involved in forming networks, out of a target group of 10 000. This helped make networking a part of the Danish business culture. Most participating firms expressed that networking increased their ability to compete. Some aspects of the programme have been criticized but the approach has sparked widespread interest and variations on it are being tested in a number of countries. Box 4.2 summarizes the New Zealand experience.

Another example comes from Chile, where in 1990 the government SME promotion agency SERCOTEC introduced an initiative to increase the take-up of government support services and promote joint action between firms. Each initiative in this networking programme (PROFO) targets firms in a particular region and sector. Owners of small businesses in Chile are as individualistic and mistrustful of their competitors as anywhere else, and they are also suspicious of government. Brokers help to overcome mistrust by facilitating access to state support. This gives the PROFO credibility and provides a reward for participation. From here, regular meetings of participants help to build up mutual understanding. Out of this contact ideas often emerge for co-operation which would not have been considered before. The early stage is subsidized, but after three years the participating firms take responsibility for the broker's pay. The results of this Chilean programme have been promising. Most participating firms gained access to new domestic or international markets. The majority of networks also showed the capacity to be self-sustaining.

These examples highlight the following points.

○ A collective approach to SME support is a feasible one, even where existing linkages are few, or where firms are not already part of an existing cluster; they do, however, need to operate in closely related lines of production.
○ By improving the relationships between enterprises, this approach can improve the collective efficiency. Those firms that have been included in the initiatives have

Box 4. 2   Joint Action Groups in New Zealand

The Trade Development Board of New Zealand (TRADENZ) has promoted networking in order to boost the country's exports. The motto is 'Co-operating to Compete'. The initiative involves the promotion of joint action groups (JAGs); these are sector based and exist in 26 industries, ranging from wine and textiles to engineering and consultancy services. TRADENZ, the sponsor, hopes that through the JAGs government assistance can be more effectively allocated and monitored, compared with project-by-product assistance to individual enterprises.

Previously existing industry associations confined themselves to information diffusion and lobbying, had little strategic orientation and a membership unwilling to commit resources to industry development. JAGs, in order to qualify for support, must demonstrate commitment to common goals, such as the promotion of a specific product or the development of a particular overseas market. TRADENZ bears up to 50 per cent of the costs and provides specialist staff to support the initiatives. This public contribution is expected to decline over the agreed life of the initiative (usually 3-5 years) with the private sector taking increasing responsibility for organization and funding.

JAGs differ enormously, some concentrating on the organization of trade fairs and missions, others on regulating the quality of the sector's output (for example, phasing out the exports of low-value wine). Not all initiatives have succeeded, and some JAGs have ceased functioning altogether. There have also been conflicts between TRADENZ and industry over the direction which particular JAGs were taking. Overall, however, it seems that the good experiences outweigh the bad. New Zealand is – with exceptions – an economy of SMEs. The recognition is gaining ground in the country that co-operation helps to compete in a globalized market. The TRADENZ–JAG experience also underlines that there is a role for public policy. Co-operation between SMEs can be promoted. For this approach to work, however, it needs to be sector specific.

Perhaps the main limitation of the JAGs was that their initiatives were not specific and focused enough. This is why TRADENZ has started to complement support for JAGs ('soft networks') with support for groups of three to six enterprises ('hard networks'). Over 100 people have been trained to become independent brokers who are available to assist enterprises in developing 'hard networks'. With the help of such a broker, five of New Zealand's smaller wineries from the Canterbury region have joined forces in 'The Cellars of Canterbury' and have significantly increased their sales at home and abroad. The broker is paid by the enterprises participating in the network. The critical role of TRADENZ lay in drawing together international experience in network brokering and then training brokers familiar with the reality of New Zealand.

Sources: Perry (1995) and Williams (1996)

been able to increase their competitiveness and enter new markets.
- ○ Individualistic and anti-state minded entrepreneurs can be convinced that inter-firm co-operation and state intervention can be of benefit.
- ○ But, lasting improvements in competitiveness can occur only if practices are self-sustaining. There is a trade-off in this respect, between a high degree of initial subsidy,

which accelerates the up-take of enterprises, and a low degree, which has the advantage of eliciting from the start a stronger commitment of participating enterprises.

Emphasizing the collective approach does not mean that supporting individual enterprises is always wrong. In some cases there is no alternative. Whether there is or not, individual support rarely does harm and often helps the benefiting enterprise. But is it sustainable? Does it trigger cumulative change? In the approach proposed here, the private grouping (association, network) does the bulk of the work. Public intervention merely facilitates, provides an initial investment and works as catalyst. The entrepreneur's enthusiasm depends on whether participation promises more or better orders.

A customer-oriented approach

The collective approach can bear fruit only if participating enterprises are customer-oriented. The most successful policy interventions in developing countries have been those that establish the means by which SMEs can learn from the needs of their customers, thereby forcing them to tackle their key problems of competitiveness.

Three mechanisms can be identified by which intervention can follow a customer-oriented approach.

Joint participation in trade fairs

Particularly where clusters are dormant, trade fairs can have a catalytic effect: trade fairs provide an excellent opportunity for firms to market their produce, learn about customer needs, and eye up the competition. For small firms, however, the cost of exhibiting, particularly in international fairs, can be prohibitive. Such fairs can also be very intimidating. Joining forces helps to overcome these barriers. A shared stand allows producers to attract more attention and face the world's buyers and competitors with greater confidence. Joint participation also gives rise to more discussion and absorption of new ideas. Public agencies can support such initiatives by paying for part of the exhibition costs. The advantage of this kind of subsidy is that it is easy to administer and induces firms to be outward going. This approach takes into account that the initial 'sunk costs' of entering new markets are considerable.

Trade fairs played an important role in the development of the Sinos Valley of southern Brazil. As mentioned earlier, over the span of three decades, it has grown from a cluster of small shoemakers producing for regional markets, to being a major player in national and then international markets. Joint action in the early 1960s led to the setting up of their own regular trade fair which attracted buyers from all over the country. In the late 1960s, when first steps toward exporting were taken, groups of local shoe producers went to overseas trade fairs in the USA and Europe, organized by local business associations and subsidized by government. These groups played a vital role in connecting the existing cluster with international buyers and providing a driving force for improvement. Joint participation in trade fairs was also how ceramic producers from the Philippines launched themselves internationally: with external support they exhibited a range of products at European fairs.

UNIDO and other donor agencies have begun to help developing country manufacturers to exhibit in trade fairs. GTZ, for example, has launched Protrade, a programme which provides financial and technical assistance to groups of firms, enabling them to share a stall at major trade fairs.

Public procurement

New and challenging forms of demand need not come only from export markets. The public procurement scheme for furniture which is highlighted in Box 4.1 shows a demand-driven approach led by the public sector.

Upgrading of small suppliers

In recent years there has been a trend amongst large firms to focus on their core competence and deverticalize. Can small suppliers do the same? Only if they can raise their quality and delivery standards. A Brazilian agency launched a programme which helps them to do so. SEBRAE's 'Programme for the Upgrading of Small Suppliers' is aimed at small firms that provide specialized components or services. Its first key feature is that the large customer is the entry point for reaching the small supplier. The agency then works with both the large contractor and small suppliers. Issues covered are both technical and behavioural so that both sides see each other as partners. The second key feature of this programme is that what is discussed can be practised in existing orders. The cost of the programme is shared between SEBRAE and the participating enterprises. Public support for such a programme is more than a subsidy to the selected firms. After all, the small firms included are not only suppliers to the large customer through which the programme is organized; they also supply to other firms that will in turn benefit and also be challenged to improve their sourcing practices. Such cumulative effects help to raise the collective efficiency of local enterprises.

Next steps

Policy makers and practitioners worldwide search for new and effective ways of promoting local small firms. This article seeks to provide a torch shining in a new direction. The articles cited below can give further light. They also show that the sceptical reader, suspicious that collective efficiency is a European idea forced on to developing countries, need not worry. The main conclusions from recent research are as follows.

○ Clusters matter in developing countries, they can be found in many regions and sectors.
○ Clustering has helped small firms to overcome well-known growth constraints and sell to distant markets, nationally and abroad.
○ Where firms are not in an established cluster, networking can help them to overcome their limitations.
○ The collective efficiency idea has practical relevance, contributing to a policy approach which looks into enterprise networks and self-help institutions.
○ This approach is most promising where it focuses on the relationship between enterprises and their customers.

References

Humphrey, J. and H. Schmitz (1996) 'The Triple C approach to local industrial policy', *World Development*, Vol.24, No.12.

Nadvi, K. (1997) 'Cutting edge: collective efficiency and international competitiveness in Pakistan', *IDS Discussion Paper* No.360.

Nadvi, K. (1998) 'International competitiveness and small firm clusters – evidence from Pakistan', *Small Enterprise Development*, Vol.9 No.1, ITDG Publishing, London

Perry, M. (1995) 'Industry structures, networks and Joint Action Groups', *Regional Studies*, (Policy Review Section), Vol.29, No.2, pp.208–217, April.

Schmitz, H. (1995) 'Collective efficiency: growth path for small-scale industry', *Journal of Development Studies*, Vol.31, No.4.

Tendler, Judith (1997), Good government in the Tropics, Johns Hopkins University Press.

Tendler, J. and Amorim, M. (1996), 'Small firms and their helpers: lessons in demand', *World Development*, Vol.24, No.3.

Williams, I.F. (1996) 'Co-operating to compete', *Agricultural Science*, Nov-Dec.

About the author

Hubert Schmitz is a Professorial Fellow at the Institute of Development Studies, University of Sussex. This chapter draws together some of the key points of research carried out jointly with John Humphrey. For further details and more recent work carried out by Hubert Schmitz and his team, see www.ids.ac.uk/ids/global/cluster.html

5 Compromise and cheating in small enterprise development

THOMAS W. DICHTER

This paper was first published in June 1994.

When small enterprise practitioners 'help out' their client businesses by supplying their own labour and project resources free of charge, are they in reality compromising the self-help principle? In a thought-provoking paper, the author points to ways in which small enterprise practitioners gloss over the hidden flaws in their projects, and delude themselves about the long-term impact of their work. He forecasts a bleak outlook for the small enterprise development field unless advisers can learn from real businesses.

AS WE APPROACH THE MID-1990s, the Small Enterprise Development (SED) field could make the claim that it has come a long way. The larger world is beginning to accept that the poor are bankable, and our own ambivalence about whether we can be do-gooders and businesslike at the same time seems to be behind us. With these founding battles for legitimacy over, the field has begun to focus almost entirely on praxis. There has been a shift away from claims of SED as the latest developmental magic bullet to more open, albeit quiet, discussions of the pros and cons of technique. An example is Katherine Stearns' admirable and widely circulated paper (1991) 'The hidden beast: Delinquency in microenterprise credit programs', an excellent response to a statement made by a representative of a donor agency, which Stearns quotes in her introduction: 'The microenterprise credit field is getting too old to be dishonest about delinquency. How can everyone have a repayment rate of 98 per cent?' Indeed. As US teenagers used to say a few years ago, 'get real!'

These signs of maturity and transparency notwithstanding, the tendency to hide or ignore the beasts in development work is an enduring one. Stearns' key point is that loan delinquency should not be blamed on the borrowers: *they* are acting rationally. Rather the blame must be laid on flaws in the credit programmes themselves, flaws which lie in their philosophy, or the perception of easy money they create among their borrowers, or their poor management information systems, or the unrigorous formulae they use for measuring delinquency.

It is such flaws which 'permit' borrowers to delay or ignore their repayment obliga-tion. Of course, many small credit programmes do have these flaws and it is time we heard more about them. There are two sides to loan delinquency, however; if one is flaws in our programmes, the other is the fact that there are people out there ready to cheat, and it is not simply because of 'loss of respect' for the lending institution that they do it (Stearns, 1991: p.34).

Loan delinquency is just the tip of the iceberg, however, just as credit is only one part of our field. SED, more than other development sectors, centres around money: helping people get access to it to make it work for them to earn more of it. That alone should lead us to expect some cheating, but as we try to go beyond just credit – and many programmes are doing just that – cheating can become more complex and the tendency to compromise on fundamentals, observable in nascent form in credit programmes, seems to increase. Though these beasts constitute a broader threat than loan delinquency, we hear little about them.

This article sets out to demonstrate that surprisingly often our SED programmes, run by NGOs of the North *and* South, compromise on fundamentals and are cheated on both by outsiders and from within. As mentioned, one reason this happens is self-evident – money. Three less obvious reasons are explored here.

○ The very nature of our role as disinterested 'helpers' to enterprises may make such compromise inevitable.
○ Development, an 'industry' in its own right in the North for some time, has recently become one in the South as well. As a result the intensity of the industry's stake in internally generated jobs and resources has increased, and with it the compromises made in order to keep those jobs in existence and resources flowing.
○ We are naturally uncomfortable about acknowledging compromised projects and cheating, especially internal, because we generally do not like to admit the limits of our field, nor the fact that both the people we are trying to help and those who work with us embody all the varieties of human frailty, including the extremes of self-interest. As long as this discomfort persists, we tend to fantasize about how good we, the helpers, and they, our clients, are.

The strange role of the small enterprise developer

Whether our goal is to help get small businesses and microenterprises financed, started, scaled-up, better skilled, studied, better sourced, or more organized, we are and always will be once-removed from the enterprise itself. We exist, work, and function in an in-between realm, characterized by a vision that is larger than profit, and gentler than raw capitalism.

We are here, fundamentally, *to help* – a dubious prospect in reality, but one to which we are all sincerely committed.

Unlike other realms, in the world of business there is no historical precedent for this role of the disinterested helper. Thus the problematical aspects of our role are not ones we are much used to debating, though for many an SED practitioner at the end of a hard day, beer in hand and feet up, questions about our strange role do get asked: 'When does "our" help cross the line to taking responsibility for "them"?', 'When does our help engender their dependency?' 'How do we know when we are being told what we want to hear?' 'How can we ensure broad-based poverty alleviation through SED when business development schemes emphasizing entrepreneurship lend themselves to hijacking by those who are already better off?' 'Can we really be kind-hearted *and* tough-minded in the face of hard-luck stories that often make us cry?' And (most privately), 'Do I really believe that last hard-luck story anyway, or is someone trying to put one over on me?'

The dilemma of being here to help: of wanting to facilitate others' path to becoming small business people, almost demands that we continue to skate on the old thin ice of do-goodism. Unprotected by the mantle of religious motivation, most of us are vulnerable to deep disappointment. Thus we do not talk much about the ways we compromise our own principles, much less about the cheating that goes on. When we do acknowledge these things, we tend to think there are technical solutions. Or we think that compromising our principles or cheating do not happen often enough to worry about, as if they were simple gnawings at the edges of our profession. They are more than that, however; they are an increasing part of the reality of daily SED practice, so much so that they should lead to a fundamental questioning of the SED endeavour: is our field, with all its variety of practice, on the right track?

Case 1   A small livestock enterprise in West Africa

A West African NGO, an early proponent of the sub-sector approach to SED, helped a rural community begin a small commercial livestock operation. It held many long meetings with the community and virtually all voices were sought and heard. The NGO had a clear sense of who would take responsibility for what. The NGO's initial role was to enable access to credit. The community, for its part, guaranteed the loan and agreed to pay commercial rates of interest. Community labour went into the construction of the necessary storage sheds and preparation of the land. Shares were issued. A management committee was elected. The NGO in turn worked to instil the principles of management and good business planning; created linkages between government extension workers and this community group, and in the initial period, helped to source equipment.

These interventions were undertaken with care; steps were not skipped. Furthermore, expectations were unusually realistic, so much so that one of the 'what if' scenarios in the final business plan's sensitivity analysis turned out to be uncannily accurate. In the first six months of operation, bad weather caused a higher than normal disease rate among the livestock, and resources had to be diverted to containing it. Income was seriously delayed. Cash flow suffered. While everyone was disappointed, however, no one was surprised. In short, the project was a model of a mature approach to SED at the community level; a tribute to project staff and their accumulated years of experience.

The NGO's SED adviser responsible for this particular enterprise visited the site one day a week for the first year. A native of the region, he spoke the language, and had the knack of communicating business concepts clearly. Moreover he had been to several SED training workshops, in which he had absorbed some important philosophical and practical lessons. One of these was the notion of 'teaching rather than doing'.

He had seen that his task was not to run the business, but to help others become business people. He had thought that the good teacher helps the student to think through her lessons, raising questions the student may not have thought about, playing devil's advocate, being tough on her just when she may be self-satisfied, praising her when she is overly discouraged. The SED adviser knew accordingly how much easier it is simply to do than to teach, to say to the student: 'See, here is the answer, copy it and memorize it'.

Some months after livestock production had got back to where it 'should have been', the SED adviser arrived for his weekly visit. The enterprise's own vehicle had broken down. He was asked by the manager to take a load of animal skins into the market and, since the enterprise's vehicle would probably be out of service for several weeks, to bring back some needed supplies from the capital on his next visit. The SED adviser agreed.

By the time the project was evaluated by its major donor 18 months later, the SED adviser had repeated this service very often, and added others. In looking at the books, the outside evaluators had seen a good balance sheet. However, when they visited the project and noted that the SED adviser had a load of animal feed in his truck, they asked whether he had costed his 'service' in the balance sheet. When he said he had not, he was politely criticized by the evaluators. He responded that he could understand their point, indeed he explained how he had often thought about the difference between being a teacher and being part of the business. Then he added with some agitation: 'Come on, these are poor people, are we not here to help? How ridiculous to hold up the progress of the project when there is a vehicle at my disposal. We have to be realistic, after all, this is Africa. There is no such thing as methodological purity when you are "on the ground". Compromises are inevitable, indeed isn't this what we mean by flexibility in development?'

There is no denouement in this story. The project continued for several years, with the adviser continuing his visits. It showed a consistent though small profit. A small dividend was paid on the shares in the second year, though none in the third. The initial loan from the local bank was paid back. The NGO had done its job, and after a fourth year of monitoring (once per quarter), it withdrew entirely. Three years later, in 1993, there was no trace of the project, the enterprise, or the livestock.

We will suspend the question of whether this project was a success or a failure, although with sustainability much in our thoughts these days it is a legitimate question. Rather, the concern is whether or not it is important that the SED adviser compromised on a fundamental principle. Do we not also make such compromises? And if they cannot realistically be avoided, how much of a difference does it really make?

Case 2 A dried-fruit venture in South Asia

In a mountainous area of South Asia, an indigenous rural development NGO is working on an appropriate technology for the uniform sun-drying of local fruits. As the technology improves, so does product quality. Marketing tests in a city south of the area indicate high potential demand, even export possibilities. Local farmers, however, who long ago organized into community associations (one of the goals of which is generating income for the community), are not terribly keen on keeping up product quality, and no matter how much the project's extension workers try to get the message across that high quality will produce high profits, farmers have other concerns, other products to sell, and increasingly, other sources of income.

By the seventh year of the programme, the sunk costs of the experiments in fruit-drying and the level of frustration about most local farmers' lack of interest in improving their product were such that it was decided to set up a local marketing association aimed only at those growers who were committed to maintaining quality control. This decision involved an ideological compromise for some of the staff, committed as they were to the idea that no one was to get rich at the expense of others, or to become richer faster than others.

Ghazi Din, one of the extension staff with specific responsibility for developing marketable products, was assigned the task of getting this marketing organization started. Ghazi Din is a member of the area's dominant tribe, university-educated and speaking three languages, including English. Personable, kind, and committed to the development of his region, his work with the NGO was his first post-degree job. Ghazi Din's boss made it known that this marketing association must be a success, since donors were watching. Ghazi Din therefore made this assignment his sole priority and worked tirelessly on it for months. Using a small 'research budget' he rented warehouse space in the local town, and hired a watchman. Then he helped form an executive committee of the three most active and also the largest of the fruit growers. An account was opened at a local bank owned by prominent members of Ghazi's tribe.

Ghazi then travelled to the capital city 400 miles away, where the main exporters of agricultural products are. There he made contact with a company interested in sun-dried fruit and a deal was made.

On his return, Ghazi visited the growers to tell them that they had a contract. The growers quickly realized that their own supply would not come close to meeting the order and so decided to approach neighbouring growers and buy from them. Transport was going to be a problem, so Ghazi offered to use the NGO vehicle assigned to him to gather up the product in burlap bags and bring it to the warehouse. For three weeks, Ghazi and his driver were on the roads bringing tons of fruit to the central warehouse.

The fruit, however, was not of high quality because Ghazi had undertaken a contract so large that the primary growers could not supply it. Moreover, because the contract had a time limit, and because the season was now over, everything had been done in such a rush that Ghazi neglected to set up the books for the association. The shares sold to members had been marked in pencil in a black notebook that Ghazi carried, as had been other of the association's transactions.

Six months later, an evaluation team came around to look at this particular operation. The 'account books', still kept in pencil in Ghazi's notebook, were examined and Ghazi was questioned about certain numbers that did not add up. Ghazi explained that some spare purchases had been pledged but not yet paid for. Yet the assets reflected these as real. It also turned out that Ghazi and his cousin had bought shares in the association, and that Ghazi had lent money from the Association's bank account to two of the richest of the growers, at no interest, with no term limit. These loans were not recorded in the black book. He was not concerned about this, however, because, as he said to the evaluators, these men were relatives of his and he trusted them.

The evaluators *were* concerned, however, and decided to pursue further the nature of the association. In the skimpy files, they saw that Ghazi had been in contact with a number of exporters and in two cases, negotiations were underway for shipments at prices that struck the evaluators as well below market price. They sat down with Ghazi and asked him how he had calculated these prices. He replied that he had simply taken the cash outlays that he needed to make from supply point to delivery and added 10 per cent for the profit. It was clear that Ghazi had not counted his own time, the time of his driver, or the use of the NGO programme vehicle. Nor had he counted the cost of renting the warehouse or hiring the guard, as these costs had also been paid for out of the NGO 'research' budget.

The evaluators asked to go out to the field and talk to the executive committee, the head of which, a distant cousin of Ghazi, also owns a local hotel. He was effusive about the help that Ghazi had been giving the association, and praised Ghazi's devotion to getting the association up and running and seeing to it that the first orders were filled.

He added that Ghazi's hard work had permitted him and his colleagues to pay full attention to their other businesses.

The evaluators reminded Ghazi Din that his job was not to make deals on behalf of the association, nor to do the work of the association's members. Ghazi Din said that he understood this, but what could he do? The leaders of the association were too busy with other things, and that's why they had left the handling of these things to him.

What do we have here? This fully indigenous 'Southern' NGO is exactly what 'Northern' NGOs say they want. It is well run by many accounts, and international donors are quite happy with it, but the project's small enterprise arm has compromised the principle of an arms-length relationship with the assisted enterprise. It has compromised its own values by allowing itself to serve the interests of the best-off farmers in the area, who see an opportunity. And Ghazi Din had aided this process by, in effect, lending the NGO as a full partner on the cost side of the association's business, while profit sharing was not part of the deal, except for himself. However Ghazi Din, while he cheated, especially in lending money to friends from the marketing association's account, is no crook. Nor was he entirely naive. In the abstract he understood the notion of 'conflict of interest'. Ghazi was acting, by his own account, appropriately opportunistically, and in the interests of his community, as he saw it. Indeed one could argue that he was being entrepreneurial in starting a business using the resources of his employer. Isn't the local NGO after all a local resource institution? Perhaps for Ghazi Din, his job with the NGO is just that, something that fulfils both his own and others' needs.

One of the evaluators, both stymied and bemused by Ghazi's attitude, later asked Ghazi Din why, given his contacts, he had not just quit the NGO and gone into a straight business partnership with the other growers. The evaluator suggested that there is a world of difference between starting a business while being an employee of the NGO, and quitting the NGO to start a business on his own. Ghazi Din saw this. But he had been afraid, he said. What if things did not work out OK? Then he would have lost his money and, more important, his secure job with one of the few large employers in the region, would be gone. It was just too risky.

Case 3 The commercial loan programme on the island of Caribea

The Febreel Beach Community Bank had been set up in 1984 in order to provide small loans to women. Febreel Beach lies on the south coast, the most impoverished part of Caribea island. Set up on the solidarity group principle, it had a record of being quite tightly run. This in turn attracted additional donor funding, and as the International Adam Smith Plan (the USA-based sponsoring NGO which was channelling the donor funds to Febreel Beach) wished to 'scale up', it began to think about larger loans for medium-scale businesses, run by graduates of its earlier programme. The ground rules for the new Febreel Beach commercial loan programme were that the recipient would have prior experience, that a community member would vouch for her, and that the loan would be for one year, at 16 per cent.

While the first impression the evaluators got was that the Febreel Beach CLP had been conceived of rationally, the fact was that it arose out of several needs, one of which was to get more money out of the donor. It also evolved in a very *ad hoc* manner, both in terms of process and implementation.

For example, in the project proposal that Adam Smith presented to its main donor, the Febreel Beach CLP was presented as a demand-driven programme, filling a gap in the local credit market. This assertion depended on being able to say that amounts in the $500 to $2500 range were not available from informal or formal sources. However, one of the evaluators knew of a survey of local enterprises which indicated that amounts in this range, and even higher, *were* regularly sourced from friends and family at reasonable rates. While the Adam Smith analysts had long held that a lack of credit was the major constraint to enterprise growth in the Febreel Beach area, the evaluators began to think that Adam Smith's real rationale for the CLP was an over-supply of credit funds from its donor.

The data the evaluators examined and the discoveries they made in their own field work suggested not only that the Febreel Beach CLP was very sloppily managed, but that the outright cheating that took place was led by local elites in two different communities, and that this was known to the directors of Febreel Beach. The evaluators also showed that many of the borrowers had previous borrowing experience, and may well have been attracted to the CLP because the transaction cost was astoundingly low. When procedures were analysed, it became apparent how easy it was to walk in to Febreel Beach, slap down a one-page loan application, and walk out with 5000 to 20 000 LCUs (Local Currency Units). Of the application forms reviewed, 5 per cent had no description of the proposed activity on them; and 9 per cent had no revenue stamps on the promissory notes (required by Caribea law). Furthermore, the instructions to the officers who were charged with the task of vetting the loans, were extraordinarily perfunctory. The evaluators concluded: 'It is no wonder that 500 000 LUCs passed through the door so quickly!'

When the evaluators brought some of their findings to the attention of Febreel Beach's board of directors, they were surprised that two board members dismissed these as of little importance since it was clear to them that returns to the borrowers had ranged from 25 per cent to 1000 per cent per annum, and therefore that the CLP had been successful in fostering wealth in the village economy, which was after all Adam Smith's main objective. The evaluators pointed out that the high end of this range was dominated by loans to shopkeepers (43 per cent of the CLP portfolio), whereas it was Adam Smith's intention to invest in local productive enterprises, as opposed to retail trade. The wealth generated by these shopkeepers was neither productive nor local since all the wholesalers from whom they had to buy their stock were located in Boomtown on the other end of the island.

Are compromise and cheating fatal tendencies?

The above stories are true – names and places have been fictionalized, since presumably none of the NGOs involved wants to be identified. What is important is that these are not exceptional accounts: I believe the traps described in the case examples will be recognized by many with SED field experience.

As these accounts show, the disinterested helping role in business is at best problematic and at worst contradictory. The SED adviser who carried the enterprise's supplies in the NGO truck, Ghazi Din who ran the business of the dried fruit marketing association on behalf of local bigwigs, and the International Adam Smith Plan,

wanted for the most part to help. Too stringent an adherence to SED principles, especially the idea that people should manage their own affairs and not be sheltered from
the real world, or tight financial controls, struck these projects or their advisers as
short-sighted, or unkind. 'After all', their actions seem to be saying, 'why not get the
job done?' The real job is not done, however; merely glossed over and kept going long
enough to fulfil a donor's timetable or pass an evaluation with a gentle slap on the
wrist.

There may be examples in the world of real capitalism where marriages between
social goals and profit are successful, but the ones I know of (South Shore Bank in
Chicago comes to mind) are businesses run by primary actors with a real financial
interest in outcomes, and where there are no secondary actors. I know of no long-term
successes, however, where the marriage is between those who are disinterested helpers
and those who actually run a business. Somehow the do-goodism on the part of the secondary actors gets in the way of the marketplace. In short, either we own and operate
the enterprises ourselves, or we let them (the small enterprises we wish to help) do it
on their own, without subsidy and without our direct assistance.

'But what's wrong with subsidies anyway', one could argue. 'There is evidence that
business transformation and growth take place in a variety of culturally different ways;
there is no such thing as a pure up-from-the-bottom route where success came about
entirely through the entrepreneur's own will and gumption. Shouldn't the Third World
entrepreneur enjoy the same lucky breaks as the First World one? Why should she be
subjected to tougher standards when she is in a tougher environment to begin with?
Shouldn't it be the other way around? Why not then, give them a break?' Well, we
could if we were a bank or a government. In those cases we'd have to bear the long-
term consequences of such a 'break'; but being enterprise helpers with no financial
stake in the enterprises we help, 'giving them a break' risks getting us even further
away from reality.

The obstacle of organizational imperatives

The problem of our helper role has become exacerbated by the rise of SED as an industry in its own right. The more we in the North and the more our colleagues in the South
have been riding the wave of donor interest in SED, the more we have become victims
of the imperatives that come with being an industry. In such an industry we must, in
order to survive, compete with each other to get donor attention, donor grants and
donor contracts. The more we do that, the more we are forced to follow some if not all
of their bureaucratic imperatives. Inevitably, we take on staff, we develop systems and
procedures, we hold more meetings and circulate memos. We too become bureaucratic.
We too enter a world where writing the proposal and bidding for work can take up
almost as much time and energy as the eventual work itself. Then, once launched, our
projects are subject to constant review and evaluation. No sooner has one evaluation
been completed than another team is preparing to arrive.

The cycle continues, all in the good name of accountability. The stakes, and the
focus in all of this, can imperceptibly shift to our own jobs and our own organizational
survival. And in the South, where the development industry (and its SED sub-set) has
grown phenomenally in the past decade, the stakes are closer to home. A job in such an

NGO for a young local graduate means the difference between stagnation on the border lines of poverty and full-blooded success in his world.

These increasingly internal stakes in our industry get in the way of our goal – helping enterprises become viable businesses. For a business nowadays, even at the small scale, things are moving fast. Integration, internationalism, information, innovation and flexibility, are increasingly the challenge for *all* businesses at the end of the twentieth century. As the SED field becomes an industry, the helpers become too slow for the world we are trying to help. By the time we have finished studying a particular sub-sector and wringing it dry of possibilities, the big world of international commerce and trade has cut some of our basic assumptions out from under us. The real world of business has moved on, while we have not, because it has to do so for survival, and we, plain and simply, do not.

This is not to say that business acts in a totally free market: we know things are much more complex than that. The real world of business is by and large a world where primary actors are in charge, however, and it is our once-removed role which is incompatible here. In fact it may be that as business gets more and more innovative and fast on its feet, it may be better suited to undertake social goals directly than we in SED are (see, for example, Avishai, 1994).

The obstacles to seeing reality clearly

Finally, there is a tendency to fantasize about our work and our clients. A human tendency which we see in virtually every industry and every sector of life, in ours, it is more dangerous because there is little to puncture it. We in the SED industry have less stark reality to face than such companies. We do not have a bottom line beyond which we cannot go, nor a time beyond which it is 'too late'. We seem to have, always, more time.

Nor do those of us who are field practitioners get much reality therapy from our donors. The donor too does not want to entertain the possibility that the entire effort may be miscast; there is also the oft-lamented fact that the donor needs to get money out of the door. So when there are problems, both donor and practitioner prefer to see them as isolated, as manageable, as practical matters of tinkering that any field of endeavour may face. On the other side, we have expectations of the recipient. Because the SED business deals in tangible and attractive resources, such as money, when evaluators speak to the clients of the SED organization, the 'customer' has every reason to suggest to the evaluator that he or she is very satisfied with the 'product', and indeed could use more of it. Thus the fantasy of self-help is fed.

It is true that 'everyone does these things', but there may be reasons why we should be different. A privately held company can live in illusion, can hide its numbers, and fool itself all it wants to. It does not need to tell anyone about how it does its business. If it is dishonest, it may get away with it. If it fails because of its dishonesty or because its illusions are too far from reality, well, it and its employees will bear the consequences. Should not our profession, a helping profession, be different? Not because we are more moral – we are clearly not – nor because we are more righteous; but because our mandate is fundamentally different. Our purpose, especially that of the NGOs, less so that of the bilateral donors, is to be disinterested helpers.

But can we be honest and transparent to our donors and to our ultimate clientele?

For we are simply not in a position to make claims of enduring success in SED and are not likely ever to be. We are not in a position to promise anyone anything except an honest effort to try to solve problems. Our field, given the limitations outlined in this article, can in the end only be experimental. But can we say that openly in the present climate? If we talk about self-help and then offer our help under the table, are we not cheating on our clientele's eventual dignity? If we say we have the guru of popular participation guiding us, and are thus the instruments of the people's will, when all the while the people are telling us what we want to hear, are they not in collusion with us in our delusion? Given the realities of our role and our industry can we avoid these and similar tendencies? I think not.

Can anything be done?

Can better monitoring make a difference? In the accounts cited in this article, the monitoring of staff, tighter controls, and more general oversight might have avoided the compromises and the cheating. But control and oversight are contrary to the principles of institutional development in our field. More practically, the reality is that oversight, control and monitoring will probably have their own negative consequences by destroying confidence and morale. Finally, monitoring costs money, and at some point the cost-effectiveness of the whole network of SED organizations has to come into the calculus.

In conclusion, we have to question the entire direction the Small Enterprise Development field is taking. I believe that direct action to assist microenterprises and small businesses will show itself increasingly to be a dead end. I do not think the characteristics of our industry discussed in this article are going to change soon. It is unrealistic to say 'stop being the way you are', or 'go home', or 'go out of business voluntarily'. There is too much at stake. Therefore, if we proceed from the realities of our industry and accept them for what they are, there may be some hope (and it will be small) in a shift in emphasis. There are two possibilities.

First, I believe it would make sense either for some of the organizations in the SED field to begin doing business themselves rather than trying to help others do it, or to enter into alliances with real established businesses and develop small enterprises from within their structure and with the self-seeking motives of that particular business (just as some large companies today are teaching reading and maths to their workers so they will be more productive). A shift of this kind of course means a change in our status from teachers to doers. Counter-intuitive as it may be, such a change may lead to more effective and lasting enterprise development.

Second, for the bulk of our industry that is not going to take up the latter challenge, a shift from direct action to indirect is warranted – particularly policy work and services for the benefit of small businesses and microenterprises. The case for policy work has by now been accepted in the field in general; but the SED field has not really taken up services, particularly information services, in part because the service approach is unsexy and seems too unspecific. There *is* a need for services, however latent, in many sub-sectors. As the direct value of information becomes apparent to businesses, the need will become explicit and demand is likely to grow. Services in technical areas (accounting, business planning, technology development, equipment sourcing, and general advisory services, and so on) exist now and are not new. Whether tried by NGOs or governments, they have had low status because they have often been given away. That would change if these services were set up on a sub-sector-specific basis, to be paid for by the enterprises that use them in a given industry.

These two possibilities are very modest proposals; but at the short-term cost of a wrenching shift in status, and an SED field significantly reduced in size and importance, they may serve to pre-empt tendencies which could be fatal in the long run.

References

Avishai, Bernard (1994) 'What is business's social compact?' *Harvard Business Review*, January–February.

Stearns, Katherine (1991) 'The hidden beast: Delinquency in microenterprise credit programs', Document 5 in Discussion Paper Series, ACCION International. Cambridge, MA.

About the author

Thomas Dichter is a small enterprise consultant.

6 Towards success: impact and sustainability in the FIT programme

JIM TANBURN

This paper was first published in March 1996.

The FIT programme is working to strengthen local capacity for action research, specifically in the field of non-financial services for micro- and small-scale enterprises (MSEs). High priority is being placed on the development of services which can be self-sustaining in the long term. If the services are self-sustaining, it is argued, then they are presumably in demand by the beneficiaries. They could also achieve considerable outreach in a cost-effective way, if they can be copied by others.

At the same time, monitoring the impact of those services has been of great importance to both FIT and its partners, to understand what is actually happening, and in particular, to ensure that the ultimate effects have indeed been beneficial, for example in the creation of high-quality opportunities for employment. This article gives a brief description of the FIT programme; it then considers the demands of MSEs for services, and the impact achieved by some pilot activities to meet those demands. The needs of the end-users of MSE products, and the situation for the partner organizations, are also discussed. Finally, conclusions are drawn about demand, impact monitoring and the design of future activities.

THE FIT PROGRAMME is a collaborative technical assistance programme between the International Labour Organization (ILO) and TOOL (the Dutch NGO); the programme is funded by the Netherlands Government. FIT aims to strengthen local capacity for the development of innovative 'mechanisms', through which non-financial services can be provided sustainably to MSEs. Local partner organizations, including NGOs and groups of MSEs, are implementing a portfolio of action research activities, in close collaboration with FIT. FIT is currently working in Ghana and Kenya, but this article focuses on FIT's experiences in Kenya, since the author has been working most closely with those activities. In both countries, FIT is working to establish national networks, for the dissemination of the results of pilot activities. It is expected that through the exchange of ideas and information, new action research initiatives will result.

'FIT' stands for 'Farm Implements and Tools', since FIT is taking a sub-sectoral approach, focusing on the capacity to meet the needs of MSEs in the metalworking and food-processing sub-sectors. By enhancing the ability of metalworkers to supply appropriate equipment to farmers, it is expected that agricultural capacity will be boosted. Similarly, by assisting food processors (and particularly women), it is expected that the demand for agricultural produce will rise, stimulating farmers to increase agricultural output. While new approaches are introduced in these two sub-sectors, it is also expected that the lessons learned will also be relevant to MSEs and organizations working in other sub-sectors.

The demand by MSEs for services

MSEs often compete in saturated markets, lowering their prices to gain sales, to the point where profitability is very low. Working conditions may be hazardous, and product quality is generally poor, meaning that customers are not happy with their purchases. The response by development practitioners to this has often been to provide support services which are to some extent scaled-down versions of services designed originally for larger companies. While helpful to the MSEs that benefit, such services will probably always require some external subsidy, and their outreach is therefore limited by the size of the subsidy available.

Meanwhile, the private sector is already providing almost all of the services that MSEs need, such as the provision of raw materials, commercial information and distribution channels, in self-sustaining ways; could these ways be enhanced and made more effective, possibly without the long-term involvement of any of the traditional MSE support institutions? Could new services be provided, which MSEs already want, but have no access to, at present? These questions already imply some important indicators of success:

○ the willingness of MSEs or other private sector participants to pay part or all of the costs of the service
○ the willingness of MSEs or others to continue participation after external input has come to an end
○ the interest of other MSEs to participate, or to initiate similar activities.

One such service, which is currently not available in Kenya, is the opportunity to visit other enterprises, elsewhere in the country, and even in neighbouring countries. MSEs would like to be able to visit other MSEs, a facility referred to as 'exchange visits' by FIT; they are also interested in visiting larger enterprises, dubbed 'host visits'. Such visits are sufficiently attractive that MSEs may be willing to pay all of the direct costs, particularly once the new concept has been demonstrated. Thus, in a collaboration with PRIDE (Promotion of Rural Initiatives and Development Enterprises), visiting MSEs paid for about half of the direct costs of the first visit (the total direct costs being about $10 per day). After the visit, 85 per cent said that they would pay more next time, covering all of the direct costs, if required.

Similarly, a collaboration with KIC-K (Kisumu Innovation Centre, Kenya) facilitated exchange visits by MSEs from Kisumu to others in Nairobi; the visiting MSEs again paid half of the direct costs. Subsequently, MSEs near the ones which had made the visits saw the effects on the businesses of their neighbours, and organized their own exchange visits, to Eldoret and Kakamega, without any outside input at all. This indicates the delicacy of the process whereby initial demand for a new service is first registered: MSEs are unlikely to ask for (or pay for) a service until they become aware of it as an interesting possibility.

The format of the service also seems to have a major influence on the willingness of MSEs to pay for all of the direct costs. For example, no subsidy is needed where MSEs can form their own group for the visit, even when the visit is to a neighbouring country (and is therefore more expensive). In contrast, some subsidy may be required, if entrepreneurs are invited to make visits to new places on their own (Craig and Oneko, 1995, p.22).

It is not always evident why MSEs are asking for a particular service. PRIDE noted that its clients were keen to visit other enterprises, but had difficulty in defining what the objective of such visits would be, for the individual enterprise. PRIDE therefore collaborated with FIT to mount a workshop, the aim of which was to define the objectives for future enterprise visits. The event brought together PRIDE clients from five different branches around Kenya; what emerged was a strong desire on the part of MSEs to broaden their horizons, and specifically to develop networks of business connections. It also became very clear that the participating MSEs had much to teach other, and indeed the workshop became a service in itself, subsequently referred to as a 'brokering workshop'; participants expressed a willingness to pay for at least part of the costs of future workshops.

Another demand for MSEs is for facilitation of more direct contact with the people who ultimately use their products. One format now implemented in Embu and Kisumu has involved the facilitation of a sequence of meetings and exhibitions between groups of MSE metalworkers and groups of farmers, in a process of 'participatory technology development' (PTD). The farmers were initially more enthusiastic than the metalworkers about this facility, paying for their own transport, even from quite remote locations. The MSEs were initially more reluctant, even though participation cost them less, perhaps because they expected (rightly) that much of the initial feedback about the quality of their products might be negative. After this hurdle had been overcome, however, the MSEs were very keen to continue the meetings, both to learn from their customers, and to market their products to them.

A related service in demand by MSEs has been help in identifying new markets for their products. It has become apparent to some that they have taken a passive approach to market research, often diversifying only after a customer has taken the initiative to ask them to make a new type of product. In a methodology dubbed 'rapid market appraisal' (RMA), FIT has provided training for MSEs in how to carry out market research (Burger and Haan, 1995). Participants in that course have subsequently trained other MSEs.

Thus, there is evidence that non-financial services can be provided to MSEs, in ways which they perceive to be meeting their immediate needs; they are therefore committed to continue the service in some form, albeit not necessarily the original one. But what impact has been achieved by the provision of these services? The following sections outline the lessons learned in this area, considering both quantitative and qualitative aspects.

Quantitative impact on MSEs of the services provided

Monitoring the impact of pilot activities is incorporated into the activity itself, so that all involved can know what progress is being achieved. At the same time, it has proved valuable to commission local consultants to evaluate the impact of individual activities; these commissions, often collecting much of the quantitative data, aim to strengthen local capacity in external evaluation. The methodological experiences gained in this way have been presented as guidelines, which include sample questionnaires for the various stakeholders in the activity (Wesselink, 1995). In practice, consultants have used these guidelines as a basis for their work, adapting them to the individual service being evaluated.

One such evaluation, of the enterprise visits facilitated by PRIDE/FIT, found that participating MSEs had each hired an additional three employees, on average. Of those interviewed, 80 per cent felt that their profits had increased by more than 45 per cent, but this was rather a subjective measure, since the MSEs had not kept accurate records. Similarly, an evaluation of the brokering workshop with PRIDE found that, on average, participating MSEs were now employing an additional 0.4 paid employees; relating this to the total cost of the workshop of $89 per participant might indicate a cost per job created of $225. This compares reasonably with the range reported by other projects of $25–$5500 (Harper, 1995). However, it is not possible to validate it totally, since there was no control group; PRIDE did not have sufficient non-participating clients in the FIT sub-sectors.

An evaluation immediately after the seven-month PTD sequence with KIC-K in Kisumu found that MSEs had made and sold agriculture-related equipment, to the new designs developed during the PTD sequence, worth an average of $700 per MSE. This may be related to the only input by FIT which could not currently be borne by the participants locally, namely the assistance to purchase raw materials with which to make prototypes.

Most MSEs felt initially that, despite receiving high-quality information on market potential from the farmers, the purchase of raw materials for the construction of prototypes was too risky for them. FIT therefore provided $70 per participant, and the MSEs decided to form their own group, subsequently investing a further $100 of their own funds, on average; in addition, they contributed their time for design, development and manufacture of the prototypes. Thus, the provision of a small initial amount by FIT persuaded the MSEs to invest more, from their own resources; ways should now be explored to make this part of the methodology sustainable, perhaps by offering 'loans for innovation', which could further enhance the group dynamics.

In general, however, FIT evaluators have not placed great emphasis on the quantitative data; participants often seem vague about the financial performance of their business, and a preference for working only with those MSEs which do keep records would presumably exclude the poorer (and less literate) entrepreneurs. There may be data which would be more easily memorable by the MSE, such as working schedules and wage payments, which could subsequently be translated into more reliable income and employment data (Haggblade, 1992); FIT has now drafted a manual to incorporate such ideas. It is expected that the manual can now be tested in a future evaluation.

Furthermore, the timescale of the evaluation is often not that of the local economy; MSEs expect a lag of up to three years between the time when a farmer notes the availability of an improved plough (for example) and the time by which he has saved sufficient funds with which to purchase it. In addition, the MSE metalworker will probably need some time, even when in good communication with his customers, to develop appropriate implements; in Machakos District, for example, the ox-drawn plough has evolved over a period of about 70 years, passing through many design iterations to reach its current form (Mortimore and Wellard, 1991, pp.23–5). Thus, it can be argued that any additional sales by participating MSEs during the first seven months after the start of an activity constitute a significant achievement.

Many FIT evaluators have noted a wide variation in impact between different MSEs; some MSE participants have used the experience gained during the pilot activity to expand their business and product range very substantially; others, however, are still hoping for more assistance, before they can realize such benefits. A further obstacle has proved to be the identification of a suitable control group to isolate the effects of other factors, such as liberalization and seasonality; it is hoped that an approach using the level of economic activity locally as the 'control' (Haggblade, 1992) can also be tried by FIT in a future evaluation.

Thus, while FIT will continue to collect quantitative data, they do at times seem only to prove that pilot activities have not harmed participating MSEs. In the long term, quantitative indicators such as outreach, cost-effectiveness and financial sustainability may become important. In the short term, however, it may be concluded that qualitative indicators are probably the most interesting ones to investigate, and these are discussed below.

Qualitative impact on MSEs of the services provided

Qualitative aspects covered during monitoring have essentially included any change in business practice which could be attributed directly to the provision of the new service. Such changes might include improvements in the procurement of raw materials and other inputs, in management or technical skills, and in marketing strategies; they might also include the adoption of new technologies or product designs, or access to new markets. Essentially, the evaluation process required some alertness on the part of the interviewer; however, it was also much easier to attribute a specific change to a specific activity, and the qualitative benefits were often the ones which were perceived by the MSE to be the most important ones. Illustrations of the qualitative benefits could be given at length for each pilot activity, but there is space in this chapter only for some conclusions about the trends.

In general, MSEs that had participated in visits to other enterprises (other MSEs, or larger enterprises) were found to have benefited particularly in the following ways:

○ improved technical skills, and knowledge about improved equipment (having seen them in operation during the visit, many MSEs purchased new tools, such as scales, a thermometer, an improved stove, etc.)
○ improved linkages with suppliers (particularly for the supply of spare parts and raw materials)
○ ideas for new or improved products (food processing entrepreneurs, in particular, learned many new recipes and techniques of food preparation)
○ improved management skills, particularly in customer relations, record keeping and employee relations.

After noting the value of the brokering workshop to participants, FIT sponsored a small evaluation of the impact of other meetings, where MSEs from different locations had had the opportunity to exchange business information informally among themselves. For example, some NGOs bring their clients together from time to time, to give particular training, or to present prizes to the best clients. This study found that MSEs that participated in these group fora (including the brokering workshop) reported the following, particular benefits:

○ new product designs (metalworkers learned about new designs for mills, stoves, hoes and water heaters, for example)
○ feelings of increased self-confidence, ability and recognition (particularly appreciated by women entrepreneurs, for example when dealing with male customers, suppliers and employees)
○ improved management skills, most particularly in the efficient organization of production, but also in the skills listed above
○ improved linkages with existing and new markets.

It is possible that the differences outlined above between the two formats (visits vs. fora) are in some cases a function of the relatively small sample sizes; larger samples may be needed to draw definitive conclusions about the nature of the potential benefits inherent in each mechanism. Nonetheless, these findings do show that MSEs take every opportunity offered to them to develop their skills and ideas, if the opportunity is in a format to which they can relate. A further illustration of this was provided by a FIT evaluation of the MSE shows in Kenya; this evaluation found that nearly half of the participants had gained new product ideas while at the show, which they had subsequently used in their business (Esbin, 1994, p.27).

Similarly, the PTD experiences in Embu and Kisumu showed that MSE metalworkers can indeed respond to the needs of their customers, by developing new or improved products. Thus, the range and quality of their products were enhanced, and additional sales resulted. After the course in RMA, the proportion of MSEs that were actively marketing their products increased by 32 per cent; in addition, 27 per cent of the participants introduced new, improved products as a direct result of improved communication with their customers.

In general, MSEs often described the pilot activity as 'an eye-opener'; it seemed to enable them to move from traditional ways of doing business, to a more modern approach. For example, the traditional marketing strategy was described during one evaluation as 'you either buy or leave'; once the benefits of adopting more modern business methods have been demonstrated, MSEs seldom look back.

However, the demand by MSEs for services is ultimately financed by sales to their customers, and it is the demand and perceptions of these customers which are therefore the origin of all sustainable activities with MSEs. Furthermore, improving the products and services provided by MSEs can generate important benefits for their customers; in FIT's case, the benefits accruing through such linkages are an integral part of the project design. This aspect is therefore considered in the following sections.

The demand for improvements, from the end-users of MSE products

As mentioned earlier, the end-users of MSE products (smallholder farmers, in this case) have demonstrated their interest in providing feedback to MSEs about their products, to the extent that they will pay their own transportation costs, to participate in meetings with MSEs. At one rural meeting where improved implements were displayed by MSEs from Embu, 300 farmers attended; in both parts of Kenya where such meetings were initiated (Embu and Kisumu), they have continued in the subsequent months, without further input from FIT. The additional sales achieved by the MSEs in Kisumu as a result have already been referred to. These indicators show that end-users are very interested in the process, and respond to apparent improvements; however, it is also important to consider the impact of their operations on the end-users of the improved MSE products.

Ideally, FIT would monitor and quantify increases in agricultural productivity, as a result of pilot activities. Since it is not clear who will choose to purchase the improved implements, however, the final end-users cannot be predicted before the start of the activity. Thus, no baseline data can be collected for later comparison. Add to this some large swings in climatic conditions, and recent liberalizations in important areas, such as the transportation of maize, and the quantification of impact on the farmer as end-user becomes apparently impossible – at least within the time-frame of the project as it currently stands.

Nonetheless, the opinion and experience of the end-user can still be sought, and representative samples have therefore been traced and interviewed. This is inevitably costly, since it can involve substantial transport costs. Furthermore, it may be time-consuming, when end-users are scattered in remote, rural locations; it has become apparent that MSE products are distributed through wide-ranging networks of traders (Ngau, 1995; Waithaka, 1995).

In general, the end-users' opinion of the improved implement has been very positive, and the farmers are happy that it represents an improvement on what was available before. For example, the recent mid-term evaluation of FIT found, in Embu, that neighbouring farmers had seen the new tools in use, and had purchased them also from the metalworkworkers who had developed them. Not all of the feedback from end-users has been so positive, however. In some cases, the product which had been 'improved' through PTD or RMA was found not to be very durable, and the customer was therefore quite unhappy. This has raised the issue of tool testing: it seems that MSEs can respond to the needs of the customers for improved technologies, but without achieving 100 per cent success, in the first iteration of development. Options such as product guarantees, and the testing of prototypes in ways which can be self-sustaining, should now be explored.

At the same time, it may be questioned whether a process of technological improvement, which will ultimately rely on local resources, can be expected to satisfy every customer, all of the time. Innovation has historically been a process of success and failure, with entrepreneurs building on the lessons which they have learned from their mistakes. It may also be observed that MSEs tend to appeal to their customers, on the basis that their products are cheaper than the competition; thus, to some extent, the customers should expect to get what they are willing to pay for.

It may also be relevant to wonder whether the end-user has enjoyed qualitative benefits as a result of purchasing improved products; for example, have farmers been able to adopt new agricultural practices as a result of improved access to equipment? In practice, this has apparently not yet occurred. As with tool testing, the MSE does not generally have the resources to demonstrate the application of new or improved tools in any detail. Where farmers felt that the tools should enable them to adopt new practices,

they tended to be waiting for further demonstration and adaptation, perhaps by extension officers. Again, FIT is interested in exploring ways in which new tools could be
demonstrated, sustainably, so that their potential can be fully realized.

Since the majority of smallholder farmers and food processors in Kenya are
women, it is also particularly important to consider the involvement of women in the
process. In Kenya (and apparently also in Ghana, where participatory technology
development sequences are currently running), many of the farmers participating in
meetings with MSEs were men, even when women farmers had been specifically and
individually invited. This trend was most apparent when the meeting was advertised
as relating to tools, probably since the man in a couple is generally the one responsible for tool purchase; this tends to be the case, even for tools which will subsequently
be used by women (e.g. weeding tools). Some steps have already been taken to
address this situation; at PTD shows where improved tools have been judged by a
panel of farmers, for example, FIT has ensured that 50 per cent of the judges were
women farmers. Further work is needed to involve women farmers and food processors more in the process of developing appropriate equipment.

The providers of support services

The experiences outlined above indicate that local organizations can develop innovative mechanisms for providing non-financial services to MSEs, in ways which could
become self-sustaining. Through such experiences, it is expected that this capacity is
being strengthened, and one indicator of that would be the ability of local partners to
replicate and expand on the pilot activities. Here, there are some promising signs;
PRIDE, for example, is now working to facilitate the concept of enterprise visits
throughout East Africa, and other organizations are also interested in incorporating it
into their SED programmes in Kenya. Similarly, a local consultant is offering courses
in rapid market appraisal, in both Kenya and Tanzania.

Another important indicator for each mechanism is the extent to which pilot activities are scaled up, so that they achieve national outreach; this would ultimately imply
that the service becomes available to any MSE in the country, at least in principle.
Development agencies, however, tend to focus on their own clients and areas of geographical concentration; they may not aim to provide a service nationwide. Many
development agencies do not currently consider 'innovation' as part of their core mandate, although this may now be changing, partly as a result of the activities of FIT and
others. Furthermore, development agencies tend to rely on external funding, while the
ultimate goal is for service provision to be internally self-sustaining (i.e. with all of
the costs being met from local, commercial sources).

For these reasons, FIT is continuing to explore the potential for the provision of new
services through the private sector, perhaps with no formal partner agency at all. For
example, could larger companies which supply MSE inputs be assisted to meet the
needs of MSEs more effectively? Indeed, one could hope to monitor the impact of MSE
promotion on those suppliers. In practice, however, it may be difficult to measure this
impact in the short term; even in scrap steel, for example, MSE metalworkers form
only 10–15 per cent of the total demand in Kenya, and substantial increases in overall
demand will appear, therefore, only in the long term. Nonetheless, many suppliers may

see MSEs as an important source of future demand; some are sufficiently interested to pay for advertising in bulletins, aimed at MSEs, currently being 'test-marketed' by FIT. Indeed, there seems to be a great potential for the promotion of such linkages, since the possibilities extend far beyond the sub-contracting mode, which has tended to be the favoured format of many development initiatives to date (Mead, 1994).

The development of individual services is only one objective for FIT; however, a major indicator of success in the long term is whether the mode of 'action research' in this important field is continuing and expanding. Are more 'mechanisms' being developed to provide non-financial services to MSEs in sustainable ways? Essentially, it is too early to say whether this has yet been achieved. FIT is currently working to establish a National Network of collaborators and partners in Kenya; this network will bring together people from a wide variety of backgrounds, who are enthusiastic about the potential. It is expected that, during the next two years, their common interest will enable them to form a self-sustaining stimulus for local innovation through action research.

Some initial conclusions

It is widely accepted now that services for MSEs should be demand led; it is also increasingly acknowledged, by both development practitioners and by the MSEs themselves, that the most important demand, in this context, is the demand of the final customer of the MSE. The money paid by the final customer enables the MSE to pay for services to improve his or her business, and the MSE generally provides the most accessible entry point for such interventions. Nonetheless, the final customer may also be willing to contribute to the costs of activities, which will ultimately lead to improvements in MSE product quality. This willingness to pay for the service is one of the most important indicators of achievement.

It is also apparent that services may not be self-sustaining because a small adjustment is needed in their format. For example, MSEs may be reluctant to try a new service, at full cost, if they must apply as individuals; however, if they are allowed to try it as a group, they may be willing to pay the full costs. Similarly, MSEs which did not participate in the pilot activity may nonetheless benefit, through spontaneous replication of what they have observed.

Efforts have been made to quantify the impact of FIT activities on MSEs, and some promising data have been collected, for example indicating that additional employment opportunities have been generated. Improved methodologies for collecting data are being developed. There are, however, considerable obstacles to ensuring that these data are totally reliable, and qualitative indicators have therefore been given greater importance; in addition to being valued by the MSEs themselves, they can often be directly linked with the individual services which have been provided to the MSE. Qualitative evaluation has shown that MSEs have benefited in many areas of business operation from the services provided.

The response of MSEs to FIT's pilot activities has been very encouraging, as have the signs of replication by development agencies; however, FIT has not yet achieved extensive, private sector replication of those services which have now been demonstrated on a pilot basis. Finally, it is too early to tell whether the local capacity for innovation in the provision of new services for MSEs has yet been strengthened; the initiation of a network of such organizations is a significant step to meeting that challenge.

FIT is keenly interested to hear from any other organization working in similar or related fields elsewhere in the world, so that experiences may be exchanged in more detail.

References

Burger, Kas, and Hans Haan (1995) *Rapid market appraisal for MSEs*, FIT/TOOL Amsterdam, FIT manual.

Craig, Kim and Mike Oneko (1995) (ed. Hileman), 'Strengthening the Kenyan informal sector through exchange forums', PRIDE Nairobi/FIT working document.

Esbin, Howard, (1994), 'Marketing channels for MSEs in Kenya: analysis and strategic plan', Nairobi/FIT working document.

Haggblade, Steven (1992) 'A proposal for monitoring small enterprise promotion,' *Small Enterprise Development*, Vol.3, No.4, London.

Harper, Malcolm (1995) 'Small enterprise development: value for money?' Cranfield School of Management, for ILO Geneva.

IL0 (1981) *Procedures for the design and evaluation of ILO projects*, Geneva.

Mead, Donald (1994) 'Linkages within the private sector: A review of current thinking', Michigan State University/FIT working document.

Mortimore, Michael, and Kate Wellard, (1991), 'Environmental change and dryland management in Machakos District, Kenya, 1930–1990,' ODI Working Paper No. 57, London.

Ngau, Peter (1995) 'A study of traders servising MSB metalworkers of farm implements and tools in Kenya: a case study of Kisumu and Vihiga Districts', University of Nairobi/FIT working document.

Tanburn, Jim (1995) 'Pointers to success: A framework for evaluating the impact of the FIT programme', FIT/ILO Geneva.

Waithaka, Daudi (1995) 'Thika town SME metalworking and services study', Matrix consultants, Nairobi/FIT working document.

Wesselink, Bert (1995) 'Guidelines for evaluating FIT activities, including Evaluation Forms', FIT/ILO Geneva.

About the author

At the time of writing this article, Jim Tanburn was employed by the ILO. He currently administers www.bdsknowledge.org and works as Coordinator for the Committee of Donor Agencies for Small Enterprise Development.

7 Franchising: a vehicle for entrepreneurship development in Singapore

CHONG LI CHOY and MARK GOH

This paper was first published in June 1997.

This chapter argues that business format franchising is a form of entrepreneurship development that provides the franchisee with the necessary knowledge and practice as well as supplies and service support to run a viable business. It discusses the various scenarios under which a franchising arrangement may help develop entrepreneurship successfully and provides case illustrations. The first relates to the modernization of traditional local retail businesses which enables them to hold their own in the face of competition from the entry of larger international retail businesses into the Singapore market. The assistance given to such existing small businesses is equally relevant in developing the business knowledge and skills, as well as the much-needed business contacts, of a new entrepreneur. The second case relates to overseas business expansion which involves the development of franchisee entrepreneurs abroad. The sprouting of copycat entrepreneurs resulting from such franchises can also be seen to have a developmental effect on entrepreneurship. The third case relates to the promotion of intrapreneurship, which in practice resembles a franchising-type arrangement.

FRANCHISING IS INCREASINGLY being seen as an effective vehicle for promoting economic development. Although there are different manifestations of the franchising model and concept, effective franchising is needed to contribute towards the growth of an economy (Alias, 1994). Recently, franchising is also viewed as an instrument for small enterprise transformation (Chong, 1994) and entrepreneurship development.

This chapter looks at how franchising is used to help small local retail businesses upgrade and to help the overseas business expansion of local small businesses, particularly those in non-manufacturing industry. Franchising, as a business instrument, has no fixed definition, since franchising arrangements in practice always have to vary according to the needs of the franchisers and franchisees. However, franchising and franchising-type arrangements normally involve the owner of a proven business granting the right and providing the necessary assistance and support to another party to replicate his or her business (or to establish another business), elsewhere, in another geographical location. This is a common arrangement for many chain stores around the world. In some instances, such arrangements have taken place as a form of co-operative venture among small businesses. In other instances, joint venture partners were sought for such arrangements. In yet other instances, the managers and other employees of a company's chain store seem to have taken the place of franchisees.

Such arrangements are essentially a form of entrepreneurship development. Here the franchiser provides the franchisee (entrepreneur), not only with a business format, well-established brand names, equipment and supplies or raw materials, but also training for the entrepreneur and his staff, support for the operations and the set-up and layout of facilities, as well as consultancy and trouble-shooting if needed, to ensure the business success of the franchisee. Such transfer of business experience, resources, knowledge and skills, which often includes the sharing of a business network as well, are certainly developmental in nature, particularly in situations where the entrepreneurs are new. Such entrepreneurs normally lack the relevant business experience and networking, as well as the requisite knowledge and skills to run a business successfully.

Franchising development in the ASEAN region

Franchising in Europe is well established and progressing (Williams, 1994). In some countries, like the United Kingdom and France, it is an industry which has already reached maturity. In other countries, like Denmark and Sweden, it is still in its infancy. In Australia also, franchising has achieved considerable growth and maturity since the 1980s, and a number of franchises have begun to expand internationally (McCosker, 1994).

The confidence of established Australian franchisers is attested by the growing number of franchisers choosing this path of international expansion. For instance, 19 franchisers had 273 outlets overseas in 1988. In 1992, 21 franchisers were reported to have 286 outlets overseas. Further, an Australian task force study found that the franchise sector had a beneficial and significant impact on the growth and development of small business in Australia.

Within the ASEAN region, it is extremely difficult to quantify the size and rate of growth of franchising accurately, owing to a lack of comprehensive statistics. However, visual observation on the rate of proliferation of franchise outlets, in Malaysia, Indonesia and Singapore, suggests that the home-grown franchise sector is a sunrise industry in this part of the world.

For example, in Malaysia, Alias (1994) reports that the government's franchise development initiatives had been initiated only in the 1980s. By 1990, the franchise industry in Malaysia had an estimated turnover of US$214 million and an annual growth rate of 9 per cent. This growth rate is coincidentally the country's economic growth rate too (Fatimah and Zamri, 1992). A similar situation has been reported in Indonesia.

In the case of Singapore, Walker (1994) recently reported that Singapore has 69 home-grown franchises in the food, fashion, gas stations, hotel, retail and service sectors. Singaporean entrepreneurs have also become local or regional franchisees for 79 foreign franchisers within the past three years. Part of the reason for this sudden and recent growth is the effective and determined promotion by the Singapore National Productivity Board's (NPB) Franchise Development Centre and Singapore's Trade Development Board's (TDB) Franchise Development Assistance Scheme. We now turn our attention to some of the various scenarios under which a franchising arrangement has helped develop entrepreneurship successfully in the context of Singapore.

Local business co-operation through franchising

Forming a franchise system as a co-operative effort among small businesses is certainly unusual if not novel. Normally, franchises are given by established businesses to others who wish to replicate them elsewhere. However, in the case of the Provisions Suppliers Corporation (PSC) and the Econ-Minimart chain in Singapore (Chong and

Goh, 1992), the franchise was initiated as a coming together of small retail stores (provisions shops) to compete against larger businesses (see next section). The chain store has been so successful that the NPB, which is responsible for helping small retail stores in Singapore upgrade themselves to become more competitive, cites it as a model for business co-operation which other local small businesses can emulate.

There is little doubt that such franchise arrangements involve not only the transformation of the business, but also the entrepreneur, his knowledge and undertaking of the business and its environment, as well as his management methods and system. This entrepreneurship development constitutes the modernization and upgrading of the traditional entrepreneur. This model of co-operation through a franchise system is being introduced to other small businesses, such as bakeries and hair salons. PSC also shares its experience and expertise with others through its subsidiary company, the International Franchise Pte. Ltd.

PSC and Econ-Minimart

PSC was initially set up by members of the Singapore Provision Shop Friendly Association as their central buying agency, in order to benefit from bulk purchase. It is jointly held by the owners of small provisions shops. In 1982, the Econ-Minimart chain was launched as voluntary chain under a local franchise system to upgrade the traditional provisions shop, with the PSC acting as the consultant and supplier to their franchisees (Foo, 1993). The Econ-Minimart chain must, however, agree to follow certain guidelines in management set by the PSC. These are mainly in areas such as shop fittings, lay-out lighting, merchandising and pricing. The stores continue to be owned by the original business people, although they now bear the common identity of the chain, with corporate advertising to give each shop promotional opportunities and consumer awareness equal to that of larger stores.

The setting up of the Econ-Minimart chain is an exercise in the modernization and upgrading of provisions shops in Singapore which came forward to join the voluntary chain. The shops were accepted into the chain on a first-come-first-accepted basis, with no membership requirements. Care was taken in the selection process to ensure that no two Econ-Minimarts would be placed too close to one another to avoid unnecessary and unhealthy intra-chain competition.

All these represent revolutionary changes to the traditional provisions shops. Before the transformation, the shops were characteristically poorly lit and poorly ventilated, with broken and unhygienic floor surfaces, and were cluttered by large quantities of all kinds of goods used in households, ranging from open sacks of rice and flour, to stacks of eggs, to cans of cooking oil and paint, to packets of soap powder and cereal, to jars of instant coffee and jams, and to bottles of soft drinks and kerosene. Goods were often stacked to impossible heights. The cash till was normally a tin suspended from a high point in the shop with poor accounting and inventory control.

Since the transformation, these shops have become well lit and with good ventilation, including fans or air-conditioning for some shops. The floor is properly resurfaced and the goods are properly displayed on open shelves for customers to inspect and serve themselves. Electronic cash registers were introduced to provide receipts for customers and to help the owners with their accounting. Products are now price tagged electronically. Training is given to the participating owners, both in the classroom and more importantly at their stores, to help them manage their stores better. On-the-job training and guidance is an important and ongoing activity for participating stores.

Encouraging franchise-type co-operation among local businesses

Given the need to upgrade the small retail and service businesses in the government's housing estates (HDB) and elsewhere in Singapore to combat increasing competition, the Singapore Government, through the NPB, is currently encouraging co-operation among local businesses. The Franchise Development Centre of the NPB helps small retailers organize themselves into economic groupings to benefit from economies of scale. This centre helps companies form suitable business alliances, by making available consultants to assist in setting up operations and procedures, to formulate appropriate training programmes, and to obtain government grants for the development of economic groupings and training (Singapore Enterprise, 1992).

Since the setting up of this centre, the NPB has been active in bringing together small retailers in different industries, such as the travel industry, to co-operate within their industry. Larger local retailers, like Metro (a local department store chain) and Times Bookstores, have also been requested to consider franchising their operations to small retailers in the .HDB estates. Even established firms, like Prima Flour, have developed and launched a successful Prima-Deli franchise chain of cake shops and cafes. This represents a strategic alliance between a larger established firm and its small franchisees. Like the Econ-Minimart, these franchise developments involve entrepreneurship development and transformation in Singapore.

Going international through franchising

With increasing foreign competition and a small domestic market, it is inevitable that many local businesses are expanding their operations overseas. This is also being encouraged by the government. To encourage local businesses to expand overseas through franchising, the government, through the TDB, operates a Franchise Development Assistance Scheme. This scheme, launched in 1991, helps 'proven entrepreneurs' in Singapore globalize their businesses. It offers qualifying businesses a grant of up to 50 per cent of the costs for consultancy and marketing abroad. The beneficiaries of this scheme have since included Mido Textiles, Goodvine, Noel Hampers and Gifts, Cold Storage Holdings, Informatics Holdings, Microskills Services, Palm Beach Seafood Restaurant, Seoul Garden Korean Restaurant, and Ken-Air Leisure Group.

Informatics Holdings, for example, with a worldwide turnover of $40 million last year and a total of 23 computer training centres in Singapore, Malaysia, Indonesia, Thailand, Taiwan, India, Oman and Bahrain, expects to increase its turnover by 20 per cent annually based on its plans to double its international network of training centres to about 50 over the next three years. Microskills, which spends about $1 million every year on R&D to remain competitive as a franchiser, and has two centres in Jakarta, intends to set up seven more new centres there in the near future.

The Seoul Garden chain, which currently has four outlets in Indonesia, hopes to set up 15 new franchise outlets there. Besides the advantage of smaller start-up costs for each new outlet, franchising will also allow the group to take advantage of greater economies of scale in central purchasing and in R&D. Palm Beach, which operates two restaurants in Singapore, is negotiating with an Indonesian party to open at least five new outlets in Indonesia. The franchisee's knowledge of local conditions will help Palm Beach cushion the risks of breaking into an unfamiliar foreign environment in Indonesia (*The Straits Times*, 1992).

Like local franchising in Singapore, international franchising by small home-grown companies also helps to develop franchisee entrepreneurs in a similar manner. We look at one such company in detail, Noel Hampers and Gifts.

Noel Hampers and Gifts

This is a local company which specializes in selling gift items, including gift hampers and flower arrangements. Over the past 17 years of its existence, it has developed considerable business expertise to become a pace-setter in the gift business and is well known for its creative value-added ideas. Its turnover currently exceeds S$20 million. Recently, it has franchised its business to another party in Malaysia. In return for the franchise fee and royalty, Noel provides total support for its franchisee from start-up to product development. Anything that has worked at Noel will be shared with the franchisee. Periodically, Noel sends people over to the franchisee to provide training for the franchisee's employees. Noel also receives people from the franchisee for training at the company in Singapore. Regular meetings are also held with the franchisee to find out how best to help them. The arrangements also involve Noel buying in bulk from the suppliers and supplying to the franchisee. Noel hopes to gain market entry into eight countries within the next three to five years.

'Copycat' entrepreneurs

The success of international franchise chains such as McDonald's and Kentucky Fried Chicken has certainly spawned many 'copycat' entrepreneurs in Singapore. These entrepreneurs copy the established foreign businesses in various ways. They may copy the products or methods of one or more successful franchises either with or without modifications.

In Singapore, even the hawkers at public food centres and coffee shops have started to sell Western fast foods, copying the products of these franchise businesses. Other copycat entrepreneurs may copy the methods of these franchises. In Singapore, some hawker entrepreneurs have even adopted the methods of franchises by franchising their hawker stores. Examples of these include the Koo Kee 'Yong Tau Foo' food store, 'Odeon Beef Noodles' and 'Old Chang Kee' curry puffs. These business developments have taken place at the initiative of the entrepreneurs, even before the government started to encourage franchising.

Promoting intrapreneurship

While franchising and franchise-like arrangements have been made to promote entrepreneurship development in Singapore and abroad, they have also been used to promote intrapreneurship, that is entrepreneurship development within a company. Here, the company has a chain of stores like any franchise, except for the fact that these stores are all owned and managed by the same company. A family-type culture, emphasizing sharing and joint ownership by the employees, is cultivated in the company's chain stores. A good illustration is that of the Hour Glass franchise.

The Hour Glass

The Hour Glass started as a small firm with a new concept of up-market watch retailing in 1979. Today it is a publicly listed company with nine watch boutiques in Singapore, two in Malaysia, two in Australia, and one in Indonesia (under sub-licensing arrangements). Along with these, it has also three Mondial jewellery shops and eight Milano restaurant outlets.

Like a franchise system, the company trains people to be their own boss. Staff members are given generous performance-related incentives in addition to their salary, to encourage them to meet the company's sales and profit targets for their branch (outlet), through which they are made to feel that they are working for themselves. Where sales and profit targets have been exceeded, the incentives for the employees concerned are even more generous. If a branch does well, employees can also expect bonuses of between one and six months of their salaries, in addition to the above incentives. Additional bonuses are also paid for the company's overall good performance. Everyone is therefore sales and profit oriented, and is well motivated by the financial rewards.

In spite of all these financial rewards, the company still continues to look into further ways to reward its staff and to think of more things that the company can do for its employees. This is because the company wants employees to think of the company as 'their' company, and that they are building a future for themselves. The company has a 'give, care and share philosophy', and believes that the more the company gives to employees, the more the company is making in terms of profits. The response of the employees has been highly positive. Like entrepreneurs working in their firms, many employees in this company come back to work at weekends on their own. With the implementation of the incentive scheme in the company in 1987, sales have also increased by 100 per cent since that year. Like a franchise system, each outlet is responsible for its bottom line. The managers are given a free hand under guidance from the head office to meet and to exceed the required sales and profit targets set for their outlets. Training is provided for all staff. The managing director of the company (who is the entrepreneur) also gives personal coaching to her chain stores' managers as well as two of their assistants, to help them become more entrepreneurial in their thinking and to free them from various 'mental blocks'. They are in turn expected to coach their employees similarly and to build up their teams in their shop. The management system and culture of the company are to be replicated in every branch and shop.

Conclusion

The above cases are good illustrations of the effectiveness of franchising or franchise-like arrangements in entrepreneurship development in Singapore. Franchising or franchise-like arrangements are not only beneficial to both franchisers and franchisees, they are also excellent vehicles for the co-operation and development of entrepreneurs both internationally as well as within the same country. An example is that of F&B Pte Ltd, a coffee shop franchise that has decided to delegate the warehousing of its purchases and the bulk buying to the franchise. As a result, it has five coffee shops operating throughout Singapore. It is expected to operate 200 such coffee shops within the next two years. Such a business pattern transfers business knowledge, skills and methods to upgrade and thus develop the franchise entrepreneurs. It also promotes enterprise and hence entrepreneurship among franchisees or employees by allowing them to maintain some sense of autonomy in their business. This has stimulated, in the case of Singapore, what is known as intrapreneurship, which motivates employees to commit themselves to work for the firm as if it belongs to them. A recent NPB survey reports that nine out of ten retailers involved in the 30 local franchise schemes surveyed have thus far reported higher profit margins compared to non-franchises. This can only testify to the fact that franchising improves the small business survival rate in Singapore and promotes entrepreneurship development.

References

Alias, A. (1994) 'Developing local franchise: strategic perspective and model', *Journal of Enterprising Culture*, 1:3–4, 437–8.

Chong, L.C. and M. Goh (1992) 'SME development in Singapore: intra-industry co-operation among SMEs', *Public Enterprise*, 12:1–2, 41–8.

Chong, L.C. (1994) 'Franchising as an instrument for business transformation: the Singaporean experience', *Public Enterprise*, 14:1–2, 115–119.

Fatimah, H. and S. Zamri (1992) 'Franchising in Malaysia', paper circulated at the International Franchise Conference, Hong Kong, October 13–14.

Foo, D.R. (1993) 'The Econ-Minimart (Singapore): the concept and its applicability to developing countries – a case study', *Public Enterprise*, 13:1–2, 70–80.

McCosker, C.F. (1994) 'Australian franchising: from international invasion to international expansion', *Journal of Enterprising Culture*, 1:3–4, 39–65.

The Singapore Enterprise, August 1992, 1–2.

The Straits Times (1992) 20 July, p.40.

Walker, J. (1994) 'More Singapore entrepreneurs franchising their way to success', *Business Times*, 5 September.

Williams, R.G. (1994) 'The development of franchising in Germany', *International Journal of Management*, 11:1, 609–619.

About the authors

Chong Li Choy is Professor at Singapore Management University. Mark Goh is Associate Professor at the National University of Singapore Business School.

8 The role of markets in delivering BDS to the poor

ALAN GIBSON and MALCOLM HARPER

This exchange was first published in March 2002 as a 'Crossfire' debate on the proposition 'markets alone cannot be relied on to deliver BDS to poor people'.

Dear Alan,

Sustainability can be defined in many ways, but I suspect we are agreed that in the field of small business development it usually means 'ability to cover all its costs with fees paid by its clients'. I think we also agree that a market can be said to have been created in a given commodity when two or more providers, not being in connivance with each other, are able to cover their costs by selling it to clients who pay for it.

The current enthusiasm for markets and sustainability, at least in the subjects covered by *Small Enterprise Development*, arises mainly because some providers of microfinancial services appear able to cover all their costs, including in rare cases even the cost of inflation, with the interest they charge on their loans. Here, at last, is a form of enterprise assistance which does reach poor people, and which need not depend forever on subsidy.

Providers of non-financial business services, or BDS as they are now called, want to show that their product can do the same. They are emboldened in this attempt by their 'discovery' that there has always been a thriving market in BDS; businesses have always bought training, advice and marketing assistance from other businesses. Donors have only to discover and remedy the market imperfections that prevent these services being made available to poorer people, as they famously have with microfinance, and small businesses will be able to select and pay for BDS in the same way as they are beginning to be able to with financial services.

The problem is that there are some critical differences between finance and non-financial services. When you lend money, the main cost is the money, and it is a variable cost. You also have transaction costs, which are not fully variable, but microfinance institutions have cleverly designed ways of making their customers take on many of these through groups, such as loan appraisal, collecting repayments or covering risks. When you provide advice, or training, or marketing assistance, you have no variable costs; it is all labour, and it may actually be more difficult, and thus more expensive, to advise or train a micro-business owner than a larger-scale entrepreneur.

Often, too, the most valuable service you can provide is advocacy, to reduce official harassment. Better-off entrepreneurs are in associations and chambers of commerce, and can pay for advocacy, but poorer microentrepreneurs cannot. BDS for the poor cannot depend on markets, and if we try to make it do so the providers will inevitably 'drift' towards larger business, which can pay. Yet again, the poor will be left out.

Yours,
Malcolm

Dear Malcolm,

Delighted to hear of your interest in BDS. Slightly less pleased that you appear to have missed the point entirely in relation to recent thinking. By way of an initial response I thought it might be useful to lay out a few fundamental points that lie at the heart of BDS market development.

Why markets in BDS? Because the best environments for enterprise development are ones in which markets for business outputs and inputs (financial services, BDS, etc.) are working effectively. To a large extent, SMEs' growth and development depends on their ability to get answers to core questions of 'how to', 'who with' and 'where to'. As services that are fee-based, embedded within other commercial transactions or offered informally through other business relationships, BDS offer answers to these questions.

Of course, agencies have been engaged in support for BDS for years. But let's be clear: rather than facilitating markets for services, the final result of much of this has been to debilitate SMEs with the expectation of welfare, distort incentives, reach not very many, and cement SMEs' disconnection from the wider private sector. Candidly, much of the problem here stems from an intellectual half-light that shrouds SME development; in this context, market development offers a clear framework to guide BDS interventions, and indeed to shape the role of government.

Why is financial services' experience relevant? Because we've learned from financial services that SMEs are discerning consumers who don't want charity but do want useful services delivered in a transactional manner. Yes, BDS are different – they're diverse, they're offered in different ways by a range of providers, the scale economies of financial services may not be achievable, but the core objective for both should be the same.

Why is sustainability important? Because we're interested in longer-term, substantial change and that means, again, thinking at the market level. Providers obviously have to earn a buck, but the primary focus of agencies intervening in BDS (or in financial services) should be the wider market institution of which they're a part. It's the sustainability of this that counts. Here your definition doesn't help at all. On the contrary, by focusing only on organizations you blur the crucial distinction between providers, who should be creatures of the market place, and facilitating agencies, implementing market development interventions with donor resources.

Yours,
Alan

Dear Alan,

Thanks for your guidance; I wish that the undoubted quality and clarity of your writing would help to make some poor small business owners less poor, but I fear it won't.

It is nice to talk of 'making markets work for the poor', but the evidence from the past 20 years in the UK and the USA, and from much of the rest of the world in the past 10 years, suggests that they don't. Markets increase aggregate wealth, but they also increase the inequity of its distribution. Surely the major role of foreign aid, which is a non-market activity if ever there was one, is to mitigate this marginalization.

No services of any kind 'flow naturally' to the poorest people. Primary education and health care, clean water and decent housing – all these 'basic services' have to be subsidized if they are to reach the poor. Business development services are surely no different.

Part of the problem lies in the term 'BDS'. I never heard a businessman or woman bemoan the lack of 'BDS', in any language. They tell me that they cannot get loans from banks, and that they cannot buy affordable and reliable insurance, and these difficulties can indeed be blamed in part on market failures. Business people also know that they need more customers, more technical skills, more modern machinery, or, sometimes, better records, but only donors and those who work for them try to lump all these problems under the one catch-all term 'BDS'.

This meaningless generalization conceals the differences between 'embedded' services such as the training that is provided with sewing machines or welding equipment, information about markets, advocacy to remove irrelevant restrictions or management consultancy. All these can be called 'BDS', but there is little to be gained by putting them under the same label. If the term leads us to believe that all of them can be 'sustainably' provided by markets that work, it may do a lot of damage.

Markets become imperfect because sellers and buyers lack information, or because prices are distorted by subsidy. You say that SMEs are constrained by their lack of answers to critical questions. Maybe we are thinking about different types of businesses, but I cannot imagine what answers, to what questions, would enable a rickshaw puller in Calcutta, or a vegetable vendor in Nairobi, to escape from poverty. They need better basic services for themselves and their families, and they need the authorities to get off their backs, but I don't think better markets are going to solve these problems.

Yours,
Malcolm

Dear Malcolm,

It's good to start with a couple of points of agreement. Yes, I too can't recall having come across hordes of indignant business people marching purposefully beneath the banner 'We want access to double-entry bookkeeping services (and any other BDS going) – and we want it now!' And yes, the term 'BDS' is hardly perfect. It is, of course, a development agency (or perhaps consultants') creation, designed to put a label on a disparate set of activities and interests of agencies (what's left after finance and policy work are taken out) and therefore slightly artificial, not being sourced in the 'real' world of businesses and markets. I think 'business services' is much better, but BDS is what we've got and I'm loath to start inventing new terms at this stage.

Let's not mistake confusion over the language of the development community with any doubt over the importance of business services. Without any placard waving from disgruntled entrepreneurs, business services offered by private sector providers have been the fastest growth sector in most high-income economies for the past 10 years or so. Driven by very real competitive pressures, SMEs' consumption of communication, marketing and production business services have increased hugely, markets for these services have developed and economies become more efficient in the process. There's nothing artificial about this: SMEs demand these services because they help them answer key questions and perform better.

Now, you might think, he's wittering on about a world a million miles away from the one that really counts. Well, the context may be different but the pressures are the same.

I wouldn't expect small-scale handicraft producers to engage an Italian designer to keep them abreast of fashion trends; but appropriate design information passed to them through suppliers, acting in their own interests and in the context of a commercial transaction could be useful. SMEs may be unlikely to engage a 'Big 5' accountant but a small-scale bookkeeper and trainer – possibly. The point is not that business services are irrelevant – they're critically important – but what they are, and the market mechanisms through which they are delivered, varies.

Market development is obviously not a panacea, nor does it imply that government is unimportant. Commonly, people mistake the hard rigour of market development arguments as wild-eyed, anti-government zealotry. This is nonsense. A balanced view of development understands the unique roles that governments should play in providing public services – preventive health care, children's education, infrastructure, law and order and basic welfare. All of these are necessary for development – not least to build the capacity of poor people themselves to participate in markets. However, these public services – entitlements – are very different from BDS or financial services that are best offered within a market context (private services).

Yours,
Alan

Dear Alan,

Let me start where you finished. Yes, we should all have learned by now that most BDS should be provided by businesses, probably small ones, and not by government (nor by NGOs for that matter). But this does not mean such provision must be entirely market driven, paid for by users, any more than private provision of basic services such as education or health care means that the costs must be fully covered by fees paid by the children or the patients. Subsidy, or even full payment, is necessary for some services, to some clients, and will continue to be so. Governments, or donors, will have to pay, regardless of who delivers.

Of course it would be wonderful if the business people who need subsidized services today were able to pay the full cost tomorrow, as they do in the 'high-income economies' to which you refer. But, we have to be realistic, and to recognize that only a small proportion of the millions of microenterprises of the poor will ever evolve into the famous 'growth businesses' that are supposed to be the engines of development. Most of them will continue to be survival or subsistence businesses, undertaken not by choice but because there is no alternative.

I am not suggesting that it is necessarily wrong to try to stimulate the development of service providers, and the provision of embedded services, in an attempt to foster the development of growth businesses. This should, I suspect, be done more subtly and less expensively than it appears to be in the examples that I have observed, but it is not a bad thing to do.

What worries me is that this type of BDS development is coming to be seen as the main or even the only form of non-financial assistance for microenterprises. We were meant to have abandoned the earlier naïve expectation that assistance to the less needy would somehow 'trickle down' to the poor. But if we focus only on the development of sustainable markets in business services, we shall by implication be reverting to the same belief.

If we do this, some businesses may grow a little faster, and a few of the more skilled poor may find jobs in these businesses and thus be able to abandon their micro-enterprises. But the client profile of BDS providers will drift ever further up-market, in response to donor pressure for sustainability, and the microenterprises that support far larger numbers of poor people will gain nothing.

It is very difficult to figure out how to assist the mass of microenterprises, and to design and implement cost-effective (as opposed to sustainable or profitable) ways of delivering what they need. Surely, however, if we are trying to alleviate poverty we must face it head on, and try to assist the poor direct, with subsidized services when necessary, rather than fooling ourselves that 'markets' can do the job.

Yours,
Malcolm

Dear Malcolm,

I sense you're wavering slightly – and would like to think that there's some hope for you after all! But your response is worryingly close to that which I've often encountered in recent years, and which can be characterized as the 'OK, but' school. Key 'arguments' put forward by OK Butters include:

'OK, it's all very well, but this market development thing can't work here – we're different.'

'OK, that's fine for bigger businesses, but SMEs need our help.'

'OK, I don't have a valid counter vision or argument, but I don't like the implications of what you're saying: I'm familiar with our approach, our partners, our development treadmill, the acceptable ambiguity of our results – and it's a way of spending our budget.'

All right, the last one might be a bit more subliminal than the others. I am conscious that there's often a dissonant clash when rhetoric meets reality, but if we're to make progress with this stuff some radical change is required. Beginning with revisiting some disparate ideas that unfortunately still have considerable (but diminishing) support. For example:

BDS as a public service. We don't think of financial services as a public good now and we shouldn't think of BDS in this way either. The mythology that somehow these have equivalence to real public services reaches its most perverse pinnacle in some African countries where governments and donors agonize over whether businesses should pay anything for aid-funded services while primary school children are required to pay school fees.

The poor can only self-develop out of poverty in their own microenterprises. Yes, people escape from poverty through their own efforts, but are often enabled to do so through wider improvements in economies and in markets, rather than targeting resources at the poor direct. Can anyone doubt the poverty reduction impact of, for example, the million or so jobs created in the Bangladesh garment industry without any significant donor poverty-focused input?

SME development should be separated from private sector development. Excluding SMEs from 'big' private sector development marginalizes, minimizes and cements their disconnection from the mainstream. With honourable exceptions, one cumulative result of classic SME interventions over many years is that SMEs have developed in a parallel world with different (lower) standards, aspirations, disciplines and capacities, and often an expectation of welfare. This is especially the case in Africa; indeed in South Africa, whose wealth and political context has allowed it to throw more resources at 'SME development' than most, this dual nature of the economy has, if anything, been strengthened in recent years.

Of course, there remain many important questions, especially: how should agencies go about facilitating market development? I've no illusions about the level of our knowledge here. But equally, I've no real doubts that in market development we have the right focus at least. Why? Because it's in the best interests of the poor, and ultimately that's what counts.

Yours,
Alan

About the authors

Alan Gibson is a partner of the Springfield Centre for Business Development, UK, and Malcolm Harper is Emeritus Professor of Enterprise Development, Cranfield University, UK.

9 The training market for MSEs in developing countries

AKIKO SUZUKI

This paper was first published in March 2002.

Training is commonly regarded as a BDS which it is difficult to provide sustainably since MSEs are unwilling to pay the full costs. This chapter takes the starting point of private sector training which is provided without public subsidy, and draws out some lessons about how this operates and covers its costs. The author then examines the demand side of MSEs as trainees, to identify major key obstacles for market development. Finally, a hypothetical model is suggested for the development of a training market for MSEs, which leads to key recommendations for future interventions.

ALONG WITH OTHER BDS, training is an important means to help MSEs improve their skills both for business management and production. Governments and donors have been actively involved in the area of training, usually funding public training institutions and trainers. The new BDS approach, however, attempts to identify and enhance private sector service provision, rather than providing a publicly funded alternative, and it is worth examining how applicable this approach is to the training market for MSEs. The purpose of this article is therefore to share findings on what already exists in terms of private training supply, and how this might be built upon.

Private training is defined as training services which are provided on a fully commercial basis. Private training is therefore by definition sustainable without subsidies as far as the demand for and the supply of training can successfully meet in the market. There are two categories of private training: courses offered by training businesses and training offered based on business relationships.

Training as a for-profit business: stand-alone training

This type of training is a means for trainers to make a profit. Trainees, therefore, pay the full costs of training. This category includes registered training institutions and non-registered private micro-trainers. Clients include anyone interested in training and willing to pay the price. It is worth pointing out first that the quantity of this type of training is far from negligible (Box 9.1). For instance, in Harare, Zimbabwe, registered private trainers teach more than three times as many students as government vocational education and training (VET) institutions (Bennell, 1998a). In Tanzania, private trainers accounted for around 60 per cent of total VET enrolments throughout the 1980s and 1990s (Bennell, 1998b). Second, although the quality of for-profit trainers varies, there is evidence that it is better than generally expected.

There are three observations to support this. First, the content of private sector training courses are more likely to be relevant to MSEs' needs than public training. This is largely because private trainers are much quicker to respond to the market changes than public training institutions (see, for example, Bennell, 1998b). Second, trainers are

---

Box 9.1 Examples of training by training businesses

Training by registered trainers

○ A private college in Harare offers courses in both business and technical skills, which last from 2 to 3 days. The fee is Z$6000 (US$110). The college trains 2000 to 2500 clients per year, most of whom are employed by SMEs and large companies, and their employers pay the fees. Equal numbers of men and women are trained. Trainers are invited from outside, and are in relevant businesses; academics are avoided. The college has established an association of trainers and at present it includes around 100 trainers.

○ A cooking college in Bangkok offers a course in Thai cooking skills. The director herself is the main instructor, with 40 years of experience. The length of the training can be adjusted to the trainees' convenience. The fees are B8000 (US$180). The college trains 300 clients annually and 90 per cent of them start businesses after the courses. The director introduces trainees to possible employers in Thailand and abroad.

Training by non-registered trainers

○ A trainer in Bangkok teaches clients how to make crispy fried sticks. This is a one-day course with a fee of B1500 (US$30), and he trains 150 clients per year. He started offering training after he had been in the business of selling crispy fried sticks for 10 years, and now the training is his side business. He is not registered because the fees are too expensive. When asked about the level of his fees, he said that he would consider offering a 30 per cent reduction in the fee if he had more trainees as a result.

○ A craftsman in Uganda with his own metal workshop offers training in business management skills. His courses include: Rapid market appraisal and User-led innovation, which are two FIT-developed training modules which he learned when attending a 'training of trainers' course three years ago. He trains around 60 trainees per year. An RMA course takes three afternoons and costs 10 000 Ugandan shilling (US$6). He said that he did not have to compete with private or public trainers, as his courses had been tailored to metal work.

---

quality conscious. For micro-trainers in particular, word-of-mouth is the major means of marketing, so if trainers wish to attract as many clients as possible, they need to ensure the quality of their training. The comment of a Thai trainer underlines this point:

> The technique is to knead the dough perfectly. There are certain skills in kneading better, which no one teaches but I. I make sure that trainees have learned these skills well enough to be able to use them after training. This is important, because my reputation as a trainer depends upon the results of my trainees.
> *(A trainer who gives instruction in how to prepare crispy fried chicken, Thailand)*

Third, trainers are better paid in the private sector than in the public sector, which implies that better-qualified people go to work in the private sector. In Thailand, for example, a trainer can earn 800 to 2500 baht (approximately US$18 to US$56) per course in a private institution. If the trainer delivers the same course at a public institution, she can earn 100 to 150 Baht (approximately US$2 to US$3) per course. Comparing salaries between not-for-profit private training institutions (presumably publicly funded trainers, such as NGOs and churches) and for-profit private training institutions, the latter paid higher salaries than the former. Bennell concluded that this largely reflects the greater demand for the private training courses (1998b). Field research conducted in Kenya also supports this: it shows that private trainers have better educational attainment than those in the public sector (Mung'oma, 2000). Although there is little research available that comprehensively compares educational background between trainers in the public and private sectors, the facts here clearly do not support the notion that private trainers and therefore private training are always lower quality than public training. When the greater work experience of private sector trainers is taken into account, this seems even less likely.

To summarize, training offered by for-profit businesses comprises a significant part of the supply, and the quality is probably better than is generally assumed. Thus, it is worth considering how donors can make the most of the training already existing in the market.

Training based on business relationships: embedded training

This type of training is a means to develop the business concerned. Examples include: training offered by a manufacturer to its subcontractors, and training by a franchiser to its franchisees (Box 9.2). The trainer has a business interest in developing the client, such as ensuring the quality of its supplies, expanding the business, and so on. Trainees are not expected to pay the full costs of training, as part of the return on the training investment will be improvements in the business relationship in future.

Embedded training deserves greater attention because of its strengths. First, embedded training is more affordable than stand-alone training. As this type of training is a means for a trainer to make greater profits eventually, the costs are partly or even sometimes entirely borne by the trainer. For example, a manufacturer in Thailand offers free training to its future subcontractors. After completing the course, subcontractors buy their raw materials from the manufacturer, and sell their products via the manufacturer. This means that the manufacturer can get commission from the sales as well as profits from supplying raw materials to the subcontractors, which is how the manufacturer is repaid for the free training.

Box 9.2 Examples of training 'embedded' in business relationships

○ *Training by buyer to supplier.* International textile buyers provide design and product improvement training to weavers and small tailoring businesses (Vietnam).

○ *Training by franchiser to franchisee.* A company offers free training in beauty treatments to salons interested in using their products. This course can also be offered to individuals who want to open beauty salons (Thailand).

○ *Training by manufacturers.* A company offers free training in how to bake Thai-style crispy waffles to customers purchasing their portable waffle machines (Thailand).

○ *Training through subcontracting.* An institute teaches clients how to construct water tanks in return for a fee of 100 000 Ugandan shillings (US$60). The institute runs a business selling and assembling the tanks. Trainees can be subcontracted to construct the tanks, and thus earn 150 000 Ugandan shillings per month (US$90) (Uganda).

The second advantage of embedded training is direct links to a market. Because skills are provided partly to benefit a business relationship, there is an almost 100 per cent guarantee that skills are saleable after trainees obtain them. This point is crucial and cannot be emphasized too much. For those in businesses, obtaining relevant skills is necessary, but not sufficient: they also need to have markets to sell the skills.

Lastly, embedded training involves clients in a business that a trainer has established, and which clients can envisage being a part of. The benefits of training are usually difficult to communicate to people, because skills are highly intangible. It also takes time for trainees to see improvements in their businesses. Embedded training may be much more attractive to MSEs that are not familiar with the concept of training, since the benefits are more plain to see and quickly realized. This is, therefore, a strong marketing point for embedded training.

We can learn a number of key factors for successful training from embedded training, where training delivery, payment for the training and marketing of the skills are all embedded in a business relationship. These factors are:

○ affordability, because costs are not wholly borne by trainees
○ relevant and saleable skills taught by people in the business
○ tangible benefits to show to potential trainees.

Frequently asked questions about private training

Outreach to disadvantaged groups

Private trainers are actually reaching women very well. For example, 60 per cent of enrolment in private institutions was female in the case of Tanzania (Bennell, 1998b). When interviews were conducted in Harare by the author with five randomly selected trainers, four of them reported that they had equal numbers of women and men. Nonetheless, it should be noted that female participation varies significantly among training courses. Courses for textile design and baking, for example, usually have almost 100 per cent female trainees with just a few male trainees. On the other hand, training in metalwork has almost no female trainees. Outreach to young people is also well achieved, both by private training institutions and by traditional apprenticeships.

Outreach to MSEs in rural areas, however, is a problem. Although trainers do exist in rural areas, it is doubtful if the supply fully meets the demand, for private trainers usually live in cities. Trainers in cities often claim that it is difficult to deliver training in rural areas in a profitable manner. They may also not wish to deliver training there because of travel time, language differences, etc. There is clearly much room for improvement in both the quantity and variety of training available in rural areas.

Affordability

The main challenge is how a commercially based delivery mechanism can be used to bring services to people with low incomes. There are a number of possible ways to improve affordability. For instance, trainers can offer lower prices if they have more trainees, and are thus able to spread the fixed costs. Interviews with trainers reveal that they are interested in offering price reductions of 10–30 per cent if this would lead to more trainees. There are also ways to reduce the size of the upfront costs that trainees have to meet. For instance, interested MSEs can form a group and invite a trainer collectively, which means that the trainer can save on the costs of marketing. The trainer can then charge lower fees. This is a method typically used by business associations in both rural and urban areas.

Key challenges facing private trainers

When asked what they need to improve their services, trainers often mention: capital, opportunities to upgrade their skills, promotion and governmental policies (Pejerrey and Tueros, 2000). Two of these requirements are important for the market development approach: promotion and governmental policies.

Effective communication for promotion

There are two issues relating to training promotion: a lack of affordable communication channels and a lack of communication skills. In many cases, micro-trainers currently rely on word of mouth to publicize their training courses, which is not always effective. Placing advertisements is often costly, and trainers are doubtful that the benefits justify the costs. As a result, people often do not know what training is available. In addition, when small trainers use media, such as newspapers and radio, to promote their training to the public they often use the wrong sort of language for MSEs. They use terms such as marketing, stock control, and customer care, and although MSEs may be familiar with these activities in their day-to-day businesses they are unfamiliar with the formal terms. Moreover, advertisements consisting of names of courses, trainers and their contact details may not be enough to win the confidence of MSEs. In terms of developing the training market, assuming that there is demand, the first essential step is to send effective signals from the supply side to the demand side.

Unfriendly business environments

Regulatory environments are not always favourable to trainers. In the case of Zimbabwe, it is said to take six to 12 months to complete the registration process (Bennell, 1998a). Micro-trainers are also often faced with inappropriate regulations: those who run training activities in their workshops are required by local authorities to have a licence equivalent to that of a training institution. When trainers therefore avoid registration, they face greater problems marketing their activities (Mung'oma, 2000).

Another key issue in business environments is market distortion. It is hard for private trainers to compete with free or nearly free training subsidized by the government and donors, and it takes time to change people's perception that training should be free. This is illustrated by the words of a carpentry trainer operating in an area where an international NGO funds free training in the same sub-sector.

> After I went through TOT (training of trainers), I marketed my training. People were not convinced of the training benefits. I then concentrated on improving the quality of my products and people understood that my training would deliver

certain benefits. People then started coming to me. But they still wanted me to provide free advice. It is difficult to convince people that they should pay while free training is available in my area.

(A carpenter trained as a master trainer by a UNIDO project in Uganda)

An Indonesian survey shows, for instance, that 60 per cent of MSE users of training services got them for free (FIT, 2001a) – though it is not clear how much of the 60 per cent is due to public subsidies. Since public training is limited in its outreach, it is possible to overestimate how much competition has occurred between private and public training.

Issues on the demand side

Some of these issues overlap with what has already been said about the supply side, but they bear repeating. During a market research exercise in Indonesia, of 400 MSE respondents who were interviewed about technical skills training, 65 per cent answered that they had not used this kind of training because they had not felt the need for it (FIT, 2001a). Another 13 per cent said that they had not used training because the prices were too high; and 8 per cent pointed out that the course was too long.

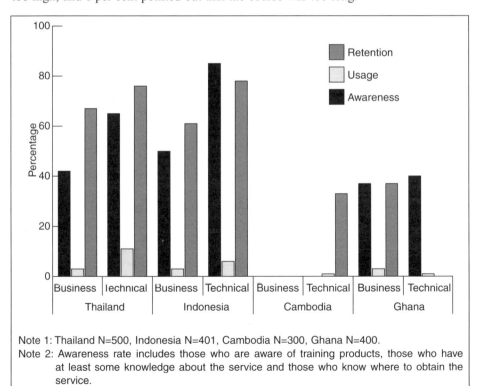

Note 1: Thailand N=500, Indonesia N=401, Cambodia N=300, Ghana N=400.
Note 2: Awareness rate includes those who are aware of training products, those who have at least some knowledge about the service and those who know where to obtain the service.
Note 3: Usage rate: those who have ever used training services in the past two years.
Note 4: Retention rate: of those who used training, percentage who used the service more than once.

Figure 9.1 *Entrepreneurs' awareness, usage and retention for training (percentage).*

MSEs' difficulty in associating training with their businesses

What is implied by this is, first, 65 per cent of the market is lost because MSEs cannot see the importance of training for their businesses. Trainers report that MSEs commonly do not recognize the problems they have in their businesses, and even after they have realized that there is something wrong, they still cannot identify what it is. Besides not recognizing their need, another challenge relates to MSEs' understanding of 'training'. Although many MSEs have informal networks from which they get advice and information, they do not regard this as 'training'. This is presumably the reason why, when market research was conducted in Cambodia with 300 MSE respondents, it was only 17 respondents who understood what was asked about when it came to training-related questions. It is also the case that there are training products on offer that do not fully meet the requirements of MSEs for training, which has presumably discouraged MSEs from attending courses.This is a typical picture of the lack of demand in the training market that affects the supply side, i.e. trainers are not willing to make investments to be MSE-oriented or to market their products to MSEs. This will, in turn, affect the demand side negatively (see Figure 9.1). This vicious cycle needs to be broken if market development is to be pursued.

However, there is a very positive sign from the market research as well: once MSEs try training, many tend to be repeaters. In the case of Indonesia, among those who used training in the past two years, 78 per cent had used more it than twice. Apart from the Indonesian case, other market research shows a similar trend, i.e., a relatively low awareness rate, a very low usage rate and a high retention rate (Figure 9.2).

Demand side	Supply side
○ MSEs can benefit from training products	○ There are good-quality trainers in the private sector
○ However, awareness of training available/ benefits is very low	○ However, they are not convinced of the potential of the MSE market
○ Some may have heard of or experienced low-quality training	○ Therefore, they do not invest enough to adapt and market training to MSEs
○ Therefore there is weaker effective demand	

Figure 9.2 *A hypothetical picture of the training market.*

Training products not meeting MSEs' requirements

The second implication from the Indonesian research is that 21 per cent of the market is lost due to poorly designed training. We therefore need to understand requirements that MSEs have for training. There are six requirements, as follows:

- ○ the duration and timing of training should be manageable
- ○ training should take place near to MSEs' workplaces
- ○ the local language should be spoken
- ○ practical skills, not general skills nor theory, should be taught
- ○ certificates should be issued upon course completion
- ○ post-training services, such as marketing linkages, should be offered.

In relation to the last point, post-training services are regarded as crucial by trainees. At a popular training course for MSEs in Thailand, trainees often mentioned that marketing their products to other trainees was one of the most important gains from participating in the training.

Case study: a publisher offering training

An example demonstrates how a training business has developed, from awareness raising, trial and retention up to sustainability (Box 9.3 overleaf).

*1. To raise awareness: information flows from trainers to MSEs.*The first step is to inform MSEs about the training available. In this example, magazines are used to promote information from trainers to MSEs. However, effective information channels may differ from country to country. For example, the major information source for MSEs in Uganda is radio, but in Cambodia it is TV.

2. Devices to encourage MSEs to try training. In the example, discounted fees were offered. There are several other ways to encourage MSEs, including training exhibitions, effective marketing tools such as success stories of ex-trainees, etc. Trial-related devices may not be necessary if the information itself has enough pull or people already see the benefits of training. For example, in Uganda, a radio station broadcast training opportunities for bee-keeping and water tank construction, which resulted in significant increases in the number of trainees, and many of whom were later hired by the businesses that offered the training.

3. To raise retention rates: information flows from MSEs to trainers. Assuming trainers offer a variety of courses of interest to MSEs, retention rates depend mainly on how satisfied trainees have been with the courses attended. If retention rates are low, something is probably wrong with the training. By getting feedback from MSEs, trainers can adapt existing courses and/or invent new ones (Haan, 2000; Rogowska, 2001). This direction of information flow is important for market development, as it helps improve training, thereby deepening the market. Another way to ensure training quality is to run training of trainers (ToT) courses. In the context of MSE development, this sometimes means training existing trainers to instil MSE-oriented business skills. The following comment was made by a trainer who participated in ToT for this purpose.

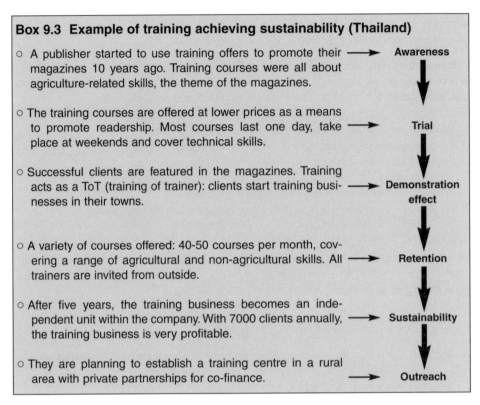

Box 9.3 Example of training achieving sustainability (Thailand)

○ A publisher started to use training offers to promote their ⟶ **Awareness**
  magazines 10 years ago. Training courses were all about
  agriculture-related skills, the theme of the magazines.

○ The training courses are offered at lower prices as a means
  to promote readership. Most courses last one day, take ⟶ **Trial**
  place at weekends and cover technical skills.

○ Successful clients are featured in the magazines. Training
  acts as a ToT (training of trainer): clients start training busi- ⟶ **Demonstration**
  nesses in their towns.   **effect**

○ A variety of courses offered: 40-50 courses per month, covering a range of agricultural and non-agricultural skills. All ⟶ **Retention**
  trainers are invited from outside.

○ After five years, the training business becomes an inde-
  pendent unit within the company. With 7000 clients annually, ⟶ **Sustainability**
  the training business is very profitable.

○ They are planning to establish a training centre in a rural
  area with private partnerships for co-finance.   ⟶ **Outreach**

Before I attended the ToT I had already delivered training to businesses, but not to MSEs. I was not sure whether MSEs could be viable clients for my training. During the ToT, I realized that there was a huge potential in the MSE segment but that communication to MSEs required specific skills. It is four months since the ToT and I am confident that training MSEs can be very profitable.

(Trainer in Kenya)

There are two key lessons about ToT from the FIT experience. First, the selection of trainers is crucial. They themselves should be entrepreneurs with a strong interest in running a training business. Second, new trainers need continuous marketing support during the initial period after ToT, especially when they have to market themselves to people who are unfamiliar with training, or who are used to getting training for free.

Interventions may be aimed at any of these three stages. One possible intervention aimed at all three key elements is a voucher programme. It can promote two-way communication between trainers and MSEs, with vouchers offering a temporary discount. There are several reports describing voucher programmes (see for example, Goldmark et al., 2001), though there is no consensus yet on whether voucher programmes can successfully create a sustainable training market.

Conclusion

The training market for MSEs in developing countries is characterized by 'uneducated' potential customers on the one hand, and sceptical suppliers on the other. By taking the role of facilitator, donors can help private trainers discover how much further they can penetrate the grey zone of the market, and at the same time identify areas where subsidies are justified. Donors should also adopt the role of advocate of the new BDS approach so as to bring about a more enabling environment for training.

References

Anderson, G. (2000) 'The hidden MSE service sector: research into commercial BDS provision to micro and small enterprises in Viet Nam and Thailand' SEED Working Paper No. 5, ILO.

Bennell, P. (1998a) 'Vocational education and training in Zimbabwe: the role of private sector provision in the context of economic reform' IDS Working paper 74.

Bennell, P. (1998b) 'Vocational education and training in Tanzania in the context of economic reform' final report from the VET Study Group.

FIT (2001a) 'Use and demand for commercial non-financial services among MSEs in Semarang, Indonesia' prepared by Taylor Nelson Sofres Ltd. Indonesia, the FIT project, International Labour Organization.

Goldmark, L., C. Botelho and P. Orozco, (2001) 'Key issues in the design, implementation and monitoring of voucher training programmes' SED Working Paper no 2, Swiss Agency for Development and Cooperation (SDC).

Haan, H. (2000) 'Training for work in the informal sector in 2000', a report compiled for the International Labour Organization.

Mung'oma, J. (2000) 'Market development intervention: market appraisal and sensitization report', a report compiled for FIT Resources Ltd. Kenya.

Pejerrey, G. and M. Tueros (2000) 'A study of private providers of Business Development Services for small and micro enterprises in Lima'.

Rogowska, L. (2001) 'Results of the East Java Voucher: BDS providers' presentation by Swisscontact.

About the author

Akiko Suzuki wrote this paper while working with the IFP/SEEDs department of the International Labour Organization, Geneva. She is now employed by a private Japanese company in the IT/mobile industry.

10 Assessing markets for business development services: what have we learned so far?

ALEXANDRA O. MIEHLBRADT

This paper was first published in September 2002.

How can an organization decide in which BDS markets to intervene? This article draws on market assessments from all over the world to help managers decide when and how to launch such programmes. SEs are found to use BDS much less in some countries and for some services, but generalizations are unreliable, and it is usually necessary to draw up a profile of a market before it can be determined if a strategy that is effective in one country is appropriate for another. The chapter goes on to examine under what conditions of supply and demand for a service intervention will be most effective, and gives examples of appropriate interventions. Common assumptions, such as that business women use BDS less than men, or that price is a deciding factor in the choice of BDS, are examined.

OVER THE PAST THREE YEARS, a number of donors and other organizations have conducted assessments of business development services (BDS) markets. Comparing the results of these market assessments can help the BDS field address a number of practical questions in the design and implementation of BDS market development programmes, such as:

○ How can an organization decide in which BDS markets to intervene?
○ How can a programme manager determine the appropriate time at which to exit a market and leave it to develop on its own?
○ When are strategies that have been successfully used in one market appropriate for another?

This chapter aims to contribute to answering these questions by comparing data from 13 different market assessments. The chapter addresses the following issues:

○ How developed are various BDS markets?
○ What are the key similarities and differences across a number of BDS markets?
○ How can market assessment data be applied to programme design?
○ How can organizations assess the potential for development of a BDS market?
○ Are the common preconceptions about BDS markets – on which many programmes have been built – valid?

The chapter draws on the following market assessments: International Labour Organization in Thailand, Cambodia, Ghana and Indonesia, GTZ in Nepal, Swisscontact in Bangladesh, Mercy Corps in Azerbaijan, and six market assessments conducted as part of the Performance Measurement Framework field research sponsored by USAID: CECI/MARD in Nepal, FAIDA in Tanzania, IEDI in Nepal, SEEDS in Sri Lanka, Swisscontact in Peru and Swisscontact in the Philippines (see References for full details). These market assessments used consumer research – surveys and discussions with small enterprises – as the main method for gathering market information. The assessments gathered information from small enterprises using tools adapted from private sector marketing research. These tools are beginning to replace conventional needs assessments as a more effective way of understanding the demand for services, current usage of services and the supply of services from the perspective of small enterprise (SE) consumers. They focus on SEs' demand and actual use of services rather than only expressed needs.

The 13 market assessments were conducted with somewhat different goals. Not every assessment used exactly the same methodology. The chapter examines those aspects of the studies that are comparable. However, it is important to keep in mind that the assessments examined somewhat different markets – bounded by a service, a consumer group and a geographic area. While the consumer groups studied are overlapping, this paper does not examine exactly the same markets in different countries but somewhat different markets in different countries. Table 10.1 overleaf summarizes the market assessments.

How developed are various BDS markets?

Market penetration is a bottom-line indicator of the level of market development. It shows what percentage of all enterprises have purchased a service either in a given time period or ever. Figure 10.1 shows the market penetration of a similar group of services from market assessments of Ghana and Thailand, which are chosen as examples from each end of the market penetration spectrum. In Thailand, enterprises have used a wide range of services, whereas in Ghana only a few services have been used by a reasonably large proportion of SEs.

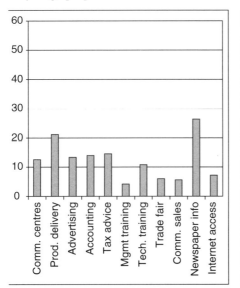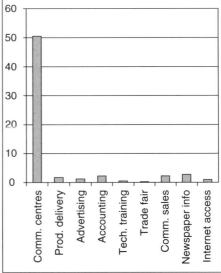

Figure 10.1 *Market penetration percentages for various services in Thailand (left) and Ghana (right).*

Table 10.1   Summary of market assessments

Organization, country and geographic area	Consumers	No. of services	Methodologies	Sample size
ILO; Cambodia 2/3 urban (Phnom Penh) 1/3 rural	SEs with 1-20 workers; all sectors	12	Consumer survey	300; 400
ILO; Ghana urban, peri-urban, rural			Informal market research	401
ILO; Indonesia ½ urban; ½ rural				500
ILO;Thailand; urban (Bangkok, 2 smaller cities)				
GTZ; Nepal, urban	All enterprises; all sectors (except agriculture)	13	Consumer survey Consumer focus group discussions Provider interviews	504
Swisscontact; Bangladesh urban	SEs with 1–50 workers; all sectors (except agriculture)	10	Consumer survey Consumer focus group discussions	410
Mercy Corps; Azerbaijan urban, peri-urban, rural	SEs with 1–50 workers; all sectors	16	Consumer survey Provider survey	335 consumers 121 providers
CECI/MARD; Nepal rural	Microenterprises with 1–10 workers; all sectors	4	Consumer survey	182
FAIDA; Tanzania urban and rural	Microenterprises with 1–10 workers; all sectors (except agriculture)	4	Consumer survey	288
IEDI; Nepal urban, peri-urban	SEs with 1–50 workers; all sectors (except agriculture)	1	Consumer survey	200
SEEDS; Sri Lanka rural	SEs with 1–50 workers; all sectors	2	Consumer survey	100
Swisscontact; Peru 2 urban areas	SEs with 1–50 workers; all sectors (except agriculture)	2	Consumer survey	307
Swisscontact, Philippines small urban and peri-urban	SEs with 1–50 workers; services and manufacturing	2	Consumer survey	110

Despite the differences, some generalizations are possible. Basic services such as telecommunications and product transport generally enjoy higher market penetration than higher end services such as training and trade fairs. Most services have market penetration under 25 per cent and the majority under 10 per cent. Some countries have generally better-developed BDS markets than others. However, a country with generally weak markets may still have one or two strong markets.

This analysis can also be applied to individual service markets across countries. Figure 10.2 shows the market penetration of technical training purchased by SEs in a variety of country markets (for Ghana: purchases made in the past 12 months only; for Cambodia, Indonesia, Thailand: purchases made in the past two years only).

The figure provides a frame of reference for judging the relative level of development of technical training markets. Comparing these figures with those for countries and markets which are considered well developed – for example medium-sized enterprises in urban areas of developed countries – will begin to show at what point a training market can be considered reasonably well developed and thus donors should exit.

A comparison of the technical training markets with those for advertising is instructive. Figure 10.3 shows the market penetration in a variety of countries for the advertising market. In almost every country, more SEs use advertising services than technical training services. This shows that the level of market development which would signal a donor to exit may vary for a number of different services. It also shows that cross-country comparisons for the same service can be helpful in establishing benchmarks for market development.

Understanding the level of market development can help with programme design. Weaker markets, such as those in Ghana and Cambodia, will likely need longer, more intense and more multifaceted interventions than stronger markets such as those in Indonesia and Thailand. The level of market development must also be the context for judging programme performance. What can be considered good programme outreach in a weak market, might be considered modest in a stronger market. As more data are gathered, it may be possible to establish benchmarks for what constitutes a 'strong' market based on the particular country, consumer group and service. This will help programmes determine when to exit a market.

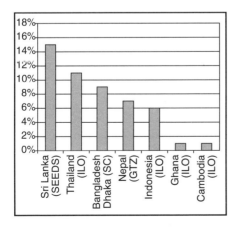

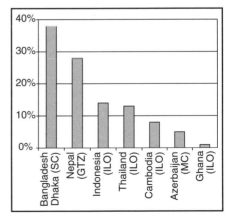

Figure 10.2 *Market penetration of technical training.*

Figure 10.3 *Market penetration of advertising.*

What are the similarities and differences in BDS markets?

Are there common issues that run across many BDS markets in developing countries? Identifying similarities and differences in BDS markets may help the BDS field develop profiles of various markets. This will help practitioners determine when a strategy that has been successfully implemented in one country is applicable elsewhere, and when it is not.

Four important challenges in BDS market development are: making SEs aware of services, helping SEs understand services, persuading SEs to try services and ensuring that SEs continue to use services. Not all of these issues are present in every BDS market. In some markets, the primary problem is a lack of awareness. In others, the primary problem is getting SEs to try a service. Market assessment data can help pinpoint which of these issues exist and their relative severity. This information can help a programme manager target programme activities to address the key problems in a market. There are four ratios in use by the private sector to pinpoint these market issues. They are described in Table 10.2.

Comparing the markets in the studies based on these four issues yields only a few commonalities. Reach is a common problem across many BDS markets. Even when SEs understand services, only a few actually try them. Therefore, a key challenge for the BDS field is to develop effective strategies to help suppliers design more appropriate service products and more effective marketing campaigns. It would be useful to study those markets that have a relatively high reach rate, for example, the markets for sales on commission in Cambodia and advertising in Nepal. Learning why SEs are

Table 10.2   Key market issues

Ratio name	Definition	Question the ratio addresses	Possible market weaknesses
Awareness	The percentage of SEs aware of a service out of all SEs.	What proportion of SEs know a particular service exists?	○ Suppliers are not adequately marketing their products. ○ SEs are not interested in information on services.
Understanding	The percentage of SEs who can correctly define a service out of those who are aware of it.	Even if SEs are aware of the service, do they understand what it is?	○ Suppliers' marketing does not convey the meaning and benefits of services. ○ SEs do not see value in seeking information about services.
Reach	The percentage of SEs who have tried a service out of those who understand it.	Even if SEs understand a service, do they try it?	○ Suppliers are not offering products that SEs want. ○ Suppliers do not have adequate marketing to induce trial. ○ SEs are too risk averse to try services.
Retention	The percentage of SEs who have used a service more than once out of those who have ever used it.	Once SEs have tried a service, do they come back for more?	○ Products in the market are poor quality. ○ There is not sufficient range of products in the market to encourage repeat sales.

willing to try these services and identifying the mechanisms used to persuade them may help BDS practitioners improve reach in other markets.

Beyond this, markets differ. While awareness is a key problem in some countries and markets, it is not in others. For example, in Cambodia, the awareness level for seven out of 13 services is below 10 per cent. But awareness of most services in Indonesia is high. Looking at these market issues for specific consumer groups within countries highlights priorities for particular groups of SEs. For example, in Nepal, GTZ found that the lack of understanding of services was particularly acute among smaller enterprises. In countries where awareness of services is generally not a problem, it may still be a problem for specific consumer groups. For example, in Indonesia awareness among traders about some services, such as advertising and business tours, is less than among other sectors.

The studies show few predictable similarities among markets. Therefore, a programme strategy that effectively develops a market in one country may not be appropriate for the same service market in another country. Instead, a more detailed profile of a market must be drawn before it can be determined if a strategy that is effective in one country is appropriate for another.

How can market assessment information be applied to programme design?

When designing a programme, it is helpful not just to know if a market is weak or strong but if demand is weak or strong and if supply is weak or strong. For example, in a market with strong supply but weak demand, a voucher programme is appropriate to help persuade SEs to try the service. But in a market with weak supply and strong demand, technical assistance to suppliers, product development and/or efforts to help start up suppliers are appropriate to increase and improve available service products. Table 10.3 provides illustrative suggestions for the types of interventions that might be appropriate in the four different types of markets.

Market assessment data can provide information for categorizing market demand and supply as strong or weak. It is possible to roughly categorize markets based solely on quantitative consumer research. Qualitative information from SEs as well as information from directly assessing the supply of services can help fine-tune the categorization. Figure 10.4 categorizes the markets in Thailand by demand and supply using only quantitative consumer research data. It shows the relative strengths of demand and supply in the Thai context only. Percentage market penetration is provided for reference.

The level of demand relies on the following three variables:

○ SEs' awareness of services
○ SEs' assessment of how important each service is for their business to be competitive
○ the percentage of non-users whose reasons for not purchasing the service could be 'actionable' by a programme (e.g. responses other than 'Do not feel the need').

The level of supply relies on the following three variables:

○ each service's retention rate (the percentage of SEs that use a service more than once out of those that use it once)
○ SEs' stated satisfaction level with services

Table 10.3 Illustrative interventions in different types of markets

| | | Supply | |
		Strong	Weak
Demand	Weak	No intervention	Technical assistance to suppliers. Product development. Help start-up new suppliers. Promote supplier franchising.
Demand	Strong	Voucher programme. Provision of information to consumers. Promote 'third party paid for' services. Promote trial-inducing marketing (e.g. coupons, one free trial, demonstrations). Promote customer-referral marketing.	No intervention. Multiple interventions on both demand and supply side. Promote embedded services.

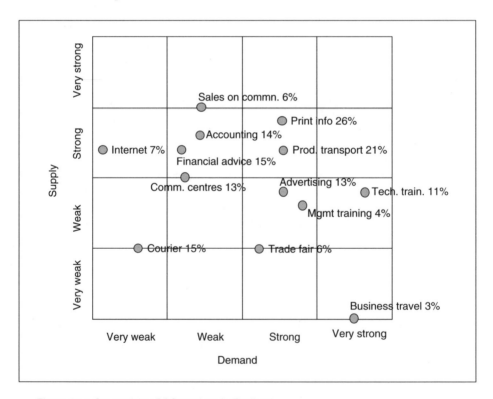

Figure 10.4 *Categorizing BDS markets in Thailand.*

○ the percentage of SE users that said they chose their supplier because it was the only one they knew; this is a negative point because it shows a lack of choice and a lack of competition among suppliers.

Each of these variables was given equal weight in the calculation of a rating for demand and supply in each market.

The graph describes each market in terms of the level of demand and supply in the Thai context. It shows, for example, that there is strong demand for technical training but somewhat weak supply. Therefore, this market could benefit from interventions such as product development and technical assistance to suppliers. While the supply of internet access services is strong, demand at the time of the survey was very weak. Therefore, this market could benefit from interventions to stimulate demand, such as demonstrations, coupons and free trial offers.

Are the same services usually in the same category in different countries? A comparison of the markets in Thailand and Indonesia using this analysis shows that the same service market is not usually in the same category in these two countries. While more research on other countries is needed, this comparison shows that practitioners cannot assume that a market development strategy that worked for a particular service in one country will work for the same service elsewhere. It may be more helpful to apply a strategy that worked for a market with similar demand and supply characteristics, even if it is for a different service.

It is helpful to use a matrix like the one above as a starting point for programme design. The matrix is not meant to provide a formulaic prescription for interventions but rather to be used as an aid, together with other information, in programme design. Using both other market assessment information and first-hand knowledge of a market to identify the specific reasons for weak demand or supply in a particular market will help pinpoint areas for programme intervention.

How can organizations assess the potential for development of a BDS market?

In order to determine which services to promote, organizations are interested in the potential for market expansion. Many of the market assessments conducted have attempted to quantify the 'gap' between potential demand and current purchases. Potential demand has been determined in different ways, such as:

○ the percentage of SEs who say they would be willing to pay for a service
○ the percentage of non-users who say a service is important for the competitiveness of their business
○ the percentage of SEs who say they would definitely or probably buy a service in the future
○ the percentage of non-users whose reason for not purchasing the service can be addressed by the programme.

For example, in Indonesia, awareness of services is reasonably high, but usage is still modest. In order to determine the potential demand for services among the non-users, the survey asked SEs which services they thought were important for the competitiveness of their businesses. They found that those with the most potential are advertising, technical training and information (51, 43 and 42 per cent respectively of SEs thought that these services were important for their competitiveness). Of course, the fact that an entrepreneur thinks a service is important is no guarantee that s/he will purchase it. Nevertheless, when combined with other information, it does provide a starting point for judging the relative growth potential for different service markets.

Despite the different techniques used, several services emerge frequently among the studies as having potential for market expansion: management training, technical training, information and advertising. Services which help with marketing, such as links to new customers, sales on commission and new product development, also show potential in several countries. However, there are some services which appear to have strong potential in one or two countries but not others, such as internet access and legal advice.

As these studies were only recently completed, there are no available data yet to establish how helpful this type of analysis is in determining the potential for market expansion. Nevertheless, they do provide some basis for managers to decide which services to promote.

Are the common preconceptions about BDS markets valid?

Many BDS programmes have been designed based on particular ideas about demand and supply in BDS markets. While more evidence is needed, the available studies provide some early indications about the validity of these preconceptions.

All BDS markets in developing countries are weak

Is it valid to intervene in any BDS market in developing countries because it is assumed they are all weak and need outside assistance to develop? While the BDS field does not yet have a complete picture of what is a 'strong' or 'weak' market, the wide range of levels of market development in the studies indicates that not all markets are weak. It would be hard to call a market with over 50 per cent penetration, such as the SE market for advertising in Bogra, Bangladesh, weak. Assessing BDS markets before starting a programme can provide information on where they might have most impact.

There is a mismatch between demand and supply in most BDS markets

A key rationale for organizations to intervene in markets is that there is a gap between the demand and supply of services. Is this in fact the case? The studies do appear to indicate unmet demand in many BDS markets. All of the techniques used to quantify unmet demand rely on SEs' thoughts, perceptions and intentions. Marketing researchers have found that estimates based on intentions usually overestimate the actual market potential. However, even if half or more of those SEs classified as potential users in the various studies are not, there is still significant unmet demand for many services. The BDS field must be careful, however, not to assume that all SEs are potential users of any given service. The studies also show the potential additional users of a given service are usually less than 50 per cent of the current non-users.

Rural BDS markets are weaker than their urban counterparts

It is often stated that providing SEs with access to business services is more difficult in rural areas than in urban areas. Only two studies provided comparative information on urban and rural markets. Both found that urban BDS markets were somewhat stronger than rural BDS markets for most services. The ILO's study in Indonesia compared rural and urban BDS markets on a service-by-service basis, and found that most urban BDS markets are more developed than their rural counterparts, except for communication centres and package/parcel delivery services.

SEs want management training and consulting services

For many years, the services most often sponsored by donors and government agencies were management training and consulting services. The studies provide conflicting evidence: these two services are often among the least purchased by SEs; however, management training is one service with considerable unmet demand in a number of countries. Consulting services, to a lesser extent, have potential for market expansion in some countries. There are, however, several other services which SEs appear to demand as much or more than these two: advertising, information and technical training.

Women and microenterprises are the key underserved groups in BDS markets

The studies reveal that women are underserved in some markets but not in others. For example, in Ghana women use significantly less communications centre services, advertising and bookkeeping and accounting services, but more print information and sales on commission services, than men. Across all the studies, women-owned enterprises often acquire services to the same extent as or only slightly less than men-owned enterprises.

The evidence on microenterprises is similar. While microenterprises are underserved in some countries and markets, in others they access services to the same extent as other enterprises. For example, the study in Indonesia found that BDS purchases were not correlated with enterprise size. However, in Thailand, the survey showed that smaller enterprises did use services less than larger enterprises.

Although the data appear to show that women and microenterprises are often not an underserved group, it is necessary to look deeper before making a final conclusion. Several of the studies found that although women and microenterprises are getting services to the same extent as other SEs, a greater proportion of their usage is free or subsidized services. Further research is necessary to determine whether women and men are accessing full-cost services from private providers at similar levels.

Are there other groups of enterprises that are typically underserved with business services? Many of the studies disaggregated their results by enterprise sector. The results show that some sectors use services to a greater extent than others. For example, in Peru, manufacturing enterprises dominate the market for training while other sectors are underserved. In Thailand, the trading sector spends the most on BDS, whereas in Bangladesh traders are often underserved. The implication for programme managers is that it is important to assess the market before assuming any particular group is underserved.

Most SEs are not even aware of many BDS

In the past, many programmes have assumed this and have conducted awareness-raising activities as a component of market development.

The studies show that awareness of business services varies widely. In some countries, such as Thailand and Indonesia, awareness is high, whereas in Ghana and Cambodia awareness is low for many services.

When disaggregated by sex, geographical location and sector, awareness is much higher among some consumer groups than others. For programme managers, this means that awareness-raising activities are essential in some countries and for some groups but not for others.

BDS markets for SEs are characterized by low-quality services

In the past, the rationale for starting new BDS providers was that any existing services were of very poor quality. One useful method for evaluating service quality is to measure SEs' repeat purchase of services. This measure relies on the assumption that if an SE is satisfied with a service s/he will purchase it again. While this may not be true for a few service categories, it appears to be applicable for many service categories.

The studies show that for various service markets in different countries retention is high across almost all services. Training and trade fairs are the only services that show somewhat lower retention. This appears to indicate that SEs are, on the whole, happy enough with the BDS they purchase to purchase them again. However, in order to get statistically significant figures, retention has been calculated only for those services that enjoy reasonably high usage, and less is known about those services that SEs use less. Despite the bias, the data seem to indicate that many services are of reasonable quality in the eyes of the SE customers. For programme managers, this means that it may often be worth working with existing suppliers of services, rather starting new suppliers.

The main reason SEs do not purchase services is the price

In the past, it was assumed that if free services were available, SEs would line up to use them. But what are the other factors inhibiting purchase?

Many of the studies asked non-purchasers why they had not purchased various business services. The most often-cited reason is that they do not need the service or the service is not relevant to their businesses. This may result from a combination of two factors. First, many business services may be irrelevant to some SEs. Second, some SEs may not understand how a particular business service could benefit them.

There are a variety of other factors that inhibit purchase of services in some markets:

○ *Expense.* For example, in Ghana the most-often cited reason for not purchasing information in print, bookkeeping and accounting services, technical training and trade fairs was expense.
○ *Time.* In the Philippines survey, 33 per cent of non-users stated a lack of time as the key reason that they did not purchase training services.
○ *Lack of information.* For example, in Peru, 28 per cent of SEs stated that they did not use technical assistance services because they did not know any providers.

It is important to find out the key reasons why SEs do not purchase services in a particular market in order to target those reasons with programme activities. While it would be foolhardy to ignore price as an important issue for SEs, it is not the only factor or often even the key issue in SEs' purchase decisions. It is also important to realize that not every SE needs or wants the particular service a programme is promoting. Identifying appropriate segments to target will increase the effectiveness of programmes in expanding the use of BDS.

SEs' main criterion for their choice of service provider is price

Once an SE has decided to purchase a service, is price an important factor in choosing a provider? The studies show that price is rarely the key criterion in an SEs' choice of service provider. Rather, BDS markets tend to be driven by quality characteristics such as providers' reputation, recommendations from others and the types of services available.

Does this mean that free services offered by donors and government are not distorting the markets for BDS? Not necessarily: the studies show that free services may depress SEs' willingness to pay for services. For example, in Nepal IEDI found that 31 per cent of non-purchasers stated being able to get management training for free as a key factor in their choice not to purchase it.

Conclusion

Market assessment results must be examined in the context of a country, a consumer group and a particular service. While there are some similarities among markets, there are many exceptions. Conducting a market assessment in the particular markets a programme will target is essential to understanding those markets.

The next steps in using the growing number of market assessments to help programme managers design effective programmes are to:

○ compare the results with formal sector data to improve understanding of what level of performance to expect in business services markets

○ develop benchmarks for market penetration and other indicators of market development for various services in different country circumstances

○ compare market assessment results over time to improve understanding of how business service markets develop

○ develop a framework that describes different types of markets from the perspective of demand, supply and different market issues

○ document what market development strategies work in markets with particular characteristics.

References

Market assessments from which the data in this chapter are derived:

Consumer Research Co. Ltd (2000) 'MSEs business service demand in Thailand', for the International Labour Organization, FIT Project.

Ghosh, Sandeep (2001) 'Awareness and usage of BDS in Thailand', for the International Labour Organization, FIT Project.

Ghosh, Sandeep (2001) 'Awareness and usage of BDS in Indonesia', for the International Labour Organization, FIT Project.

FAIDA-SEP (2001) 'PMF market development indicators survey report', supported by USAID.

Indochina Research Ltd (2000) 'Project FIT in Cambodia', for the International Labour Organization, FIT Project.

Lang, Hans and Muhammad Matondang and Taylor Nelson Sofres (2001) 'Use and demand for commercial non-financial services among MSE in Semarang, Indonesia', for the International Labour Organization, FIT Project.

Market Access for Rural Development (CECI/MARD) (2001) 'Market Survey Report Business Development Service CECI/MARD', supported by USAID.

Mercy Corps (2001) 'Small and medium enterprise and business development service market survey', Baku, Azerbaijan.

Miehlbradt, Alexandra O. (2001) 'Business development services in Nepal: report on BDS markets assessment', for GTZ Private Sector Promotion Project, Nepal.

Munasinghe, Chintha (2001) 'Performance measurement framework for Business Development Services outreach and market development survey report', for Support for Small Enterprise Development SEEDS (Guarantee) Ltd. Sri Lanka and ITDG South Asia, supported by USAID.

ORG-MARG QUEST (2001) 'Awareness and usage of business development services by the private sector of urban Bangladesh', for the Business Development Services Programme (BDSP) Swisscontact, Bangladesh.

Pentax Management Consultancy Services Limited (2000) 'MSEs business service demand in Ghana', for the International Labour Organization, FIT Project.

Swisscontact, Philippines (2001) 'Performance measurement framework outreach and market development survey report', supported by USAID.

Rivera, Cecilia (2001) 'Performance measurement framework for business development services market survey report', DESIDE Program Swisscontact Peru supported by USAID.

Shrestha, Binod K. (2001) 'A report on outreach and market development survey of business development services (business management training)', IEDI, Nepal supported by USAID.

About the author

Alexandra Miehlbradt is an independent consultant. This chapter summarizes a paper written for the International Labour Organization IFP/SEED on the results of market assessments conducted in 1999–2001. The full paper is available on the BDS information sharing website: www.ilo.org/dyn/bds > Market Assessment > Global Market Assessment Documents. The author expresses her thanks to Jim Tanburn at the ILO and the people and organizations who conducted the market assessments described in the chapter.

11 The market-based approach to enterprise assistance: an evaluation of the World Bank's 'market development grant funds'

DAVID A. PHILLIPS

This paper was first published in March 2002.

When technical assistance to enterprise development is justified then instead of subsidized central facilities, which have often been ineffective, the assistance should aim to develop the market for business know-how. Grants targeted to firms that want to buy business services are more likely to achieve this aim because they can stimulate a competitive response from independent providers of services. 'Matching grant funds' have been used to develop the market by targeting small, efficient firms with the potential for growth, but lacking information or know-how. The World Bank has completed and evaluated eight projects of this type.

The net impact of the eight projects, as described in this chapter, has, however, been uncertain. While their direct output benefit (in terms of increased exports or sales) appears to have been good, sustainability and development impact seem to have been weak. Operating costs have in some cases been high and implementation has been delayed, raising questions about their ability to mobilize the services market. In one case, a project in Mauritius, the first evaluation claimed outstanding results in terms of rapid response and increased output, but a subsequent study shed doubt on the market impact, showing that most firms would have purchased the business service anyway, without the grant.

For such programmes, emphasis should not be on the growth of exports and output, but on the growth of the market for services. Grant funds have to be carefully justified in terms of development impact, and better designed, if they are to be cost-effective and to achieve their potential market-making objective.

AID POLICY IN THE 1970s tended to assume that governments generally acted in the public interest, enhancing welfare through eliminating market failures and redistributing resources. Accordingly, the technical support for enterprise in general and SMEs in particular tended to be channelled through public sector agencies. Then government failure came to be seen to be as important as market failure. For example, enterprise export support through the use of public sector service suppliers is considered largely to have failed in all but a few cases. When 27 World Bank enterprise and export projects approved between 1980 and 1990 were reviewed, most of the results were found to be unsatisfactory both in terms of exports and institution building, (Keesing and Singer, 1990). In the exceptional cases of Hong Kong, Taiwan and Singapore, state agencies were also helped by strong export environments and a dynamic private sector, so the attributability of success to state support is difficult to assess.

Even given an appropriate policy environment, experience suggests that state institutions are likely to be effective only as long as they enjoy the support and participation of the business community, are well funded, have staff experienced in relevant technical areas, and have a significant degree of autonomy from bureaucracy and political interference. These conditions have generally not been met.

To try to find ways of assisting more effectively, donor agencies have tried new approaches to supporting enterprise and exporters outside the state. One way has been to establish autonomous semi-public business support institutions, which provide assistance in a more market-sensitive way. Such interventions remain essentially supply-side. Another approach has been to try to expand the market for business development services directly, by providing incentives to purchasers of services. The resulting increase in demand is expected to stimulate service provision from existing and new private service suppliers. Another version of the demand-driven, decentralized approach to enterprise support, but more experimental, has been based on vouchers, mainly in microenterprise support.

Apart from the problem of how to build local markets, in business services and elsewhere, development aid to the poorest economies is also being seen increasingly as justifying grants rather than loans (for example the World Bank has started to move more towards grant funding for the poorest countries). It is therefore critically important to find ways to make subsidies or grants work to create sustainable development impact rather than simply temporary palliatives that do not improve capacity and may entrench dependency.

The justification for public assistance to private business services

Public (subsidized) intervention is justified if it accelerates early-stage market development. The intervention needs to be in some sense proportional to the market problem being addressed. More costly interventions (i.e. larger subsidies) need to be justified by 'larger failures'. In general, subsidies should:

o   be small enough to just offset the distortion or market failure (which implies being well targeted)
o   achieve their objectives within a limited time (otherwise the targeting may break down)
o   be transparent (to minimize abuse, and to allow their impact to be easily monitored)
o   not have significant macro/fiscal effects
o   involve limited administrative cost.

Box 11.1 outlines some sources of market failure in business services.

Many earlier schemes of centralized and subsidized provision of technical assistance to enterprises were insensitive to demand, created a monopolistic supplier that could undercut competitive private suppliers, discouraged market entrants, and over-invested in services that were not necessarily needed nor of high quality. Such approaches did not adhere to the rule of minimizing the distortion created by the intervention, and they were neither temporary nor transparent. Even if they managed to increase services, this was not by itself an adequate justification for public technical assistance intervention, and could actually be harmful if it did not lead to sustainable development of the market. An illustration of this type of problem is from Tanzania (Box 11.2).

To justify public intervention in general, and public support for business in particular, it is not enough simply to show that the intervention successfully produces an

Box 11.1   Market failures that justify public support to business development services

Demand-side failures may result from a lack of knowledge by firms of what business services are available, and how they can be of use. Information on export potential is particularly lacking for SMEs. There is also a problem of 'short term-ism' as a result of uncertainty about the value of outside advice or training, which makes the cost of services seem too high compared to its benefits. Training is particularly difficult to value because it is an 'experience good'. The benefit is difficult to value prior to completion of training, at which point the incentive to pay is reduced.

Supply-side failures are linked to the demand side – an underdeveloped market results in low expected returns to business service provision. First mover transaction costs may be relatively high. Foreign competition (e.g. in external trade, accounting and auditing services) may put up barriers to local entrants, or, on the other hand, local protection may reduce the demonstration effects of foreign competition. There may also be a lack of/inappropriate professional training infrastructure to produce advisers – or a relatively high threshold investment in such training.

Linked market failures may occur in, for example, banking. SMEs are seen as risky borrowers due partly to lack of a track record. Lack of access to finance could reduce activity and demand for business services, such as in the case of exporting firms where lack of pre-shipment and post-shipment finance may reduce output.

increased output. Many projects have been judged in terms of how much they increase output. The fact that they do so is a good start, but more is needed. Indeed, if current output is inefficient then an intervention might produce a benefit by reducing it! To be justifiable the intervention must lead to the provision of additional efficient output over and above what private suppliers intend to produce, or believe they can profitably produce. But to sustain efficiency improvement, a 'one-shot-deal' (i.e. a single injection of technical assistance) may not be enough. To ensure sustainability (and

Box 11.2   Tanzania: state support bypassed existing local capacity

Despite the adverse environment for private enterprise in the 1970s, the commercial district of Dar Es Salaam still hosted many small private business service firms: book-keepers, accountants, forwarding and courier agencies, procurement and marketing agents, and training establishments. These small businesses seemed to be invisible to the donor agencies and to the government, which preferred to set up high-profile centralized promotion facilities. Yet these micro-firms were profitable commercial businesses; they understood the market and the business environment.

To the outside observer it seemed that the small accountants' offices, if stimulated by increased demand and with some technical help, could be the seed-corn of future accountancy, business advice and consultant service firms. But instead they had to compete with donor-financed business development facilities working out of expensively staffed and equipped offices, and providing free services. Fortunately for them, the local knowledge and the marketing efforts of these state-sponsored bureaus were weak, so that the local service suppliers were not seriously damaged and they largely retained their traditional 'invisible' customers. However, it was an opportunity wasted, because it was these existing fledgling service firms themselves that would have benefited from advice, training, and incentives to upgrade.

development impact) the intervention should build the market for business advisory and technical services through better market information, expanded demand and lower entry costs, which is a system that can sustain itself.

The market for business development services is often divided into strategic and operational services. Operational services are routine activities such as freight and mail forwarding, printing and publishing, and bookkeeping. The market is usually well functioning for routine services. The market problem (failure) is more likely with strategic services which are outside the regular experience or conception of small firms, such as diagnostic analysis, financing, reorganization, specialized market planning (e.g. exports), identification of investment partners. It is in these areas that a subsidized intervention may be justified, for both local and foreign advisory services. Some economists would argue that a subsidy that directly supports trade transactions is less efficient than a non-transactional subsidy (e.g. for public information, research or technical upgrading) because it 'distorts' sellers' and buyers' decisions. However, market creation is a dynamic process and a market transaction carries an inherent learning-by-doing benefit different from that of, say, pure information provision. Giving incentives to directly boost transactions may therefore produce as great or greater benefits as non-transactional subsidies.

If a grant is used to boost demand, then the initial effect might be to encourage suppliers to raise their fees for services. But if the increased demand also reduces the supplier's risk (e.g. the risk of not being paid), it might encourage new entrants, which would lower fees in the longer run. A rapid change in conditions of supply (e.g. through better information) is key to market growth with lower fees. A change in user firms' perceptions must also take place (e.g. through greater certainty about the value of services), so that demand remains elevated even after the subsidy has been removed. This means that user firms should be prepared to pay for services at or nearer full cost in subsequent rounds. Otherwise, after the subsidy is removed the market would contract back towards its initial size as suppliers exit, and the whole exercise would have been a costly waste of time and resources. To help lock in the essential changes in market perception the subsidy should be phased over time.

One method of targeting demand, through a partial subsidy, has been through a matching grant fund (MGF). These have been used increasingly by the World Bank, IADB, and other donors for creating consulting and training capacity. The MGF has been used mainly to boost demand but it can also be in the form of a general 'market development fund', upgrading service providers to meet more sophisticated demand by user firms. It could fund both non-transactional and transactional services (and both local and foreign service providers) ranging from free information to business services.

Another demand-side approach is to use vouchers. Vouchers are a partial transactional subsidy like a matching grant, but they provide a currency of payment for services that might further reduce the risk of the transaction to both service supplier and user. Some voucher projects have had good results. For example, in a Paraguay training voucher project, the evaluation claimed that 'instead of the empty classrooms and lack of enthusiasm for the supply-side approach even with private providers, demand for training services picked up strongly'. Voucher schemes may be administratively complicated, however, and more liable to collusion and forms of corruption than grant funds.

The World Bank's market development grant funds

Figure 11.1 depicts the essentials of a donor-supported market development grant fund. The donor assistance flows not to a provider but to a facilitator (the fund manager). The purpose of the facilitator is not to provide technical services to enterprises but to mobilize the market, which could consist of both local and foreign service suppliers, and local user enterprises. The approach would include the provision of partial grants for services, both to the demand side and to the supply side to upgrade their services in response to the new demand. Grants to service transactions are not essential to the idea: support could be in the form simply of a matchmaking information service. In any case, grant funds create demand by lowering the cost of business services compared to the user's (risk-adjusted) valuation of the service, and increased demand in turn promotes supply.

One of the first funds was set up in 1961 by the Irish Export Board as a marketing development fund. Grant funds have also been set up for business advisory services in Europe, including the UK, France, Italy, and Norway. A scheme set up by the British DTI in 1988 encouraged firms of fewer than 400 employees to use management consultants. A review of that project in 1991 showed that of 21 000 programmes that had been started for firms, 90 per cent of beneficiaries stated that they had received value for money, and 74 per cent of beneficiaries planned to use consultants again, paying the full market price (World Bank, 1995).

Between 1986 and 2000, about 16 World Bank grant fund projects for business development or export support were started. The total value of the funds was US$216 million and over 6000 sub-projects have been implemented. The number of new projects is accelerating, mainly in Africa and Latin America. The earliest significant Bank scheme was the 1986 India Engineering Export Project. This contained a consultant fund and a productivity fund, each of $10 million managed by State banks

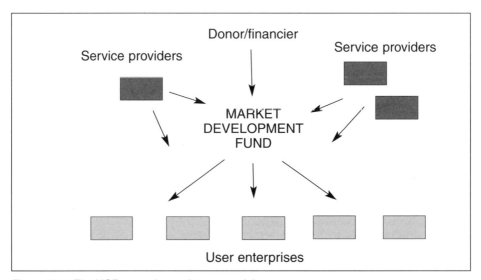

Figure 11.1 *The MGF enterprise assistance model.*

(ICICI and Eximbank). They required 50 per cent matching funds, and single firms or groups of firms could receive up to $200 000 in grants. The managing banks used decentralized, streamlined approval procedures. The project was rated a success, though there were delays and 20 per cent of the funds were undisbursed. Estimated export growth rates of the beneficiaries far exceeded the national average. This was the model for a follow-up project in 1989, with four funds totalling $20 million and maximum grants of $500 000 per firm. This project was also rated a success, with significant incremental export achievement.

A similar project for export support and SME assistance was started in Indonesia in 1986. The fund manager was the State Export Support Board. Total funds were $8 million supporting exports through marketing, production management, training, and technical assistance. The co-payment percentages were a minimum of 25 per cent. Maximum grant size was $64 000. Processing delays caused slow disbursement (68 per cent at closure) but the advisory services were considered successful and exports increased by a large multiple of the grant fund. Nevertheless, firms were not prepared to pay the full cost for the services after project completion, implying limited market creation impact.

Eight grant fund projects, initiated between 1986 and 1994, have been completed and evaluated by the World Bank. The projects are from India (2), Indonesia, Argentina, Kenya, Mauritius, Jamaica and Uganda. Most focused mainly on exports, while Uganda and Mauritius were concerned with the broader provision of business services to boost productivity. In the case of export development these services included: marketing research and planning, quality testing and certification, product adaptation, export fairs and national/international marketing tours. In the case of business support they included business strategy and planning, production management, product design, quality standards and control, productivity studies, information systems, and training.

The first projects were more oriented toward using foreign advisory services because knowledge of foreign markets was a main concern. More recent projects have addressed the building of the local services market.

The size of the grant funds varied widely, from $2.0 million (Kenya) to US$32.0 million (Argentine), approximately related to the size of the respective enterprise sectors. The average grants paid varied from about $2200 (Uganda) and $2300 (Kenya) to $43 000 (India). In Jamaica loans averaged $248 000. Payment arrangements were 50 per cent grant and 50 per cent co-payment by the recipient enterprises (except in Jamaica and Indonesia, where there was a minimum 20 per cent and 25 per cent co-payment respectively). Sub-project costs were reimbursed by the fund subject to proof of expenditure.

All projects had multi-tier governance with a government agency or autonomous government entity (e.g. a Foundation) in overall control, usually complemented by a steering committee or consultative council that approved larger grants. The type of fund managing agency varied; in India the fund was managed by state and private banks, and in Indonesia by a specially created government office (the Export Support Board). In Jamaica the loan scheme was managed by the Exporters' Association. In the other projects, management was provided by a single external specialist firm. The independence of the managing agent, both from political pressure and from ties to the service providers it was accrediting and paying, was key to achieving a streamlined and market-credible mechanism.

The indigenization of fund management varied. In the case of India the participating banks not only managed the fund but created special 'cells' to develop in-house capacity in export advisory services. In most other cases, a foreign specialist firm managed the fund, withdrawing on completion of its market-making activity.

The managing entities took some responsibility for the quality of the service providers. The extent varied from, on the one hand, proactive assistance for firms to develop proposals and select providers to, on the other hand, more hands-off support such as simply developing lists of registered providers or checks on providers selected independently by the beneficiary firms.

The enterprises selected were mainly private sector SMEs, often exporters. In the minority of cases the funds were also open to larger firms. Apart from the first project in India (engineering) there has been no product targeting. The selection of sub-projects was in all cases based on the first-come-first-served principle subject to set eligibility criteria, usually including provision by the enterprise of a marketing/business plan. In most cases restrictions were put on the number of grants per firm. Beyond establishing eligibility, appraisals were not conducted except in Jamaica.

Evaluating World Bank grant fund projects

The economic rationale for the grant fund was to increase technical and business services demand and capacity, rather than simply increase exports or output. (The increase in exports is difficult to measure because the 'without fund' situation has to be understood, and the extent to which the expansion can be attributed to the fund and not to outside factors has to be taken into account.) To justify intervention the increased exports had to be efficient (profitable at border prices without subsidies), and inherently sustainable. This required that public intervention should focus on capacity building (e.g. in the provision of export advisory services to local firms). So the development impact should be measured in terms of the development of the services industry in all cases.

Fund operating costs and grant size

Operating cost as a percentage of grants disbursed gives an indicator of cost-effectiveness. Performance ranged from 19 per cent (Mauritius) to 54 per cent in Uganda and 40 per cent (Kenya) (see Table 9.1). This is a high cost compared with typical management charges in other types of funds (e.g. in managed venture funds a norm is 3 per cent of gross assets per annum). They also exclude the costs of project committees and government implementation units. Operating cost per grant approved ranged from $1200 (Uganda) and $1300 (Kenya) to over $6000 per completed sub-project (Argentina). The Uganda and Kenya operating cost was a much higher proportion of the value of each sub-project. In Jamaica the average size of funding (in the form of loans) was relatively high, at about $250 000 per project, as it targeted a number of larger-scale enterprises, so costs per grant would have been low. However, overall if governance costs and project preparation and supervision costs are added to these figures there is a presumption of high and perhaps excessive overhead costs.

Table 11.1   Comparisons of grand fund projects

Project name[1] and start date	India 1986	India 1989	Indonesia 1986	Kenya 1991	Mauritius 1994	Argentina 1995	Jamaica 1995	Uganda 1995
Total fund ($million)	20.0	20.0	5.7	2.0	3.2	32.0	8.4	3.0
Number of sub-projects funded	359	449	685	603	266	1060	33	1140
Amount provided ($m)	15.6	16.48	5.17	2.0	2.52	17.8 (out of 26.6 approved)	8.2	2.4
Fund operating cost ($m)	N/a	N/a	2.42	0.8	0.49	6.41	N/a	1.3
Operating cost/ fund value (%)	N/a	N/a	47	40	19	36 excl. partial projects	N/a	54
Operating cost/ sub-project ($)	N/a	N/a	3532	1326	1842	6047	N/a	1140
Grant value per sub-project ($)	43 400	36 700	7550	3316	9480	16 790	248 000	2105
Sales-export increase: grant value	37:1 exports	50:1 exports	36:1 exports	42:1 exports	163:1 sales; 124:1 exports	N/a	N/a 45% export growth	N/a 73% sales growth
WB rating Output:	S	S	S	S	HS	S	S	N/a
Inst. dev.:	S	S	P	M	HS	M	M	
Sust.:	L	L	L	W	HL	L	L	

1. Project fund type: India 1986 engineering export; India 1989 export dev.; Indonesia export dev.; Kenya export dev.; Mauritius competitiveness dev.; Argentina export dev.; Jamaica investment export; Uganda competitiveness.
Key: HS = highly satisfactor; S = satisfactory; HL = highly likely; L = likely; P = partial; M= modest; W = weak

The speed of disbursement

Speed of disbursement is a rough indicator of the 'momentum effect' in mobilizing the services market. The most delayed disbursement over the project life was in the case of the Indian Engineering Export project (2.5 years). The participating banks took time to understand the procedures. In the case of Kenya, there was a six-month average delay in the processing of individual grants, which soured relations with clients. Start-up delays were also reported for Indonesia; in Argentina there were problems because of sub-project cancellations, government interference and weak management follow-up. The Jamaica fund's disbursement was delayed (by up to 18 months) because it was provided in the form of loans and required documentation and collateral. In Mauritius initial disbursement was reported as slow but then picked up. Overall, the speed of disbursement, even with the simplified first-come-first-served approach, has not been sufficient to rapidly mobilize the services market.

Project output

This was measured in terms of sales or export 'multiples' (sales or exports divided by grant value). Many of the projects claimed large increases in exports. The 'multiples' ranged between 37:1 and 50:1, except in the case of Mauritius where a remarkably high ratio of 163:1 for revenue and 124:1 for export sales was claimed. In Uganda a 73 per cent increase in sales was estimated, and in Jamaica a 45 per cent increase in exports, including penetration of the US market by food products firms. If these sales were economically profitable and attributable to the grants, then the grant funds performed very well. However, while a particular firm could make a breakthrough in exports as a result of a one-shot grant for advisory services, it does not seem very likely in general.

Sustainability requires capacity to support that expansion. Attributability is also important. In the case of Jamaica, 60 per cent of the firms reached through the soft loan scheme were relatively large and already had an export track record. It is therefore difficult to see why regular export finance through the private banking system could not have been used to the same effect. Another example is the first India project. Here export gains were impressive but concentrated in a few firms with strong international connections (e.g. Cummins, Ingersoll-Rand) that had access to private finance. Exports were maintained in a time of export decline; was this therefore assistance to 'new exporters'? For these reasons and others the sales and export multiples are not good measures of efficiency or profitability and it is difficult to prove that the export increase was associated with the grant.

Institutional impact and sustainability

In this regard the project documents were not helpful because they focused mainly on output, except in the case of Uganda where indicators of 'additionality' and 'spillover' were introduced later. The Uganda project evaluation showed good results in both sales growth and spillover benefits, but weaker in market sustainability (i.e. willingness to pay full cost for further services). The World Bank gave appropriately moderate scores to all projects on both counts except the Mauritius project, which was rated highly satisfactory.

The Mauritius project: the problem of additionality

The assessment of development impact and sustainability in the case of grant funds, as in similar projects, is complicated and often difficult, with confusion over the exact meaning of development impact. In the case of the Mauritius project the initial evaluation was highly positive (see Table 11.1 and Crisafulli, 1999). The positive evaluation implied that speed of disbursement was itself key to services market development (reducing transaction costs for all participants). Detailed sub-project appraisals were undesirable because they introduce bureaucracy and discretion. Subsidies result in queues and a potential for arbitrary behaviour by fund managers. So achieving streamlined disbursement through simple objective eligibility criteria was important. However, as shown in 11.3, a re-evaluation of the Mauritius project told a different story.

The re-evaluation of the Mauritius project focused on 'additionality' and sparked a contentious debate about the how grant fund projects should be designed to achieve

Box 11.3   The Mauritius technology diffusion scheme

This project received the best initial evaluation of the grant funds, based on its flexibility, simplicity of operation, management autonomy, and objective sub-project selection producing highly positive direct output benefits. The evaluation reflected a view that rapid disbursement to eligible firms would in itself stimulate the market for business services, while appraisals would allow discretion but also delay, slowing growth of the market. But a second internal evaluation focused on whether the project contributed a 'public good'. To assess this it looked at 'additionality'. The right targets were economically viable projects which did not have financial profits (so could not get market finance) and which could achieve maximum benefits per assistance input. If the wrong firms were targeted then, it asserted, the rationale for assistance was in doubt. The re-evaluation did not in fact find that the targets had been achieved.

Sub-project selection was on the first-come-first-served basis without detailed appraisal. Criteria were that firms should be within a target group; should provide an acceptable business plan; and should provide evidence of financial solvency. Over the project life only about 10 per cent of proposals was either screened out or formally rejected. To speed up disbursement, firms were declared eligible if they had already initiated projects (up to three months prior to application/approval) and in practice 81 per cent of sub-projects implemented (mainly in the larger firms) were started before approval. The majority of the 266 grants approved (average value US$9500) went to larger firms (above 200 employees) in textiles and garments, food processing and freight handling. These findings suggested that the fund may not have been able to select economically efficient sub-projects providing spillover benefits.

The report estimated that 25 per cent of projects clearly yielded low returns in terms of additionality. For example, grants went to assemblers of protected consumer products, to a monopoly foreign tobacco company, and to fund the same technology in different divisions of the same company. On the other hand, some potentially high-return projects were rejected as funds ran out, and follow-up grants were not usually obtainable for multi-phase inputs. The evaluation concluded that more targeting was needed to focus on sub-projects likely to generate spillover benefits e.g. cutting edge technology, industry clusters, and complementarities between assisted sub-projects.

The central objective of the project was development of the business services market. While the market was deepened and uncertainty reduced, this effect was limited because three-quarters of firms had already previously used outside help, including foreign consultants. While there were some new entrants, local consultants were unwilling to build up capacity knowing the temporary nature of the scheme because they feared that the market would dry up. Repeat business was limited both during and after the project life. Grants were available to build up the local service firms themselves but only three were in fact given, and so little broadening of service capability occurred. One firm that did develop a sustainable new business was foreign owned and already had diverse skills. A built-in incentive to forming partnerships between local and foreign firms would have been beneficial.

development impact (Biggs, 1999). It cast doubt on whether the project created an output beyond what the private sector would otherwise have been willing and able to provide, which was the critical test for public intervention. At the other extreme, the worst-case recipients would be ones that were both financially and economically unprofitable and needed subsidies just to stay afloat.

The key public objective was to develop the supposedly nascent market for business services through improved information about the value of those services. If a firm could more clearly see this value then the firm would start to demand services and thereby stimulate supply, in a virtuous circle. On the other hand, if for example the constraint on enterprise demand for business services was not lack of information but simply lack of finance then increased market activity stimulated by an injection of money through the grant fund would most likely fizzle out when the funding ended. The re-evaluation did not find that lack of information was the constraint.

One of the points made in favour of the Mauritius project was that it had a much better result than the traditional public sector approach, but the relevant measure is not in comparison with past deficiencies, but against the best approach available now.

Methods of selecting user firms are highly debatable. An approach based on appraisal may identify projects which create externalities but it may be more discretionary, bureaucratic and slow disbursing, thereby running the risk of failure to develop the momentum needed to create a market. By comparison, the first-come-first-served approach avoids discretionary approvals and has higher rates of disbursement – but it is less likely to select activities which are economic. Optimal design should aim to find a way of combining the best of both approaches, retaining the good access and ease of disbursement of first-come-first-served, but paying more attention to economics, possibly by including broad target groups of firms and products and by pre-identifying clusters of promising enterprises.

Improving the effectiveness of grant funds

From the mixed results found in the project evaluations and in other studies and reports for these projects, it is clear that, if MGFs are to fulfil their market creation and institution building potential, their design needs to be more carefully worked out and their operating guidelines improved.

There is likely to be a window of time in which the public external benefits of intervention are greatest, i.e. when the market is in its infancy and its development is constrained by uncertainty and lack of information. The subsidy should be temporary, to be phased out as and when the market starts to expand dynamically.

To justify such projects it must be shown that the market for business services is not working because of lack of business information and know-how, and that positive net social benefits can be derived from making the market work better. Even while retaining first-come-first-served selection of sub-projects, eligibility criteria should permit targeting of firms and groups of firms in product areas and technologies most likely to generate spillover benefits, and types of assistance most likely to stimulate improved local service provision. Assistance should also focus at the SME level, since large firms have got large because they already have good information. The development of good eligibility criteria will require up-front research on enterprise sector and the functioning of the market for services.

The fund manager's role

The functions of the management team are key to the success of the fund. The team's principal business is to promote market knowledge. It must be proactive in market making, forecasting the needs and resources of firms, upgrading them and matching providers and the users using various information media. The team should have business skills and experience, but should use this experience to market the skills of the firms in the market, not to provide its own formal advisory services.

Governance

Last-resort government oversight should be included through a policy committee with limited power (e.g. general fund policy, and approval of above-threshold grants); autonomous fund management should be established either through a market entity (e.g. a financial institution) or through a specialized fund management company, allowing autonomy of decisions. Oversight by a quasi-public entity such as a foundation may increase layers of supervision if it has to report to a government department, so its autonomy must be ensured.

Fund life, size and types of grant

The life of the fund must have a sunset provision tied to specific indicators of domestic market and capacity expansion. The fund size should be based on the estimated value of incremental demand for services by firms over and above demand that would exist in the absence of a fund, and on the likely upgrading needs of new/existing service providers to meet that demand. A simple norm is advisable for grants, for example reimbursing 50 per cent of costs subject to indicative maximum per firm (allowing multiple grants per firm) but where there are relatively high-cost foreign providers this norm may have to be increased. The maximum size of grant depends on the target type of enterprise.

The approval process

Generally a reasonably streamlined first-come-first-served process should be used, but it should be subject to a set of carefully designed and clear enterprise and sub-project eligibility criteria, including broad (flexible) product group targets which increase the probability of funding economically efficient firms.

The types of firm and sub-project

The priority types of enterprises targeted should be relatively small or early stage businesses that have difficulty in accessing private finance for their business plans and little experience in purchasing outside professional services, but which are organizationally or technologically innovative and show managerial initiative and promise of future profitability. If they are working within a 'growth sector' in which technological spillovers are likely, this is a further advantage. Both user-firms and service providers should be eligible.

Performance indicators and criteria

Output and impact indicators may be built into the project design via a 'project scoresheet'. Requirement of the fund manager, service providers and user firms to provide performance data can be spelled out in project agreements. To permit monitoring of the project's effects, the market development indicators must allow for selection bias and non-attributability. Institutional and market development indicators would require information on (i) whether a project would have been fully undertaken in the absence of a grant, (ii) how it would be improved with grant support, (iii) whether it led to sustained development of the market (e.g. the rate of repeater use of services at full cost) and (iv) what spillover benefits (e.g. new marketable technical or business know-how) can be gained from the sub-project itself. It would also need information on the quality and speed of development of service supply, demand and fee rates. However, information provision may be separately organized, since it should not become a bureaucratic burden on the fund manager that adversely affects the objective of market-making.

References

Biggs, T. (1999) 'A microeconometric evaluation of the Mauritius Technology Diffusion Scheme', World Bank, RPED discussion paper.

Crisafulli, D. (1999) 'Matching grant schemes for enterprise upgrading: a comparative analysis', paper presented at Rio De Janeiro Conference on Small Enterprises.

Keesing, D.B. and Singer, A. (1990) 'Expanding manufactured exports through support services'.

World Bank (1995) 'Mauritius: technical assistance to enhance competitiveness'.

About the author

David Phillips is Director, GBRW Ltd, UK, and was formerly on the staff of the World Bank.

12 From principles to practice: ten critical challenges for BDS market development

MARSHALL BEAR, ALAN GIBSON and ROB HITCHINS

This paper was first published in December 2003.

The BDS market development field has clearly made progress in its first few years of activity. However, to advance the field further, and to address incipient signs that spread has not been accompanied by depth in understanding, it now needs to confront ten critical challenges. These are concerned with reasserting the analytical rigour that underpins the approach, with confronting the difficult issues of how to operationalize market development objectives, and with building the capacity of organizations and personnel.

This chapter highlights these challenges and, in doing so, positions BDS market development within the wider private sector development field. While neither straight-forward nor given to pre-packaged solutions, the issues identified here are relevant to all development efforts aimed at making markets work more effectively and inclusively for the benefit of the poor.

THE BUSINESS DEVELOPMENT SERVICES (BDS) field is moving beyond its period of initial novelty. It is now six years since the Committee of Donor Agencies for Small Enterprise Development first produced its preliminary guidelines (Committee of Donor Agencies for Small Enterprise Development, 1997), introduced the term 'BDS' into the development lexicon, and spawned a process of substantial analysis and reflection among the development community. It is four years since BDS market development first became accepted as the guiding thrust of donor thinking and practice within the field (Gibson, 1999) and two years since this period of case studies and conferences closed with the publication of finalized Donor Guidelines, the 'Blue Book' (Committee of Donor Agencies for Small Enterprise Development, 2001).

Now, from a position beyond this initial buzz of activity, it seems an opportune time to consider where the field of BDS market development is. What have been its achievements in its inaugural phase? What have been the key points of learning and, most important, what issues need to be addressed to push BDS forward?

This paper seeks to respond to these questions. It is structured in relation to the key challenges to be faced – and commitments to be made – if progress is to be expected in the future, each framing a specific issue emerging from recent experience. It is a position paper rather than a research study but does draw on the authors' close involvement with many aspects of BDS currently and from its earliest days. The paper takes as its starting point – and builds on – the core conclusion reached through the above process, that BDS market development should be the main focus of development agency endeavour in the BDS field.

Where the BDS market development approach came from

Two main reasons lay behind this emphasis:

The failure of direct services provision to businesses by agencies. Through a detailed process of reflection, agencies were pushed into an unprecedented reassessment of their work; BDS market development emerged from this hard (and sometimes painful) learning, not from whim.

The growth in importance of business services. Driven by the rising significance of knowledge and information in determining competitiveness, business services have become among the highest growth sectors in most economies. A few examples demonstrate the point:

○ in the EU, average annual growth of business services from 1980–94 was 6.75 per cent against 1.5 per cent for manufacturing and services overall (Commission of European Communities, 1998)

○ in the USA, 85 per cent of businesses now outsource functions once performed in-house (Corbett, 1997)

○ in South Africa, while average employment growth was 1.33 per cent over the past 20 years, it has been 6.75 per cent for business services (Ntsika, 2000), and

○ in the Indonesian furniture sector, improved export performance has been linked closely with increased use of BDS which now constitutes firms' second largest input after timber (ADB, 2001).

Currently accounting for 25–35 per cent of GDP in most high-income economies and perhaps half of this in low-income countries, BDS markets are important, and becoming more important. Agencies' reorientation is recognition of this previously little-acknowledged reality.

This paper is about the challenges that development agencies need to address in order to develop BDS markets, it is not about reasserting well-established truths about the correctness of this goal or the importance of BDS per se, nor is it intended to be a detailed 'how to' guide to implementation.

Early signs of progress but …

In many ways, the progress of BDS market development within the development sphere is as much as could be expected at this stage. There are tangible signs of progress:

Written policies and strategies of development agencies. Major multilateral donors such as the World Bank and bilateral agencies such as DFID and USAID have strategies that embrace BDS market development. IFC's (International Finance Corporation) strategy, for example, emphasizes the 'creation of a market for business development services' (World Bank, 2003) and DFID highlights 'making markets work for the poor' in its overall development strategy (DFID, 2000).

Resource allocation. The actual decisions of agencies in allocating resources to market development interventions are a more revealing indicator of intent. Here there are even more signs of change: across Asia, Africa, Eastern Europe and Latin America there are a growing number of projects that have BDS market development at their core, involving agencies such as DFID, GTZ, IFC, ILO, SDC (Swiss Agency for Development Co-operation) and USAID.

Research agenda. BDS market development is also penetrating development research agendas. Most prominent, USAID's Accelerated Microenterprise Assistance Program (AMAP) – probably the largest research programme on small business development currently supported by an agency – has BDS as one of the three main areas of focus (along with financial services and the enabling environment).

While one might argue about the pace of adoption and the volume of resources being devoted to BDS market development, there is little doubt that more is happening under the BDS banner. This is where one would expect the field to be and, to a considerable extent, this is where it is. But these signs of discernible progress need to be qualified. One obvious complaint is the comparative absence of evidence of large-scale 'success'. In some ways, however, this is not the most problematic area of concern: there are success stories, and if these are small in number and scale this is hardly surprising given that substantial resources have only recently been put into BDS market development.

More troubling are indications that the spread of BDS market development has not always been accompanied by a corresponding deepening of understanding, manifested, for example, in relevant research or in the operationalization of BDS market development objectives in project design and practice. There is rather sterile and cynical talk of a BDS 'bubble', of BDS as a development fad that, having generated a wave of interest and jargon, will fade to join the list of other such fleeting fashions. This paper is sourced in the conviction – founded on rigorous analysis – that (1) BDS market development offers a new, necessary and exciting direction for private sector development efforts as a whole that has the potential to lead to significant, lasting change, but (2) this potential can be realized only if a number of basic challenges are addressed. Ten of the most important of these are discussed below.

(1) Reaffirm the core logic

Although interventions shaped by BDS market development differ in terms of sector/market and size, their essential logic should always be the same (Figure 12.1). Given

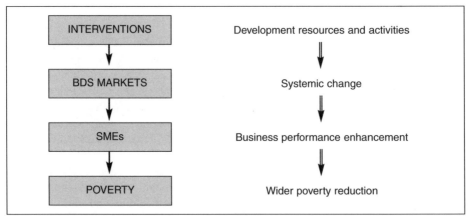

Figure 12.1. *The flow of logic in BDS market development.*

a common goal within development agencies of poverty reduction (or something similar), the focus of any BDS-related interventions should be on BDS market development in order that SME performance can be enhanced and poverty reduced. The flow is clear and should not change from one situation to another. Two related points emerge.

○ BDS market development is, like any development (as distinct from relief) intervention, about addressing causes (rather than symptoms) of underdevelopment. In 'conventional' SME development interventions, projects ask: 'what problems do businesses have and how can I help to solve these?'; a market development perspective asks: 'what problems do businesses have and why isn't the market environment providing solutions to them?' If one case is concerned with asking why the business isn't working, the other is concerned with the underlying development problem: why the market (within which businesses exist) isn't working.

○ BDS market development therefore is about systemic change. If it wasn't it would not offer the potential for large-scale meaningful impact and therefore not be of any real interest to agencies. And this is very positive news. A frequent (and sometimes justified) criticism of interventions purporting to be about BDS is that they are small and disparate, achieving isolated impact here and there but without any apparent wider significance. By focusing on changes in BDS markets we address this criticism and (see point 2) place BDS within the heart of private sector development.

Why is reaffirmation of the core logic important? First, because projects that don't have this transparent logic at their core are often irredeemably flawed. If the rationale is wrong it is difficult for anything else to be right. In particular, projects that attempt to do both – to provide services directly to businesses while also maintaining that they wish to develop markets – need to justify this openly in relation to the development challenge above: how will direct provision of support to SMEs contribute to sustainable, systemic change?

Second, because BDS market development will drift dangerously unless the rationale is affirmed consciously. The transparency and rigour of the logic that underpins the approach is a key strength. Each stage of the flow of logic connecting intervention with poverty is transparent and, while it is open to challenge, counter arguments need to put forward an equally clear alternative (see point 9). Certainly, the argument sometimes put forward – that we need to support businesses directly to get them up and running and a conducive market environment will follow – is contradicted by agencies' experience.

(2) Position BDS within the emerging market development paradigm

The above logic of BDS market development has been strengthened in recent years by the growing momentum for market development generally to be seen as an underpinning development principle to guide donor actions. Of course, in one sense, market development has lingered around development circles for many years, being a key tenet of the market-friendly approach (World Bank, 1991) to which most agencies subscribe. However, its priority has tended to be broad macro-economic frameworks and rules of international trade and, while these are important, debate has often become stuck on the wider political issues surrounding these. The more specific detail of how well (or, more often, how badly) particular markets are working – especially how the poor are affected – and the reasons for this situation are often neglected. As a consequence, contradictory signals have sometimes been sent and conflicting approaches followed. For example, while the rhetoric of macro-reform is of an appropriate role for government (the provision of public services, privatization of non-essential roles, etc.) to create the right conditions for market development, within the BDS sphere, government, NGOs and others are often supported to deliver subsidized services with little consideration for their impact on actual/potential private provision or business competitiveness (and undermining the intent of macro reform).

Other spheres of economic activity that agencies have traditionally supported are now entering their own market development debates. In the field of agriculture extension (business services for agriculture), the circumstances are uncannily similar to BDS (ODI, 2003). Here too:

○ Under an all-embracing and loose public goods justification, is a field 'traditionally' seen to be the domain of government with private sector services regarded as secondary and unable to offer the essential public service quality of the state.
○ Services are, palpably, not functioning well with limited outreach, efficacy and sustainability.
○ Services have often not brought enterprises (in this case small-scale farmers) into the mainstream economy but, rather, have cemented their disconnection.
○ The challenge is about encouraging the development of more effective markets for services and redefining a more specific role for government.
○ Previous diffidence about placing services in a market context – or even mentioning the farm business and markets – has been swept aside by irrefutable realities on the ground.

Indeed, parallel to the specific debate on agricultural extension, there are now indications that a lack of emphasis on markets is being recognized as a weakness in the sustainable livelihoods framework, an approach that holds considerable sway with many donors (Dorward et al., 2002). Therefore a common criticism – one put forward by Kate Philip in Chapter 12 – that BDS market development is valid only for larger, more formal businesses, not for microenterprises, is already receiving a response in other development arenas. The specific problems faced, the intervention approaches adopted, and the types of services required, may well differ markedly from those in a more formal business context, but ultimately the objectives remain the same. Income generation activities always take place in some form of market; the rationale for microenterprise or income generation projects must be to improve that market environment.

Intriguingly, the agriculture and rural livelihoods fields have reached these tentative conclusions essentially uninformed by the emerging experience in BDS market development. And while this is an indictment of the fragmented nature of development discussion it is significant that, through different routes, a similar destination is being reached.

Two conclusions, both of them positive for the BDS field, can be drawn from the above. First, market development offers the same clarity in conceptual framework, rationale and approach to BDS that it does in other sectors. The immediate task of private sector development is suddenly given greater focus and consistency, namely to help make markets – whether in services, finance or goods – to work more effectively and inclusively for the poor.

Second, although within agencies it is normal to divide the world of private sector development into boxes – enabling environment, financial services, BDS etc. – these are united by the market development objective. BDS market development, therefore, is neither alone nor is it peripheral. It may be perfectly legitimate not to have any intervention focused on BDS specifically, but market development should always be an underlying aim. However, because BDS has arrived at market development earlier than other areas, the lessons learned here on how to operationalize this objective (tools, indicators, processes, partners, intervention mechanisms, etc.) are of wider relevance. For this cross-learning to take place (and there has been very little to date) we need to see beyond traditional boxes.

(3) Develop a better framework for market analysis

A detailed understanding of markets shapes intervention approaches in two particular ways:

○ assessment of existing market situations, especially to identify underlying constraints, forms a starting point for intervention (answering the question 'what is the current situation?')
○ developing a detailed picture of how a market might work more effectively in the future, as a model of sustainability, sets a target for an intervention ('what could be?')

Logically, the challenge of intervention is how to influence markets to go from the first to the second.

Recognizing the importance of market analysis, the BDS field has been innovative in adapting 'standard' market research tools to the market development task. Using tools such as usage, attitude and image (UAI) surveys, product concept tests and focus group discussions, clear progress has been made in how to gain insight into what is (current use and non-use of services) and what *could be* (services that offer real benefits to SME users and to providers) (Miehlbradt, 1999). However, while the analyses emerging from these have proved useful in shaping interventions, their overall value has sometimes been limited. Commonly absent from market assessments have been any wider examination of the institutional environment for BDS and of market-supporting functions.

In BDS, as in other areas, our growing acceptance of the importance of markets has been accompanied by increasing recognition of the institutions – the 'rules of the game' – that shape their functioning and performance (North, 1990). 'Institutions' here refers both to the formal and informal frameworks within which markets operate that determine critical features of markets, such as information, incentives, values, standards and so on, and consequently govern transaction costs and access. The institutional environment pertaining to a specific market is therefore influenced by wider social and cultural norms, as well as through the actions of formal organizations, for example governments or associations. The implication here is clear: market economies (and BDS markets within these) function well only when they are embedded in a local context; any comprehensive view of a BDS market must understand this to provide insight into the underlying reasons for market performance and into the capacity for change.

The general point here is that BDS market development needs to be enriched by a more nuanced view of how markets function now and how they could function in the future. Only in doing so can the crux issue of sustainability be addressed in a serious manner (Bear et al., 2001).

(4) Define an appropriate role for the state

Within this more comprehensive view of BDS markets, the role of the state always needs to be considered. A widely prevailing misconception is that BDS market development is anti-government and 'neo-liberal' in its outlook, that in working towards more effective private markets we are motivated by an instinctive suspicion of the state. Reactions such as this are common but ill-founded and it is important to lay them to rest. In explicitly recognizing a potential role for government in BDS market development (and, incidentally, a role for publicly funded interventions to promote market development) the approach could not be more different from that of so-called neo-liberal economists.

However, BDS market development certainly is against the kind of unquestioned state-subsidized provision that has been the hallmark of government's role in many countries. The low-outreach, small-impact, high-cost, limited-sustainability outcomes of this kind of role, often pale copies of unsuccessful 'models' from the north (National Audit Office, 2003), have been well documented and epitomized the negative experience that first prompted agencies to search for a better way. The role of the panoply of state and quasi-state organizations (and not-for-profit agencies), often creations of aid, that have grown on this ill-founded basis, is therefore questioned by a BDS market analysis.

BDS market development is, conversely, in favour of government playing a role that fits with its core competence as a provider of public goods. These roles may vary, and should also be driven by an understanding of the wider market, but might include, for example, activities related to regulation, information, research and standards (Table 12.1). It might also be that the state's key role in supporting market development will be to focus on general priorities, such as education, social welfare and infrastructure, that are not specific to BDS but impinge directly on it.

Once again, the message of BDS market development is neither formulaic nor simple and, for those who like their development 'solutions' pre-packaged neatly, this, of course, might be an unwelcome message. However, to those who recognize that (1) the state is a unique and important actor within the institutional environment but that (2) its roles have to be shaped by its core competence to fit a valid picture of how markets can work effectively, the challenge is to engage with governments to enable them to define and play these roles (Hitchins, 2002).

(5) Put BDS into product markets

While agencies have usually kept BDS interventions separate from interventions to promote commodity and product markets, increasingly it is recognized that a practical

Table 12.1   Innovative roles played by government in BDS market development

Country	Issue	Action
Argentina	Low-quality standards in export sector.	Link public standards agencies with associations.
Zimbabwe/ Chile	Poor market orientation in vocational training.	Combination of financial stimuli and statutory change/liberalization to encourage private provision.
UK	High compliance costs.	Enhanced public information services to SMEs and providers of business services to provide greater clarity and guidance.
	Developing specialist information services	Government provides a public role in gathering and offering basic data on companies – tailored into specialized products by private companies.
South Africa	Disconnection between public procurement standards and SMEs	Standards organization works with BDS providers to enhance broker linkages between firms and public sector buyers.

understanding of these markets requires that the BDS within them are considered fully. It is perfectly valid to focus on those 'generic' business services that have broad application across different industries (accountancy, legal, management consultancy, etc.) but connecting BDS more immediately to strategic sectoral trends also has the potential for major impact (Figure 12.2). Several factors lie behind this:

○ In an increasingly complex world, information and knowledge are recognized to be key assets in allowing businesses to get answers to the key questions that they face. Services are a critical means through which industry-specific information and knowledge is generated.
○ Sub-sector analysis, a key tool to assess commodity and product supply chains, has commonly underestimated the importance of the service content of sub-sectors. Services have been treated as a secondary consideration, overlays to the main sub-sector map. Now, the 'arrival' of BDS market development has allowed projects focusing on sub-sectors as diverse as green beans, dairy, wool, plastics and textiles to recognize the importance of services within them.
○ Our understanding that services are often contained (or embedded) within other commercial transactions or relationships rather than paid for separately is especially important within sub-sectors – and has liberated the field from the unhelpful restriction of always thinking of fee-based services only (Anderson, 2002).

Again the implication here is clear: BDS market development thinking should be central to industry or sectoral development programmes. The same argument also applies to the 'product market' of financial services. Conventional wisdom in microfinance in particular – learning from experiences with 'integrated' finance – is that finance providers (particularly microfinance) should not stray into the delivery of BDS. Yet, strategically, BDS and finance are clearly linked. In the problematic area of SME finance especially, services to assist providers to develop products, design systems and

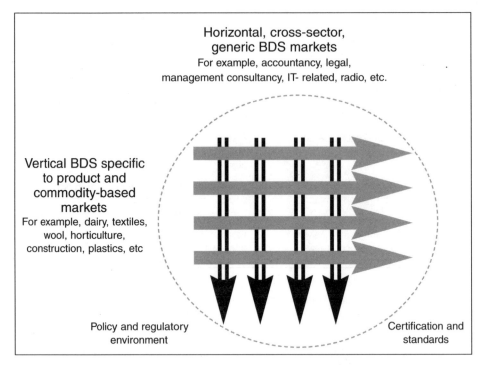

Figure 12.2 *Generic BDS and BDS within commodity and product markets.*

develop staff and help consumers to develop business plans and improve their financial disciplines are critical in helping supply and demand come together. As with other product markets, effective financial services cannot develop without relevant BDS.

(6) Making sense of the facilitation task: people and offer

The central task in BDS market development is facilitation. This has been a key change brought about by the donor Guiding Principles – that development resources should not be used to support the delivery of BDS direct but to play a catalytic role in supporting the development of markets. However, what facilitation means in practice represents a core challenge for the BDS field. Strategically, facilitators must act as a bridge between the public objectives and procedures of the donor-development world and those of businesses in private sector markets. Operationalizing this is, however, from the field's still brief experience, a more demanding and complex task than envisaged previously. In performing facilitation tasks, organizations are facing many dilemmas associated with, for example, where resources should be allocated, how much should be 'given' in interventions and in what form, and how facilitators should interact with partners. Many of these challenges are underpinned by the following two related issues.

Getting and developing people. An early mantra of BDS good practice was that facilitators needed to be businesslike: close to and able to engage with business people. This, it is now clear, means more than knowing 'about' business or having the 'right' academic qualifications. It requires relevant business experience to permit facilitators to:

○ interact credibly with market players to earn trust
○ understand and gain insight into business problems, and
○ see valid project opportunities for market development.

People from conventional enterprise development backgrounds accustomed to delivering standardized business development 'solutions' may not have these qualities. The approach of facilitators – who often intuitively understand this problem – to recruitment and staff development needs to recognize this reality.

Developing the right offer. People are at the heart of what facilitators bring, but engaging in an effective and businesslike manner requires that facilitators have an 'offer'. Borrowed directly from business, 'offer' refers to the tangible service/good that is presented, to whom, the benefits to be derived from this, and what is expected in return: the essential quid pro quo of a transaction. Facilitators' offers must be above and beyond what is already there. Informed by good market analysis, building on relevant experience – and using public resources – they are in a unique position to identify additional new ways in which they can change a market situation.

This means rather more than asking businesses what their needs are but, for example, proactively identifying new service opportunities and reasons why (existing or potential) service providers are not responding to these and consumers not demanding them, and then developing an offer to address these issues. Clearly, therefore, offers may be very unlike the standardized solutions of conventional enterprise development practice.

(7) Making sense of the facilitation task: consistency from analysis to intervention

While there is a logical coherence underpinning the BDS market development approach (from analysis of market constraints and a picture of sustainability to intervention design), there is still great scope for individual interpretation. In the crucial link from analysis to intervention there are comparatively few iron-clad rules. Rather than say, for example, 'never' provide direct subsidy for transactions between providers and consumer or 'always' work with more than one provider, the approach says 'justify' an intervention approach in relation to analysis and objectives. Does an identified weakness in the supply side of a specialized training market merit intervention in the form of improved information for existing service providers, promotion of international linkages between foreign and domestic companies, enhanced information to consumers supported by a short-term voucher programme? There may be many options, but choices need to be justified.

The nature of the approach, therefore, provides real scope for facilitators to innovate, and emphasizes again that the facilitation task demands entrepreneurial flair as much as delivery efficiency. As more is learned, guidance for facilitation will become tighter. However, what is clear is that the approach, however creatively pursued, does require that facilitators' intervention designs and implementation practices are genuinely led by analysis. The 'creativity' of justifying what agencies have always done under a new banner of BDS market facilitation is not a legitimate option. Providing services directly on the premise that 'demonstration' is necessary, for example, can become a blanket reason to repeat the mistakes of the past. It is incumbent on organizations acting as facilitators (and donors supporting them) to be true to the approach.

(8) Revise project designs to permit the required flexibility

BDS market development projects must be grounded in and shaped by market realities. Rather than arriving in a situation with a predetermined 'model', organizations must have sufficient knowledge and capacity in different intervention options to respond effectively to market constraints. This is the essence of key underlying principles – being demand-led and businesslike – yet the major implications of this for project design are often not realized. No longer can designs be developed in precise, fixed detail with limited scope for flexibility. In practice, project designs that allow appropriate flexibility may have some or all of the following characteristics:

○ Framework contracts defining programmes rather than individual projects that set out key strategic areas; the number of different markets, operating principles, overall objectives and resourcing rather than an attempt to predict specific activities or budgets for these.
○ The requirement of more detailed planning as analysis is generated throughout a project's life, including tighter budgets and indicators.
○ Provision to allow further market research as projects proceed to determine the scope for and nature of further intervention.
○ Space to permit projects to be innovative in their intervention response to new opportunities that arise, especially given the fluid nature of market situations.

Of course, this is challenging for donor agencies. Flexibility may always be desirable but always has to be countered by the need for accountability. Research can easily be seen as self-indulgent and purposeless unless tied to the discipline of intervention. Practical planning frameworks need to have indicators to define targets and incentives, bring focus to activity, and define the terms of relationship between donor and project contractor. Achieving this balance – between the public objectives and requirements of an aid project and the reality of effective engagement in private markets – is a key design challenge.

(9) Deal with poverty realistically

As with all development activities, poverty reduction is the overarching objective of BDS market development and therefore, like other activities, it is appropriate that it be considered against this goal. For some, however, BDS market development's supposedly tenuous link with poverty reduction is a persistent problem that undermines the credibility of the field. Several points can be made here:

○ The logic of the approach (see point 1) shows a clear path through which interventions should impact on poverty. While at each stage of this logic, assumptions are being made, none of these is unique to BDS. They apply equally to interventions in microenterprise and SME development generally, policy and financial services. Nor are these assumptions wide-eyed conjecture; on the contrary, they are firmly within mainstream views on how economic development impacts on the poor as employees, owners of enterprises and as consumers.

○ Proving impact on poverty is, unavoidably, extremely difficult and expensive, but again this is hardly a problem unique to BDS. Rather it is a big question for development as a whole, especially agencies engaged in private sector development, and needs to be considered by agencies collectively.

○ Although the poverty reduction criterion is important (and obvious) it also needs to be recognized that final convincing proof is unlikely to emerge easily or quickly to convince sceptics of BDS market development's worth. For some critics, the notion that (amoral) markets can serve (moral) developmental objectives is anathema – even if they are the basis of market economies – therefore 'debate' here is about more than BDS market development alone.

Given this, how should the BDS field respond? First, notwithstanding the above caveats, there is a need for improved research, monitoring and evaluation on each stage of the flow of cause and effect linking interventions with final impact (see Figure 13.1). For individual projects and organisations, their resources dictate that they should focus on impacts closest to their point of intervention, where there are comparatively fewer methodological difficulties, for example, market-level change and the link between BDS consumption and business performance. Second, develop detailed case studies on how improved business performance can impact on poverty. While these might not 'prove' a relationship with poverty reduction they should enrich our knowledge to allow improvement in interventions. Third, research aimed at proving the poverty impact of BDS market development should be the responsibility of development agencies as a whole. Importantly, however, as mentioned above, the quest to prove impact is common to all interventions related to private sector development; and BDS market development must be assessed in that context.

(10) Retire the BDS label – the future is business services

When first introduced, the business development services term was welcomed widely. Usurping the rather uninspiring title of 'non-financial services' (describing something by what it's not) that had been in use prior to it, BDS seemed appropriate and positive. And, over time, BDS has become established as the term of choice for those in the field.

Yet, it has always been problematic. BDS is a term created by development agencies and it has no currency in the outside 'real' world of business or in the economics field, where 'business services' is the normal term. So why have a different term; why have 'development' there? A range of arguments have been put forward:

○ *Objectives.* These are services that serve a developmental purpose and the name should reflect this. However, in the financial services field, agencies have not felt compelled to qualify or complicate terminology by adding 'development'. From the perspective of the consumer of services, they purchase services that are useful and are unlikely to want services that do not, in some way, contribute to the development of their business.

○ *Focus.* These are services that are of 'strategic' rather than 'operational' importance.

Yet these terms are arbitrary and subjective and not especially meaningful to business consumers, who are much more likely to define services in relation to the benefits they gain from them. Obviously, in selecting BDS markets in which to intervene, agencies do need to be guided by strategic aims such as how to make a substantial and lasting difference to the economy (and on poverty), but this could involve a wide range of different services.

o *Benefits.* These are services that have some element of public good. However, while there are few 'pure' public goods (non-rival and non-excludable) there are many which it could be argued have some public goods character, and many of these (e.g. training) are often provided on a private basis.

None of the above arguments offers a valid reason for the BDS term. But, even now, tortuous debate goes on over what is meant by the development 'bit' as if, surely in its naming, there had been some level of unique insight which has just been mislaid carelessly and only awaits recovery. The search is a fruitless one. BDS are business services. Increasingly, any benefits from maintaining the BDS label appear limited in comparison with the costs of confusion and artificial separation from the wider private sector development world.

Conclusions

The BDS – or business services – market development field has clearly made some notable progress in its first few years of endeavour. More agencies are committed to it and more resources are being allocated under its name or influence. In order to ensure that these initial, positive steps are built upon successfully, and to address inevitable signs that spread has not been matched by depth in understanding, the field needs now to address a number of key, broad-ranging challenges. These are concerned with:

o reasserting the conceptual rigour that underpins the business services market development approach (for example, the flow of logic and the market analysis)
o confronting the difficult issues of how to operationalize the approach (flexibility in project design, defining the role of the state, developing facilitation offers)
o building the capacity of organizations and personnel to undertake key tasks.

Confronting these is essential but will often not be straightforward. In doing so, however, agencies should take comfort that these issues are not unique to business services. The challenges identified in developing markets for business services are similar to those that should be confronted in the wider private sector development field. Learning here should have much wider relevance beyond the conventional 'BDS box'.

References

Anderson, Gavin (2002) 'The hidden MSE service sector: research into commercial BDS provision to micro and small enterprises in Vietnam and Thailand', presented at the BDS conference in Hanoi, available at www.ilo.org/dyn/bds>Committee of Donor Agencies for SED>Hanoi DC Conference (under market assessment).

Asian Development Bank (2001) *SME Development Technical Assistance to Government of Indonesia*, ADB, Manila.

Bear, M., A.Gibson and R. Hitchins (2001) 'A guide for agencies on the emerging market development approach to BDS', Microenterprise Best Practices, Technical Note 2.

Commission of European Communities (1998) *The Contribution of Business Services to Industrial Performance: a common policy framework*, Office for Official Publications of the European Communities, Luxembourg.

Committee of Donor Agencies for Small Enterprise Development (1997) *Business Development Services for SME Development: a guideline for donor-funded interventions.*

Committee of Donor Agencies for Small Enterprise Development (2001) *Business Development Services for Small Enterprises: Guiding principles for donor intervention*, available at www.ilo.org/dyn/bds>Committee of Donor Agencies for SED>Donor Committee Guidelines

Corbett, M.F. (1997) *Outsourcing: The US business revolution*, Michael Corbett and Associates Ltd., Poughkeepsie, NY.

DFID (2000) 'Economic well-being target strategy paper', DFID, London.

Dorward, A., N. Poole, J. Morrison, J. Kydd and I. Urey (2002) 'Critical linkages: livelihoods, markets and institutions', paper presented at the seminar on 'Supporting institutions, evolving livelihoods', Bradford Centre for International Development.

Gibson, A (1999) 'The development of markets for business development services', in Levitsky, J (ed.) (2001) *Small business services in Asian countries*, ITDG Publishing.

Hitchins, R. (2002) 'The role of government in BDS market development: a preliminary review for the International Labour Office' (SEED), ILO.

Miehlbradt, A.O. (1999) 'Applying market research tools to the design and improvement of business development services', Microenterprise Best Practices, Technical Note 1.

National Audit Office (2003) *The DTI: Regional Grants in England, report by the Comptroller and Auditor General*, The Stationery Office, London.

North, D.C. (1990) *Institutions, Institutional Change and Economic Performance*, Cambridge University Press.

Ntsika (2000) *Ntsika Annual Report*, South Africa.

ODI Agriculture Research and Extension Network (2003) 'Summary of AgRen discussion on the scope and limitations of privatised agricultural extension', synthesis paper of virtual conference on The Prospects and Limitations of Private Extension Delivery.

World Bank (1991) *World Development Report: the challenge of development*, Oxford University Press.

World Bank (2003) *Private Sector Development Strategy Implementation Progress Report*, World Bank, Washington.

About the authors

Alan Gibson and Rob Hitchins are partners with the Springfield Centre, and Marshall Bear is an independent consultant and associate of the Springfield Centre. The Centre has been closely involved with the emergence of the BDS field from its earliest days, leading the initial team that developed the Donor Committee's preliminary guidelines. All three act as consultants to key agencies engaged in BDS market development and as teaching faculty at the Centre's annual BDS training programme.

13 Putting development back at the centre of business development services

KATE PHILIP

This paper was first published in December 2003.

In this chapter examining the basis of the market development approach to business development services (BDS) a number of doubts are raised. First, the emphasis on the commercial delivery of BDS inevitably shifts the focus of interventions towards the formal, growth-oriented sector and away from poorer microenterprises, which are not so much unwilling to pay as unable to pay. Moreover, it is difficult to promote markets for BDS where the small enterprise sector is not buoyant and demand for such services is very weak. The author distinguishes between business-to-business services, which even the poorest microenterprises are prepared to pay for, and business development services, which promote growth or innovation and for which microenterprises and small businesses are less willing to pay the full costs because of the risks involved. It is argued that for such BDS, subsidy is still justified.

THE 'MARKET DEVELOPMENT APPROACH' has put markets centrally on to the agenda of the enterprise support sector. In the process, the approach has opened the way for innovation in terms of programme development, and enhanced the options and potential impacts of the sector.

At its best, the focus on market development has highlighted the range of factors that may combine to limit market access for MSEs (microenterprises and small enterprises) and to skew the terms of trade; it has located market analysis within the context of wider social and political forces.

The strengths of this approach have also been in terms of the extent to which it has located enterprise development within the context of market forces, not as a residual afterthought, where markets tended to reside previously, but as a constitutive part of the terms of viability of enterprises and sectors. Market analysis, supply chains and value chains are now part of the MSE lexicon, where they were only marginally so before. The implications of this are as relevant in programme design targeting the most marginal economic activity as they are for macro policy.

At the level of development implementation, the market development approach has also tackled many of the holy cows of traditional BDS practice and of accepted methodologies of delivery. However, in asserting its hegemony over the development discourse in the MSE sector, the market development paradigm has also developed some holy bulls and bears of its own: and it is on some of these that this opinion piece focuses.

Reaching the poor?

Within the market development paradigm, there is a focus on the development of commercial markets for the delivery of business development services, including for delivery to the most marginal of enterprises. The development of markets for BDS has increasingly become the central objective and main outcome of many interventions, and seems to have a strong tendency to become an end in itself.

In the September 2002 ILO Conference on BDS Market Development, Jean-Christophe Favre, from the Swiss Agency for Development and Co-operation, started his presentation as follows:

> The Swiss Agency does not care about business development services or BDS market development; the Swiss Agency cares about poverty reduction, through employment creation and income generation. We are interested in BDS market development only insofar as it is a means to address these issues.

He went on to outline the extent to which there has been debate within the Swiss Agency, and a challenge to the BDS market approach, in relation to its impacts and outcomes. He presented a 'pyramid' structure showing a few viable small enterprises at the top, with an increasing number of less viable and more survivalist enterprises at the base, and put forward the view that with the market approach to BDS delivery the focus has increasingly shifted up the pyramid to the more resourced, formal and viable layers of the small enterprise sector, when the mandate of the Swiss Agency is to target the base.

Favre argued that we cannot use the same strategies for BDS at the bottom of the pyramid as we use at the top, and we need to decide whom we are targeting and why. Much as this might seem to be common sense and a statement of the obvious; in fact it represents a critical fault-line within the market paradigm debate. Those practitioners targeting growth-oriented small enterprises are looking at the sector from a more macro-economic perspective, in which the aim is to strengthen it and to mainstream it as part of the private sector, where markets already exist for business development services, but need to be enhanced either on the demand or supply side.

If your target is a more robust, formal and growing small enterprise sector within a national economy, which is able to break into export or import substitution markets, then of course it makes sense to aim for the top end of the market, as many programmes are doing. And in this sector of the market, commercial, sustainable markets for business services – and even management consultancy services – are feasible, and often exist already, because they are demand driven. This is where the barriers are lowest, where the constraints are 'willingness to pay' rather than affordability and where the focus is on potential wealth creation, with its wider macro-economic spin-offs, including the expectation of trickle-down impacts, real or illusory.

There seems little doubt that the development of markets for business services has a key role to play as part of mainstreaming MSEs, and the attractions of targeting at this level are clear. However, they do not provide a justification for abandoning strategies that target the bottom end of the market, which is what a reliance on market-driven BDS often seems to lead to in practice, for predictable market-driven reasons.

Developing markets for BDS: is it a cart, a horse, a chicken or an egg?

The *Guiding Principles* (known as 'the Blue Book', Committee of Donor Agencies for Small Enterprises, 2001) define a market for business development services as: 'a well-functioning market with a diverse array of high-quality services that satisfy the needs of a large number of small enterprises affordably'. Yet such a commercial market for business services can arise only as a consequence of a thriving, viable small enterprise sector, in which there is sufficient demand for business services to sustain commercial supply. Until such demand is evident, supply will be high-risk as a commercial proposition, which is why, in marginal situations, it seldom occurs at all; and why commercial service providers will inevitably tend to target away from this sector.

This leaves practitioners faced with the same question we were grappling with before the BDS market paradigm came along: how do you build such a growing, vibrant, diverse, sustainable small enterprise sector, in a context in which the level of demand and/or the ability to afford key business development services cannot yet sustain commercial delivery?

Yet it is an assumption of the Donor Guidelines that 'with appropriate product design, delivery and payment mechanisms, BDS can be provided on a commercial basis even for the lowest segment of the entrepreneurial small enterprise sector'.

This assumption needs to be revisited. There are certainly ways of delivering BDS services that are more market driven, and that are structured to optimize the transactional and demand-led elements of service provision. And no matter how poor the constituency in which a programme operates, some level of payment, some level of contractual transaction, is key to a value being placed on the service. But in many developing contexts, this is a far cry from charging the full transaction costs for such business development services. Yet in much of the BDS literature, the issue of affordability is barely recognized as a constraint: the focus is instead on the issue of 'willingness to pay'. Poverty, it seems, is a state of mind, and all that stands between the rural poor and a wide and sustainable range of business development services is their own bad attitude.

In a context in which the aim is now for both BDS and microfinance to be 'self-financed' by the poor, the underlying assumption has to be that the poor are actually able to resource their way out of poverty. Where is the evidence to support this potential trajectory of development?

Another look at redistribution

Strategies for the reduction of poverty require an element of resource transfer, as part of a redistributive agenda: and markets alone won't do it. Even the World Bank says so (Maxwell, 2003). Many of the strategies that have attempted to achieve this in the past have failed dismally. The more direct the form of resource transfer, as a component of BDS, the greater the tendency to create dependency seems to be.

Added to this is the problem that enterprise development programmes have so often been used as a proxy form of poverty alleviation or social protection. It is partly from this developmental quicksand that the BDS market approach has fled.

MSE development and therefore BDS are not an answer to poverty, in isolation from other instruments. Sustainable economic activity in poor areas is more likely to arise where the enabling environment includes an effective nexus of forms of social protection, than where local economic development is expected to kickstart itself from ground zero. The redistributive impact of such social protection is an important part of creating an enabling environment for enterprise.

While BDS may be exempted from being a direct instrument of social protection, however, this does not exonerate it from the need to impact on poverty, nor from the challenge of targeting the base. A recognition that BDS is not an appropriate mechanism in this respect does not remove its potential to play a role in facilitating redistributive effects; nor does it solve the question of how such facilitation is resourced.

While the Blue Book appeared to propose a kind of moratorium on subsidized BDS, the achievement of commercial BDS has proved elusive at the base. In practice: 'Although the market development paradigm has challenged practitioners to get more out of each public sector dollar, and to create sustainable BDS, the era of subsidies is far from over, and the challenge of how to use them most productively has only begun' (Miehlbradt and McVay, 2002, p.102).

If that is an accepted consensus, then it needs to be clarified in the way the BDS approach is promoted. Because at present, market forces limit the extent of commercial delivery to poor local economies, and ambiguity of policy in relation to the forms of intervention and subsidy that are acceptable has compounded the vacuum, as BDS providers target areas of greater certainty to secure their own survival in the BDS, funding and consultancy market places. It is also a debate that is substantively influenced by the definition of BDS that is used.

Defining where business-to-business services and BDS meet

Identifying how strategies targeting the base of Favre's pyramid might differ from those targeted further up is further complicated by a definition of business development services that has come to include all business-to-business services. The growth of the service sector is a well-known phenomenon; but in emphasizing its implications for the MSE support sector, the BDS market approach has used it to demonstrate that commercial markets for BDS are not only feasible, but in fact, MSEs are paying for many services already. To do this, it has been necessary to conflate the definitions of BDS and business services.

At this point, 'BDS' is used to encompass everything from web-site development, fax services, freight, input supply, sales commission and a whole gamut of services that fit squarely into a normally functioning business-to-business service sector. The definition of BDS therefore now includes services that are an ongoing and necessary part of a business, as well as services that are not, and that are instead one-off interventions intended to add value in some way. Surely a distinction is useful?

The former are recurrent and core costs of doing business, and if these need an ongoing subsidy, then the business is unviable. There is probably broad consensus that even in the most marginal of areas, ongoing and direct subsidies to business transaction costs should be hard to justify. And realistically, these are costs that even the most marginal of enterprises do expect to pay.

But there is a distinction between these business-to-business services, and interventions that add value to businesses and business sectors, that are non-core, that are non-recurrent in a given business and that are aligned with a wider policy and developmental agenda. It is these interventions that should most appropriately be defined as business development services.

There will be contexts in which such BDS can be provided on a commercial basis. In practice, however, even many viable, resourced, formal-sector, medium-scale enterprises pale at the thought of spending money on non-core products with medium-term impacts, such as training, product development, innovation or exploration of new markets. Unwillingness to pay for such services – and even concerns over affordability – are not the preserve of marginal enterprises alone. The more adverse the conditions, the more risk averse businesses are likely to be: and innovation and growth entail risks and costs, whatever the size of the business.

Innovation and growth are the holy grails of economists and policy makers everywhere: the economic drivers purported to make improved social conditions and services achievable and sustainable in any given economy. Yet in practice, there is often a tension between the wider societal goals of particular types of growth and innovation that are promoted at a policy level, and the immediate and competitive interests and economic behaviour of particular businesses within the private sector.

The same tension exists in the MSE sector: between the wider societal goals of the more macro or mezzo-level 'interventionists' (whether these are governments, donors, NGOs or private sector agencies); and the narrower, risk-averse interests and instincts of particular enterprises.

It is because of this tension that even the established formal sector has to be 'incentivized' towards certain economic behaviour. If they are formal enterprises, it is called an incentive, and is an accepted policy tool; if they are marginal and poor, it is called a subsidy.

A revised definition is therefore proposed: distinguishing between business services driven solely by business interests and imperatives, and business development services, which are interventions informed by a wider developmental policy agenda, such as for growth, job creation, poverty reduction, or to make markets work for the poor.

The achievement of these goals will require an interface with specific enterprises and will have impacts on specific enterprises. The process is likely to entail benefits to such enterprises, that may profit individuals. But the aims of BDS are not to promote the interests of one client enterprise over its competitors, but to impact on a sector, or sub-sector, for a wider economic and social result. As such, there remains a core element of 'public good' involved in the definition of BDS that will also have implications for the extent to which it is able to be purely market driven, and the extent in certain contexts to which a certain degree of incentivization or subsidy or intervention in the market will be required to achieve the objectives.

In that context, BDS cannot simply be demand driven. And if it is not simply demand driven, then it is unlikely to be purely market driven either. What does this mean for the notion of a 'commercial market' for BDS?

If business-to-business services that are consumed as part of the ongoing operations of a business are 'liberated' from being defined as part of BDS, and are returned to the service sector where they belong, then we can probably all agree that a thriving, commercial, business service sector both reflects and underpins growth in the MSE sector; and that where sufficient demand does not exist to supply certain business services on a commercial basis, and where this constrains the growth of the sector, there is a key role for BDS in intervening to try to stimulate the business services sector, as a purely commercial sector, and in finding bridging mechanisms to achieve this where it is not immediately possible. While the business services being promoted should certainly be fully commercial, the BDS interventions required to facilitate this process are unlikely to be so. And while the achievement of commercial delivery of business services may be an outcome of good BDS in a given context, such markets are distinct from BDS itself.

Making markets work for the poor

Market development is a key part of economic development and pro-poor strategy. But markets, left on their own, do not efficiently supply goods and services to people who can't afford them, or where the volume of demand is not sufficient to sustain supply.

Markets are opportunistic: they always seek the best return from the most cost-effective input, and while this is the essential basis for their tendency to create economic efficiencies of certain kinds, and to create opportunities for growth in certain contexts, it is also the reason why they have a tendency to circumvent and exclude the poor. This is not a 'market distortion': it is intrinsic to the way markets operate and, as a result, it is flawed to think that simply by removing market distortions, markets will necessarily work for the poor: even if an 'undistorted' global market was a realistic goal. But there is just too much history involved: feudalism, colonialism, conquest; land appropriation, slavery, patriarchy and patronage, for a start. These 'distortions', further shaped by contestation of many kinds, and with varying outcomes, live on in the social relations of the present. In this context, where does 'market distortion' start and end? And how can these distortions be addressed without engaging the social and political dimensions underpinning them?

Power relations past and present influence the patterns of demand, supply, and the terms of exchange: not only on the macro, global level, but in any given village or household too.

Scanning the 'best-practice' BDS websites, there is scant evidence of reflection on these issues in the discourse. Instead, the BDS market paradigm seems to be in danger of an uncritical genuflection towards a notion of markets that is devoid of social context and content, as if markets operate in a privileged domain outside of social forces and relations, and are innocent of any but beneficial social impacts.

At its best, the market development approach integrates an understanding of the interface between markets, power, inequality and poverty. But to the extent that market development strategies focus merely on the internal functioning of particular markets and supply chains, and tinker with distortions internal to the workings of such markets, without engaging these wider issues, then market development is at risk of reinforcing inequalities and empowering elites: with adverse consequences for the poor.

Some conclusions and more questions

If markets tend to reinforce the powerful and reward the resourced; then the challenge, in making markets work for the poor, is at least in part how to empower and resource the poor.

Empowerment does not trickle down. Yet the focus on market development has sometimes gone along with a shift away from direct engagement with the poor, and a disengagement from organizations and institutions that give voice to the interests of the poor, in their various forms. Where is the agency of the poor in market development approaches, and where are the strategies to build it?

The challenge of resourcing the poor is also not one that can be met by markets alone. Yet market development is seldom contextualized within or articulated with a broader redistributive agenda, or the complementary policy instruments required to address issues of poverty and inequality.

In targeting the base, BDS market development approaches also have to engage with the continuum of economic activity that takes place in many impoverished areas. If BDS is not going to engage with the challenges of survivalist and marginal enterprise, who is expected to do so? And then there is the economic activity that may be entrepreneurial, but doesn't qualify as 'entrepreneurial small business'. If such activity serves simply to 'gear' income from remittances or pensions, to extend the days on which the family eats a meal, then it is contributing to the reduction of poverty. Where does BDS pass the baton to livelihoods approaches, and how do livelihoods approaches leverage off the lessons of market development – which certainly apply?

The idea of 'making markets work for the poor' implies that markets don't necessarily do so. Where they don't, intervention is going to be required to 'make' them do so. Yet intervention in markets – with however light a tread – tends to be frowned upon as a form of distortion, with market development approaches at risk of convergence with free market fundamentalism. Market development is often presented as a neutral and technical instrument: but while it can create new forms of access, it can also impoverish people. Market development strategies create winners and losers, and entail political choices. What instruments are appropriate to intervene in markets in ways that make these choices explicit, at macro and micro levels?

These issues are all reasons why the definition of business development services matters, and why the notion of BDS without development at its core is an impoverished one. Instead, if BDS are going to impact on poverty in ways that encompass the empowerment of the poor, then they need to be recognized as a development intervention, designed to achieve policy outcomes, informed by the public good, and not held hostage to markets alone.

References

Committee of Donor Agencies for Small Enterprise Development (2001) *Business Development Services for Small Enterprises: Guiding principles for donor intervention.*
Maxwell, Simon (2003) 'Heaven or hubris', in *Development Policy Review* Vol. 21 No.1.
Miehlbradt, A., and M. McVay (2002) 'Seminar reader', ILO Seminar on BDS Market Development, Turin.

About the author

Kate Philip is former Chief Executive Officer of Mineworkers Development Agency in South Africa, now an independent consultant.

14 Reflections of a gung-ho marketeer: highlights of the Turin BDS Seminar 2003

KATE McKEE

This paper was first published in December 2003.

This chapter was largely inspired by the presentations and discussions at the fourth annual BDS seminar, organized by the ILO (International Labour Organization) in Turin, in September 2003. The author considers a number of variations on the distinct roles of facilitator and BDS provider that are proving to be successful in promoting BDS market development. She also discusses the challenges of working with 'embedded services', new ways of providing BDS to poorer microenterprises, the importance of seeing BDS within larger agenda, such as trade capacity building, and the challenge of getting governments to co-operate in BDS market building.

THE TURIN SEMINAR IS A GOOD TIME to note progress in our field. When I compare our discussions here to the Rio BDS conference in 1999 or even last year's Turin BDS Seminar, we are now embracing a broader definition of BDS, which may include:

○ IT, media and info services
○ technology-related services
○ agriculture and agriculture-related services
○ both 'strategic' and 'operational' BDS (and the distinction between the two is often very context specific)
○ embedded services
○ even bartered BDS (which could be considered sustainable, albeit non-commercial)
○ and even finance.

This wider definition of BDS is healthy. Some of the earlier debate, for example, seemed to imply that all the things that might be more relevant to smaller entrepreneurs did not truly pass the test of being BDS worth working on. Now, the more inclusive definition may sometimes result in confusion and messiness, but it is well worth the greater relevance to the poor that this makes possible. And our tools, such as market assessment tools, are evolving to analyse and act better on this richer, messier picture.

There's more than one way to skin a cat

Examples from the seminar demonstrated a broader and more diverse understanding of how BDS markets actually develop than was outlined by the *Guiding Principles* (2001). For example, there may be a role for direct provision or 'jump-starting', market leader institutions which can lead to 'copy-catting', and entry of additional providers (see different approaches with three groups of microenterprises in Bangladesh described in Field and Knopp, 2003). There may be certain 'breakthrough' BDS products such as cell phone services for microenterprises or simple, local-language training

---

Box 14.1   Assumptions to challenge

We need to be careful not to make assumptions or to generalize too much regarding who are easiest to serve viably and commercially, so-called 'survivalist' businesses or SMEs. This should be a question answered with empirical evidence rather than untested assumptions, common wisdom or even dogma. For example, it might be easier to provide certain services commercially to microenterprises than to larger firms – microcredit offers but one example. Where is the border between survivalist and entrepreneurial enterprises anyway?

And there is a corollary: which scale of firms generates the most growth, employment creation and stability, or innovation, both in relative and absolute terms? This depends on the country, region and subsector. We need to investigate this more closely and update our knowledge. And even when we go back and look at the sources that we think we remember getting these oft-repeated impressions from (e.g. only 1 per cent of microenterprises grow), we are sometimes surprised by what the research actually found.

---

packages that leapfrog their BDS market to a whole new place. The concept of 'rolling facilitation' was introduced, with the emphasis on a clear exit strategy for each facilitation activity, which minimizes dependency on the facilitator over time.

Listening to these examples, I sometimes wonder if we are defining 'facilitation' as all the work that we want to do but have not yet figured out how to do commercially. Can there be commercial facilitation? Perhaps we shall find that, as markets mature, facilitation activities can either be passed on to the private sector or be provided on a commercial basis by the facilitator institution. (In either case, we seem to consider them provisions at the point at which they become commercially viable.)

The corollary of this is: what are the full costs of facilitation? The chiefs of party for GTZ and JOBS do not come cheap and we should not understate the costs of doing business in this new way. We are proceeding with these new methods on the assumption that they are less distorting in the market than their predecessors, and they certainly are. But we also need to think of the market distortion potential of international technical assistance and be very careful to outsource whenever possible and to compare the full costs of one intervention against another.

Another possibly unhelpful distinction about intervention methods has crept in: dealing with the whole subsector vs cross-cutting interventions (e.g. broadening the services of accountants to deal with the full range of microenterprises). Is it necessarily helpful to have to choose between the two approaches? The approach described by Frank Lusby (2001) might be more fruitful: select the subsector, analyse the subsector, identify critical BDS to address key constraints, assess supply- and demand-side problems in relevant BDS markets (that may be either cross-cutting or subsector-specific) and identify high-priority interventions. Does this approach not meld the two perspectives and sequence them according to the priorities identified?

Getting the best from embedded services

When these are already existing, but often not very apparent, we must ask ourselves: what can we do to strengthen supply-chain BDS, and shall we (donors and facilitators) be good at doing it? The challenges include:

○ finding embedded services
○ working out how to enhance them without making them worse
○ not upsetting the 'level playing field' between different firms or value chains
○ dealing with the power differentials between the firms at the bottom and those further up the chain. How can we strengthen the negotiating power of microenterprises, and their power in the market? How can we offer them more choice among providers of services, even embedded services? More marketing and information channels? More critical information services, especially on prices?
○ the timing issue – when is the right time to begin broadening producers' options and increasing competition between suppliers of embedded services. Field and Knopp (2003) describe an encouraging example of a larger firm, Apex, seeking out work from other larger firms to keep clusters of footwear microenterprises working, but is this the exception rather than the rule?
○ whom do embedded BDS serve? Might they serve poorer clients? Or be more relevant for rural areas? Do they have gender dimensions?

Staying on target for microenterprises

There were several remarkable examples during the seminar of BDS and interventions that seemed to have a 'down-market' bias, i.e. they are not attractive to better-off clients, and still can be provided sustainably. Examples include voucher schemes such a recent Kenya programme described by Phillips and Steel (2003), drip irrigation (IDE-India – this is another aspect of their work in developing commercial horticulture, which also includes the information activity described earlier), and group microloans.

Box 14.2   Entrepreneurs say: 'Show me the money!' and 'Show me the market!'

All entrepreneurs, and certainly those with more limited resources, prefer BDS that results in cash in their pocket in the not-too-distant future – and are more open to paying for this BDS. Similarly, BDS associated with market access is easier to sell, if not necessarily to provide. Those who are involved in this sort of intervention talked at the seminar of the energy that seems to be generated around opening new markets. Part of this is because of the interest and willingness of the entrepreneurs and other market players to be involved with these BDS programmes. Part is also due to the fact that the impact of these programmes is measurable, and those involved have clear evidence that they are making a difference. Those who spoke of increased sales, exports and producer incomes in relation to their programmes did so with justifiable pride.

   Another example of the energy around market access is that offered by the IDE-India case study, presented by Shivani Manaktala (IDEI, 2003). Here the market intermediary role was undertaken by a commercial publishing firm – information on agricultural prices and markets was packaged in a number of different ways and sold to farmers. This in turn offered the potential to make the value-adding information services a viable business model.

This is of particular interest to those of us struggling with how to provide BDS to microenterprises rather than SMEs.

The seminar continued to discuss the problems of providing BDS to the poor and in weaker markets. It is important to be clear about what we mean by weak markets: do we mean remote rural areas, very poor and even pre-entrepreneurial households or start-up entrepreneurs? The constraints, opportunities and implications for programme design and intervention are likely to be very different depending on the weakness we are trying to address.

I think this question of weak markets really has two related but different questions wrapped up in it: (1) who is entrepreneurship relevant for? If we focus on pre-entrepreneurial target groups, is there BDS that is relevant to their needs? Only if there is can we ask: (2) what are the limits of our current BDS technology and delivery methods in commercially viable, sustainable access?

Making BDS more relevant

It became apparent from conversations at the seminar that, from the World Bank to USAID, donor institutions are not very likely to be approving large amounts of funding for something called BDS, nor for the BDS market development approach. Where the action is – the real opportunity – is in integrating the BDS market development approach into the high priorities in our institutions, such as rural development in China at the World Bank and trade capacity-building, agribusiness or competitiveness at USAID. As the *Guiding Principles* are revised, this potential for the new BDS approach to find many applications in these broader programmes might be stressed.

Let me take the trade capacity-building example. A lot of examples were given during the seminar of BDS related to export promotion. As a community of practitioners, however, we need to take a more profound look at the implications of trade for our work:

o How upstream work affects it (e.g. World Trade Organization negotiations and compliance, bilateral trade agreements) as well as work that focuses more on actual competitiveness or what is sometimes called 'trade responsiveness'– the actual ability of domestic firms to take advantage of opportunities opened up by the treaties and tap new foreign markets.
o The role of BDS in helping back the 'winners' in the trade game. JOBS (see Field and Knopp 2003) and CDA (Center for Agribusiness Development, Honduras, managed by FINTRAC) are good examples of what it really takes: the package of services, the importance of timely provision or facilitation, and the demands of the market.
o We should also, however, consider how to help the 'losers' in international trade to adjust – what is the relevance of BDS to them? And does assistance to these people have a public goods aspect to it? Whose job is it? And who should pay?

Are we really looking ahead enough, to the dramatic changes in the economies in which we work that will be wrought by changes in global trading patterns? And not just in trade but also in all the aspects of globalization: have we sufficiently analysed the implications for BDS?

As Kees van der Ree of the ILO said during the seminar: 'Globalizing markets push entrepreneurs towards collective responses and partnerships.' How can we capitalize on the positive potential of globalization trends while mitigating the negative aspects?

Getting the government to play ball

Joachim Prey of GTZ gave an excellent presentation on the role of government in developing BDS markets. Governments should be creating an enabling environment for enterprises and their service providers, exiting from direct delivery and sometimes facilitating the development of business service markets. It is, however, sobering to observe how clear we are on how we wish national governments would act compared to how seldom they behave in this way. This raises several issues for me:

○ How can we make the preferred roles more appealing?
○ Do we have any examples of governments that have successfully retreated from direct service delivery and played a useful facilitative role? What were the secrets of those success stories?
○ There were some intriguing discussions on local economic development, BDS, and the potential roles of subnational governments. Perhaps next year we could hear examples of several local economic development cases and distil why they worked and how likely they are to be replicated elsewhere.
○ We also need further examination of the potential roles of business associations. I sense some unease about them serving as direct providers of BDS, arising from the fact that in the past they have often been seen as irrelevant or inefficient. But might they also have a role to play in jump-starting weak markets? What examples do we have of them successfully facilitating market development?

The role of social capital and trust

The importance of trust and the role of social capital was evident in many examples.

○ In communities, where social capital often provides a base for enterprise and for successful BDS delivery.
○ The role of trust and reputation in microenterprises' decisions to acquire BDS, e.g. Gavin Anderson's excellent examples in 'The hidden MSE service sector' (2002) or Aly Miehlbradt's many examples in her market assessment work (Miehlbradt, 2003).
○ The role of trust and social capital within business systems, value chains, and clusters.
○ The high degree of trust required for market linkage services.
○ The trust involved in the market facilitation role. The diverse market players need to believe that the facilitator will act with transparency, integrity and even-handedness.
○ The role of trust in donor agency efforts to move from old BDS approaches to those more consistent with market development principles. Longstanding partners, used to providing subsidized BDS, should not be simply abandoned as we move on to new methods. We should remember that ethics plays a role in transitions.

Trust and openness were also evident among participants at this seminar, who were prepared to tell the truth about what is and isn't working with their efforts. The ability to argue among ourselves while respecting our diverse efforts is also critical to advancing this field. Let us hope that the next year will be another constructive time of experimentation in our field, from which we can all learn.

References

Anderson, G. (2002) 'The hidden MSE service sector: research into commercial BDS provision to micro and small enterprises in Vietnam and Thailand', presented at the BDS conference in Hanoi, available at www.ilo.org/public/english/employment/ent/sed/bds/donor/member/ilo.htm

Committee of Donor Agencies for Small Enterprise Development (2001) *Business Development Services for Small Enterprises: Guiding principles for donor intervention.*

Field, M. and D. Knopp (2003) 'Business linkages and producer groups in Bangladesh – options for rural microenterprise development', *Small Enterprise Development*, Vol.14, No.4, ITDG Publishing, London.

International Development Enterprises India (2003) 'Information dissemination: Business Development Services approach' presentation at the 2003 Turin BDS seminar, www.ilo.org/dyn/bds

Lusby, F. (2001) 'The AFE experience in Mali (combining subsector analysis and BDS market development)', presentation at the 2001 Turin seminar http://training.itcilo.it/bdsseminar/Presentations/presentations.htm

Miehlbradt, A. (2003) 'Assessing BDS markets: methodology and innovations', presentation at the 2003 Turin BDS seminar, www.ilo.org/dyn/bds

Phillips, D.A. and W.F. Steel (2003) 'Evaluating the Kenya Voucher Programme', *Small Enterprise Development*, Vol.14, No.4, ITDG Publishing, London.

About the author

Kate McKee is the Director of Microenterprise Development, US Agency for International Development. The BDS Seminar is organized by Jim Tanburn and Peter Tomlinson of the ILO.

15 Business Support Centres in the transition economies: progress with the wrong model?

MILFORD BATEMAN

This paper was first published in January 2000.

During the 1990s, networks of independent Business Support Centres (BSCs) were promoted in the transition economies of Central and Eastern Europe, aimed at supporting business start-ups and microenterprises. The funding came from Western governments and donor agencies, which were largely unconvinced by the networks of business support structures that had been established by the most forward-looking local governments under late communism.

This chapter shows how the neo-liberal ideology guiding macroeconomic policy in the transition economies also very much underpinned microeconomic interventions such as the BSCs. Accordingly, the donors' preference was for market-driven BSCs that were supposed eventually to 'earn their keep on the market'. The article points out some of the main drawbacks and opportunity costs that followed from this approach. Far from ensuring their strength and sustainability, the market-driven approach has instead ensured that the BSC networks have contributed very little additionality, and most have ended up collapsing because of a lack of fee-paying clients, being privatized and abandoning their original mandate, or opportunistically converting into a new institutional format – such as a Regional Development Agency (RDA) – in order to tap into further donor funding. It is argued that many previous reconstruction and development episodes could have provided examples of local state intermediation very successfully supporting SME development structures under chaotic and post-conflict conditions similar to those experienced in the transition economies from 1990 onwards. These examples in practice were ideologically anathema to the western governments and donor agencies, but would have been a much more appropriate template to use in Central and Eastern Europe than the market-driven BSC model adopted instead.

ONE OF THE MOST WIDESPREAD FORMS of support for SME development in the transition economies has been the promotion and financing of Business Support Centres (BSCs, known in some countries as local enterprise agencies, regional business advisory and support centres, etc, but all essentially the same). The establishment of BSC networks was one of the main SME-related tasks undertaken by most of the first post-Communist central and local governments, with the overwhelming majority initially financed by the international community. The BSC networks were meant to provide basic business advice and support for start-up enterprises, potential entrepreneurs among the unemployed, small growing enterprises, and in many cases SMEs in minority communities.

Many BSCs were deliberately established in regions already experiencing, or expecting to experience, particularly high unemployment. More successful and larger SMEs were expected to tap into the growing indigenous private sector consultancy and business support services companies, incoming consultancies from the western economies, or larger-scale international assistance programmes. In addition, over the longer term, the BSCs were expected to become the focus for a wider range of SME development activities in the community. After between four and eight years of operation, the BSC networks can now be assessed for their contribution to the SME development process.

The neo-liberal origins of the BSC networks

Neo-liberalism was the most influential political project in the 1980s and early 1990s, in both developing economies and in the majority of the western democracies. It was most closely associated in the developed economies with the radical free-market policies of Margaret Thatcher in the UK and Ronald Reagan in the USA. Neo-liberalism also came to be wholeheartedly accepted as the conventional wisdom by the international assistance community, particularly by the IMF and World Bank. Given the over-arching role of the multilaterals and US and UK governments in advising and financially assisting the overwhelming majority of the post-communist governments, and notwithstanding the emerging economic, social and environmental failure of the neo-liberal project in the late 1980s and early 1990s (see, for example, Liepitz, 1992), the neo-liberal discourse not surprisingly played a key role in the design of the macro-economic policies subsequently adopted in Eastern Europe (Gowan, 1995).

Micro-economic interventions, including SME development policy, also came under the influence of the neo-liberal agenda. At its root, the neo-liberal approach to SME development essentially conflates slavish respect for the activities and freedoms of the individual entrepreneur (exemplified by the 'enterprise culture' promoted by the Thatcher administration in the UK), with the wholesale acceptance of Chicago School textbook models of perfect competition and their hostility towards all forms of collective endeavour and state intervention. It follows that the state should refrain from 'interfering' in the economy, and simply try to ensure a neutral competitive environment, property rights and the rule of law. However, owing to the especially chaotic market conditions prevailing in early post-communist Central and Eastern Europe, a number of explicit policy interventions were considered necessary, including the establishment of networks of BSCs.

The BSCs in practice

It was thus reasonably clear what the international assistance community initially considered to be the preferred model for a BSC in Central and Eastern Europe. Conventional neo-liberal imperatives were applied to the design of the BSC networks, which were structured to be driven by the private sector, to operate according to standard commercial criteria and to move towards full cost recovery, to involve minimal local government participation, and to subordinate all programmes to short-run market imperatives. The practical inspiration for the majority of BSC networks in Central and Eastern Europe was the United Kingdom's experience with Local Enterprise Agencies (LEAs) and Training and Enterprise Councils (TECs) (Bateman, 1999a).

The UK's LEA model was pioneered in Hungary by the European Union's large Phare SME support programme which began in 1990. The drive to use the LEA model in this context was initially provided by the European Union's Phare officials and advisers, many of whom had very little knowledge of the numerous small private enterprise development capacities and local state-led initiatives developed under 'late communism' (see below). But probably more important was the fact that the LEA model was the preferred choice of the consultancy companies contracted by Phare. Having significant experience in implementing and evaluating the LEA/TEC bodies in the UK, and with neo-liberal cardinal principles dominating the approach to business development in the UK, the LEA model was a pretty natural choice to make when entering the new market of post-communist Eastern Europe.

The Hungarian LEA network was established under the auspices of the Hungarian Foundation for Enterprise Promotion (HFEP), an independent body established by the Hungarian Government, business associations and the banks. The HFEP was specifically intended by both the government and the European Commission to be the implementing agency for the Phare programme. It had to link upwards with government and responsible ministries, and downwards to the LEA network. The LEAs themselves were established as non-profit-making public–private partnership bodies, with representatives of local government and other interested private and public sector bodies constituting a managing board. As NGOs, the LEAs were effectively placed alongside the myriad other NGOs competing for donor assistance, although it was planned that central and local government would assist them financially when Phare funding came to an end.

With some changes and adaptations to take account of local conditions, essentially this model became the conventional wisdom for most of Central and Eastern Europe. As in Hungary, many local governments quickly realized the way the wind was blowing and so helped to establish the sort of BSC which they knew would attract international financial support, at the same time hoping that some of this financial support would find its way into their activities.

In some cases, however, this model encountered local resistance. This was initially so in Hungary, where the Hungarian Government indicated a preference for international assistance to be channelled through the chambers of small and medium-sized enterprises linked to the Hungarian Chamber of Commerce (UNCTAD, 1993). In Slovakia, small enterprise support was initially channelled through the regional development departments located within district government offices, but heavy pressure from western consultants to build private-sector institutions was ultimately successful. And in Slovenia, the EU's Phare programme officials refused to support the Slovenian Government's plans for a network of local state-led SME support institutions linked to the Ministry of Small Business and its implementing agency, the Small Business Development Centre (SBDC), arguing instead for their own ideas for mainly private sector-led institutions to be supported. The result was an impasse, and the Phare SME programme in Slovenia effectively ground to a halt (Phare, 1996).

What have been the consequences of this business support services model so far? I would argue that there are six key interrelated issues. First, it is clear that as the international funding comes to an end the BSC networks in almost all Central and Eastern Europe countries are deteriorating rapidly, and in many cases are near to collapse. In some cases individual and groups of BSCs have actually ceased operations just before, or just after, the international funding ran out.

The main reason for this situation is that there has been a persistent shortfall of financial support for the BSC networks from the host governments, both central and local, which were meant to take over after the international financial support ceased, and before the BSCs' own income-generating capability had fully kicked into operation. Although many central governments have been reluctant to help because they were short of cash, it is clear that those governments that have most resisted offering financial support are also those which most fully bought into the idea that the 'invisible hand' was all that was needed for entrepreneurship to flourish (e.g. in Poland). Local governments have generally tried to be more supportive, but they resist offering anything more than token support to an institutional structure which they rightly perceive to have been deliberately designed to reduce their role and scope for local economic intervention, and which was very clearly meant to be driven by the private sector right from the start. And, as very much in the UK, relying on corporate largesse to finance such services has proved to be particularly difficult.

Second, as a result of the deficit of central and local government support and absence of private sector sponsorship, a major effort is now under way to transform the BSCs into fully commercial bodies capable of competing for fee-paying work with their counterparts in the private sector. The US Government's Small Business Development Centres in Hungary and Poland, where both the central and local governments were originally expected to provide some longer-term financial support, were rapidly converted to becoming revenue-generating bodies (Pricer and Blackman, 1995). The EU's Phare-supported BSCs are all becoming very heavily involved in commercial revenue-generating activities with large enterprises and incoming multinationals. UNIDO/UNDP-sponsored BSCs have also had to restructure their operations rapidly in favour of seeking out any fee-paying business prospects. Many EU Phare BSCs, for example in Hungary and Slovenia, have opportunistically restructured themselves into Regional Development Agencies in order to tap into the flow of EU funds expected from the pre-structural funding cash associated with EU accession. In fact, BSC staff everywhere are now increasingly encouraged to spend a large proportion of their time touting for virtually any sort of fee-paying business activity on offer.

This trend is compounded by the fact that the (often very high) salaries within the BSCs are increasingly becoming a direct function of the fee-income generated by the BSC, which quite naturally means there is an incentive to seek out the most lucrative clients in order to further hike up salaries. Thus, those BSCs that are set to survive into the future are doing so by becoming fully commercial and indistinguishable from conventional private sector consultancies. The BSCs are now mainly concerned with their own profitability and survival.

An interesting illustration of this comes from the county of Szabolcs-Szatmar-Bereg in Eastern Hungary, where an LEA was established in 1990. As early as 1991 Attwater (1992) reported that the LEA's managers were getting heavily involved in entrepreneurial activities in order to maximize their own performance-related incomes. By 1998, upwards of 70 per cent of its income came from these activities. It is important to note that, in the context of a 'sustainability crisis' in the Hungarian LEA network brought about by the final withdrawal of EU funding and the lack of Hungarian central or local government support, this particular BSC has recently been recommended as the 'best practice' model for the other Hungarian BSCs to emulate (and, by extension, the BSCs in the rest of Central and Eastern Europe, too, as they prepare to face their own sustainability crises as donor money comes to an end).

The result is that the majority of very small enterprises, start-ups and the unemployed, which were essentially meant to be the focus of the entire BSC network, are increasingly being squeezed out of the client frame. Worse, this increased commercialization of the BSC is having a marked 'crowding out' effect on those counterpart private sector companies competing in the same market to offer consultancy and support services to better-established and/or larger firms and incoming multinationals. This clearly reduces the extent of additionality in business support services provision being generated by the BSCs.

Third, the all-engrossing search for the most profitable business opportunities means that the BSCs are inevitably neglecting the vital wider local economic development externalities arising from SME development activities. Strategic interventions at the local level which offer little immediate financial return to the BSC, but which will benefit the local community considerably in the long run, are simply not being undertaken. In addition, local initiatives that have obvious economic development potential, such as business incubators, are routinely used by the BSCs simply to extract much-needed rental income in the short term, rather than to develop, say, technology-intensive or innovative SMEs over the longer term (Bateman, 2000). This trajectory is especially ironic in view of the fact that a major criticism of the communist planners was that they failed to understand the subtleties and nuances of longer-run, sustainable economic development strategies.

Fourth, there has been a significant opportunity cost to the current BSC network structure in the shape of the 'dumbing down' of local government. By channelling virtually all international financial support for SME development into the BSC networks, the traditional economic departments located within most local governments in Central and Eastern Europe have effectively been allowed to atrophy. In many localities there has been no more than a token 'stakeholder' involvement in SME development by the local government. In some cases, BSCs have been encouraged to resist any 'interference' from the local government (though not their financial support), even though many local governments were early on the main driving force behind the establishment of 'their' local BSC. On the other hand, some local governments are starting to contract out to the BSCs for the generation of their local SME policy, which makes it dangerously dependent upon the BSC's advice as well as its operational capacity.

Overall, this side lining of local government capacity has taken place even though there was much evidence that local governments were actually very active in promoting small enterprises under 'late communism', particularly in the former Yugoslavia, Hungary and Poland (see, for example, McIntyre, 1988; PPI/CIPE, 1993; Bateman, 1993). It thus seems most likely that a variety of local government economic departments could have used a much greater share of the international financial resources devoted to SME development to good effect, or at least no less competently, honestly and efficiently than was expected of the BSCs at that time. Increasingly, because of the perceived poor performance of the BSCs and/or their gradual repositioning as fully private-sector entities, many central and local governments are now becoming resigned to the need to have to set up 'their own' BSC networks from scratch. For example, in Latvia, where the original EU-Phare-funded BSCs have been effectively cut adrift, government support is now being directed to newly established 'field offices' within the municipalities.

Fifth, even when there remains the possibility of continuing to offer financial support from central and local government funds to support the BSC networks and their original work with smaller enterprises, the costs of such subventions are increasingly edging up towards the local opportunity cost, represented by the fees paid by their most financially well-endowed clients. Most probably, the long-term cost of ensuring that the BSCs undertake their designated support activities will rise at least to the level of the possible in-house equivalent (i.e. where such services are provided direct by local government), and in many cases it could go higher than that.

Finally, the commercial culture that has been consistently promoted in the BSC networks has undermined any growth of a sense of public duty and a real and sustainable commitment to SME development objectives. BSC staff have been given substantial freedom to push to maximize their own agendas and individual financial positions. Certainly, salaries are universally very much higher in the BSCs in order to attract the 'right people', but this has seriously undermined local governments' capacity to hold on to their best staff. In several BSCs, senior management have taken a significant personal shareholding in order to remain in control. Some BSCs have pushed to privatize their activities formally via an employee or management buy-out, or through being sold off to a related commercial organization. Of course, if this strongly entrepreneurial approach is not precluded by a variety of sanctions, and is anyway effectively encouraged by western advisers and the international agencies themselves (as by Gibson, 1997), then such deleterious developments are only to be expected.

Contrary to the official statements about the 'good health' of the BSC networks in Central and Eastern Europe, it is disappointing to report that on closer examination their operations actually look decidedly problematic. If, as seems likely, the BSC networks are eventually fully privatized over the next few years as the international financial assistance dries up, and local and central governments remain unwilling to provide financial support and strategic direction, then the loss of investment injected by the international assistance community will be very substantial. Apart from the actual financial costs involved in establishing the BSC networks, there is also the tragic loss of time and opportunity involved if the current BSCs no longer do what they were designed to do, and completely new BSCs must now be established from scratch to develop the vitally important SME sector. Further, one must also assign a cost to the relative underdevelopment of other private sector business consultancies that were not in receipt of the huge subsidy element involved in establishing what has emerged to become a very powerful competitor. Given these very tangible and, unfortunately, largely predictable limitations of the neo-liberal-inspired BSC model used throughout Central and Eastern Europe, the question now arises, was there any alternative to hand in the early 1990s? We very briefly touch upon this question in the final section.

What were the alternatives?

At first sight, the experiences of post-World War II Japan, Germany and Italy, of the East Asian 'tiger' economies since the 1960s (especially Taiwan), and of China since 1978, should have been extremely useful to policy makers in Eastern Europe.

Uniquely, these earlier historical episodes also involved a major historical and system discontinuity, corrupt bureaucracies, huge cultural shift, and the need for reconstruction and development from a very low base of economic activity. Moreover, careful analysis of these examples reveals a very successful policy model for SME development. Based around the institution-building activities, support and cajoling of local and regional government, a wide range of SME development institutions was established, operated and financed. In addition, comprehensive local and regional strategic planning was a feature of all of these successful SME development episodes, allowing for the co-ordination of scarce reconstruction and development resources and the exploitation of local and regional comparative advantages by key SME sectors. Regional governments were quick to realize that affordable finance was a desperately required item, so they fought hard to establish local and regional state-owned banks and funds which could target funds at key SMEs and SME sectors.

Fairness, equity and a commitment to social welfare were also very important aspects of these SME development episodes, creating a broad base of support and an important foundation of social capital within the local community for the necessary sacrifices and painful adjustments to be made. In total, these local and regional government-inspired policies led to an immediate, continuous, equitable, and wide-ranging contribution to reconstruction, SME development and living standards. Notwithstanding problems of replicability and cultural and geographic specificity, there is a very strong argument that these sucessful post-chaos/post-conflict experiences could, and should, have provided the starting point for the policy framework for SME development in post-communist Central and Eastern Europe.

Overall, however, these particular historical episodes played a comparatively minor role in informing Eastern European governments of the SME policy interventions on offer. One important reason was that the economic development success in these countries was achieved largely because of an extremely active local and regional state, something that was anathema to the neo-liberal agenda. In the 1980s and early 1990s, resistance to the concept of state intervention was deeply ingrained in many of the government assistance departments, consultancies and major international agencies. Many of the most respected international establishments and individuals misunderstood, or deliberately overlooked, the very positive role of the state in several of the most important post chaos/post-conflict development episodes.

The World Bank, for its part, mounted a dogged defence of the neo-liberal orthodoxy in the so-called 'Miracle report' (World Bank, 1993). This was a response to calls by the Japanese Government and others to explore more fully the reasons for the stunning industrial development success of the East Asian 'miracle' economies. The World Bank's deliberations ended up side-stepping, mislabelling as 'market-conforming', or simply 'whitewashing' nearly all the key state interventions and social policies which many believed stood four-square behind East Asian success (see Amsden, 1994). It took until the mid-1990s before the World Bank finally, and only partly, conceded that state intervention could indeed be 'efficiency-enhancing' (World Bank, 1997). By then, of course, the reform and policy trajectory was well under way in Central and Eastern Europe, where substantive central and local state-sponsored SME policies and programmes remained both conceptually invalid and financially impracticable in the eyes of many reforming governments in Central and Eastern Europe.

At the same time, the neo-liberal vision was very much at odds with the key background features of equity, fairness and the sense of 'everyone sharing the burden' which underpinned the reconstruction and SME development trajectory in the previous historical episodes recounted above. Instead, the neo-liberal project very much sees develop-ment in terms of a deliberately *increased* level of inequality and social differentiation.

The IMF support programmes were generally conditional upon cuts in the real financial and social wage in order to reduce consumption, discourage imports and improve the macro-economic situation. Other individual policies also worked in this broad direction, including the general lowering of the fiscal burden on the state, enterprises and entrepreneurs, which also reduces resources available for redistribution; dismantling the previously equal access social welfare systems; ensuring low wage rates and discouraging trade unionization which, in the short run, helps to increase enterprise competitiveness and attract mobile multinational capital flows; privatization of public services, which are then encouraged to allocate services according to ability to pay rather than need or social benefit; and privatization of the industrial sector (either through vouchers or direct sale), which facilitates the accretion of capital into the hands of a small elite. It is thus not surprising that inequality has increased dramatically in Central and Eastern Europe (Milanovic, 1998).

Finally, it was also the case that the bulk of the existing and quite creative local SME programmes and institutional support structures that had been introduced under 'late communism' were simply abandoned in the first wave of neo-liberal advice offered to governments in Central and Eastern Europe after 1990. Many of these programmes could have provided a very useful institutional foundation upon which rapid SME development could have taken place. As Stiglitz recounts (1999, p.22), the international assistance agencies and their advisers, 'seem to have seen themselves on a mission to level the "evil" institutions of communism and to socially engineer in their place (using the right textbooks this time) the new, clean, and pure "textbook institutions" of a private property market'.

Conclusion

The BSC networks in Eastern Europe, the most expensive and highly visible SME policy intervention undertaken so far, are in real trouble. Most BSCs are moving to survive by *de facto* or *de jure* conversion into private sector consultancies, with consequently few and rapidly declining links to an SME development 'mission'. It is thus very much a moot point whether a high degree of commercialization should indeed be encouraged as 'good practice' (see Gibson, 1997). Nor has sustainability been ensured by having local governments as 'stakeholders' on the BSC management boards. Meanwhile, the channelling of financial support overwhelmingly into the independent BSC networks – particularly that from the international community – has left local governments universally ill-equipped to confront the enormous challenges that face their deteriorating communities, and they certainly cannot adequately discharge the increased economic development responsibilities that have been foisted upon them by central government.

The neo-liberal SME policy discourse was heavily promoted via aid conditionality at the start of the transition by the international assistance agencies and their advisers, and it was subsequently taken on board by most Central and Eastern European governments. Overall, however, the result of this ideological imprint has been the establishment of poorly functioning, excessively commercial, short-termist, and financially unsustainable BSC networks. Tragically for Central and Eastern Europe, this poor track record is essentially a repeat of that experienced in the UK with the LEA/TEC networks, the model upon which the BSC networks in Central and Eastern Europe were established, now being restructured. In the light of the above Central and Eastern European experience, and with more of an eye to the previous successful episodes of local state intermediated reconstruction and SME development, the role of local government in SME development needs to be reassessed, and ideological and practical objections to it assuming a more strategic and developmental role in SME development cast aside.

References

Amsden, A. (1994) 'Why isn't the whole world experimenting with the East Asian model to develop? A comment on the World Bank East Asia Miracle report', *World Development*, Vol.22, No.4, pp.615–670.

Attwater, J. (1992) 'Developing relationships in enterprise support in Eastern Hungary', paper presented to the Enterprise Development in Eastern Europe Conference, Manchester Business School, March.

Bateman, M. (1993) 'Local economic strategies and new small firm entry in a labour-managed economy: the case of Yugoslavia 1950–1990', unpublished PhD thesis, University of Bradford, UK.

Bateman, M. (1999a) 'Small enterprise policy in the transition economies: progress with the wrong model?', *Zagreb International Review of Business and Economics*, Vol.2, No.1.

Bateman, M. (2000) 'The role of business incubators as local economic development tools in Central and Eastern Europe', paper prepared for Project on the Assessment of Business Incubators as Economic Tools in Development Countries, UNDP, Vienna.

Gibson, A. (1997) 'Business development services – core principles and future challenges', *Small Enterprise Development*, Vol.8, No.3.

Gowan, P. (1995) 'Neo-liberal theory and practice for Eastern Europe', *New Left Review*, 1213, pp.3–60.

Liepitz A. (1992) 'The regulation approach and capitalist crisis: an alternative compromise for the 1990s', in Dunford, M. and G. Kafkalas (eds) *Cities and regions in the New Europe: the global–local interplay and spatial development strategies*, Belhaven, London.

McIntyre, R. (1988) 'The small enterprise and agricultural initiatives in Bulgaria: institutional invention without reform', *Soviet Studies*, Vol. XL, No.4, October.

Milanovic, B. (1998) *Income, inequality, and poverty during the transition from planned to market economy*, World Bank, Washington DC.

Phare (1996) 'Framework for Technical Assistance to SME development in Slovenia (SL94) Final Report', December 1996.

Pricer, R. and R. Blackman (1995) 'A game plan for sustainability: proven strategies for Central European management development centers', in Fogel, D., M.E. Harrison, and F. Hoy (1995) (eds) *Moving to sustainability: how to keep small business centres alive*, Avebury, Aldershot.

Public Policy Institute/Centre for International Private Enterprise (1993) 'Private sector development and local government in Hungary', papers and proceedings of the PPI/CIPE Conference, Eger, 10–11 September 1993.

Stiglitz, J. (1999) 'Whither reform? Ten years of the transition', paper presented at the Annual Bank Conference on Development Economics, Washington DC, April 28–30, 1999.

UNCTAD (1993) 'A study of the emerging role and potential of Hungarian SMEs in the field of exports', internal report, 15 March 1993.

World Bank (1993) *The East Asian Miracle: economic growth and public policy*, World Bank, Washington DC.

World Bank (1997) *The state in a changing world*, World Bank, Washington DC.

About the author

Milford Bateman is currently a Principal Consultant with IMC Consulting Ltd, specialising in local economic development policy in South East Europe.

16 Case studies of BDS market development interventions in weaker markets

JIM TOMECKO

This paper was first published in December 2003.

A frequently heard comment these days, from those engaged in micro-enterprise and small business promotion, is, 'BDS, yes, well... a good concept but how can it work in practice?' One of the problems in this field is that the term 'business development service' (BDS) has frequently become detached from its sister concept 'market development'; the result has been that BDS is perceived to be a rather narrow concept applicable in only limited conditions. This chapter presents three case studies of how facilitators, using the BDS market development approach, can positively intervene in weak service markets and still avoid the distortions that appear to have characterized much of the donor or publicly sponsored projects of the past.

PERHAPS ONE OF THE BIGGEST PRACTICAL CHALLENGES to implementing the concept of market-oriented business services has been 'what does one do in really weak markets where there are no service providers and the demand from enterprises is low?' Market research undertaken in several countries in the past few years has clearly shown that the volume of business service purchases declines as the business size gets smaller. Not only is their purchasing power lower, but also their attitude to outsourcing services is still fairly negative, or at best neutral. Such attitudes are changing, albeit slowly, as the forces of competitiveness compel even small firms to look for more efficient ways of managing their fixed and variable costs. But the question for many donors or facilitators is, 'so, what are the options we can apply now in weaker markets?'

Picture yourself in the following situation. You are asked to make the BDS market development approach work in an environment where donors and government are still subsidizing a large amount of services to enterprise, all of the available service providers are, in fact, subcontractors to these publicly funded schemes so they have no incentive to offer services on a commercial basis, at the same time most small enterprises 'cry poor' as soon as the issue of raising fees to commercial levels is mentioned, and finally politicians are eager to be associated with any subsidy programme that comes their way. Does this sound familiar?

The three case studies cited below are selected from about 70 interventions (some of which were not successful) made over the past three years in situations that are exactly like the one mentioned above. While it is important to understand that the market development principles still hold true, it has to be said that the nature of the service market interventions changes as one moves progressively towards weaker markets. For example, while one may find a new service provider in the capital that is willing to develop a new and commercially viable FM radio show for small businesses, as one moves further into smaller towns or rural areas where such service providers simply do not exist, it becomes necessary to change one's partnership strategy to include co-financed interventions that tend to be more of a 'public benefit' nature, rather than the sometimes narrowly defined 'private benefit' services that were the initial focus of many BDS interventions. The partners are more likely to be business membership organizations (business chambers and associations, commonly known as BMOs) and local or national governments. In essence, as we move towards weaker markets, it appears that the broader issue of private sector or small enterprise development becomes more prominent when compared with private benefit BDS. As this occurs, one often encounters an 'all or nothing' attitude towards BDS. Either practitioners embrace the BDS market development paradigm or in fact they ignore it. This polarization has robbed the small enterprise development community of the opportunity to learn how important market development is to the way in which we promote enterprise in weak markets.

The implication of placing 'market development' at the core of small enterprise promotion is that we now have three broad categories of partners or service providers with whom we can interact: private service providers, business membership organizations and government. The term service provider is intentionally used to describe these actors, because all three of them would see themselves as providing some form of service to enterprise. They may not be familiar with the term 'service provider' and they might even be confused if you ascribed this label to them, but in a general sense this is what they are. A BMO, for example, is providing a service to enterprise when it advocates for certain policy change, a government is also providing a service when it promotes inward investment or plugs its country's products overseas (economic diplomacy). These are public as opposed to private services, but nevertheless services that are also vital to enterprise competitiveness. If carefully supported they can enhance demand for private services and can be presented as an alternative for public institutions caught in the trap of thinking that they have no role in enterprise promotion if they are not administering transaction subsidies.

So, how does one deal with different kinds of partners? Is the facilitator's offer the same or different? The answer is that one maintains a set of core principles that are the same for all partners, and then varies the offer according to the circumstances. For the facilitator, who is ultimately the donor's temporarily commissioned administrator of small grants, this, of course, involves discretion – a commodity that has been sorely lacking in many of the supply-led projects that have been much maligned in the past.

Before we get into the variation of offers for the different sets of service providers it is important to clarify how the approach works in practice. A business analogy may help clarify this. Imagine the donor to be a small investor, and the facilitator a stockbroker or a unit trust or mutual fund manager. The small investor wants to see a return on his or her investment, measured in 'impact', while the job of the broker or unit trust manager is to find suitable investments, in certain markets, that will give this desired impact. For the broker or unit trust managers to do this efficiently they have to develop a specialization in their chosen market (emerging markets, commodities, small firms, energy, etc) so that they can use their competence and contacts to the best advantage. To acquire this competence they need to investigate 'where are the markets moving?' 'what are the competitiveness drivers?' etc. Once they have this knowledge they are in a position to invest in enterprises that they think share their vision of the future. The market development approach in weaker markets is somewhat similar; the facilitator picks a few markets that suit its history, given mandate and its predisposition to risk and reward. It then studies these markets to identify commercial trends and then examines what enterprises need in these markets to be more competitive. Preliminary service gaps related to competitiveness are identified and then co-financing partners are sought to fill these gaps commercially and/or sustainably.

As part of their own overheads, the facilitators finance their own competence building through staff training and the commissioning of market research or studies of a general nature. These capacity-building investments are aimed at improving their ability to pick partners with sound ideas. The rest of the facilitator's budget is for small grants put into specific interventions.

How should facilitators intervene?

So, what is an intervention or a facilitator's investment? The definition that applies to the case studies below is as follows: 'Any significant allocation of project resources (manpower or money) invested in a well-defined project of a partner which is aimed at either improving the ability of the partner to provide better services (public or private) to SMEs or to stimulate the demand for services from SMEs.' For the facilitator, the intervention is 'where the rubber meets the road!' Each intervention should:

○ be in a weak market, defined as low demand from SMEs and inappropriate supply
○ show relevance or have 'plausible attribution' or impact on improving the competitiveness of the enterprise market selected
○ have a motivated partner that understands the service and is prepared to co-finance the intervention
○ be potentially sustainable either from a commercial perspective or as a long-term publicly funded service.

The facilitator's attitude to subsidies or small grants follows a few cardinal rules:

○ Negotiate as much contribution as possible from the partner. This will vary from case to case.
○ Use, as an evaluation criterion for all interventions, the leverage ratio of facilitator to partner expenses, plus any fees generated from the SMEs (i.e. the amount of cash the facilitator contributes over the amount of cash the partner puts in, plus revenues from SMEs that buy the service).
○ All transaction subsidies (between the service provider and SME clients) are avoided unless associated with a specific trial leading to short-term commercialization.
○ Cost sharing is administered and disbursed on a 'line item' basis to avoid cross-subsidization.
○ Clearly understanding the difference between public and private benefit, in order to avoid distortions.

The facilitator's offer to the various sets of service providers (private, BMOs and government) can now be more clearly presented and understood.

Private service providers

The co-financing of interventions is only for stimulating innovations or expanding service markets to underserved SMEs. This market expansion can be facilitated through stand-alone service providers such as accountants or through private enterprises that provide many smaller enterprises with an embedded service such as quality control. The facilitator's offer might be in the form of: specific market research related to commercialization of the service; advertising and promotion on a declining basis, to popularize the service; product development; capacity building and advisory services; and in certain cases limited transport subsidies to encourage the service provider to explore more distant markets. The emphasis is on short-term (one year) commercial viability and replicability either by the assisted service provider or by other service providers who copy the business model and provide the service on their own without any assistance.

Business membership organizations

For the BMO, the offer is different. No support is offered for developing commercial private business services, as this would compete with the private service providers mentioned above. Rather, the attention is directed to help them to provide three sets of services. The first relates to the fulfilment of their 'core' services such as advocacy, business linkages and networking, area or sector development or competitiveness, and information. The second set of services is related to fulfilling an 'agency' function where the BMO (sometimes involving a subcontract with a private service provider) offers a unique service to its members such as group insurance, bar coding, or acts as an agent for the government in matters like business registration or verifying certificates of origin. The third type of service is similar to a BDS facilitator (not a service provider) where they stimulate the demand for certain private services. This takes the form, for example, of a referral system for legal and other business issues, or promoting, among their members, the need to purchase other services that will enhance their competitiveness, such as ISO certification or advice on how to comply with World Trade Organization rules.

Government service providers

This can be a national or a local government. Again, as with the BMOs, the offer is not extended to assist the government in developing any service that would be in competition with a private service provider. The emphasis is on public benefit services, such as appropriate policies, regulations or legislation, country/regional or sector promotion, and capacity building to strengthen these services. In some cases, where the public body is clearly aware of the differentiation of the role of facilitator and service provider, the government can be encouraged by the donor's facilitator to become a local facilitator itself. Examples of how this is done will be elaborated in the case studies that follow.

Case 1 Accounting, finance and taxation services for SMEs

This first case is about expanding the market for accounting, finance and taxation services among small enterprise in small towns (average population 100 000) of Nepal. The logic of expanding this market is that the more services SMEs consume (through purchases), the greater will be their impact on the management of the businesses that buy. In Nepal, as with many countries, these services are divided into two main categories. The first is 'statutory', or the minimum services that an enterprise must purchase so that it can comply with government regulations. The second type is related to financial consultancy and includes tax consultancy, project studies, bookkeeping systems, financial management advice and training. This second type of service closely resembles the services that donors encouraged public institutions to provide for SMEs in much of the 1980s and part of the 1990s. These services are mainly designed to save the enterprise money or to improve its return on investment, and it is these services rather than the statutory ones that the facilitator, in this case, wishes to promote. The assumption is that the more that SMEs voluntarily purchase these services, the more impact there will be on the competitiveness of these enterprises.

The facilitator's market research indicates that purchases of financial consultancy services by MSEs, in the target market, are in the region of $44 per annum per small enterprise (average employment 8–10 persons), and that this figure declines as the enterprises become smaller. Research also indicates that there are about 3000 enterprises in this category in the capital, and probably twice as many outside the capital. Two interventions have been tried which are designed to stimulate increased MSE purchases of these services from private service providers: the first is on the supply side while the other is aimed at stimulating demand. In a previous intervention, the facilitator has been working with a service provider in this sector on developing specific training products related to how small enterprises in small towns can comply with the introduction of a newly introduced value-added tax. The product has done well and is now commercially viable. Based on this success, the service provider would now like to expand its outreach and franchise a series of ten financial consultancy and training packages in ten small towns outside the capital. While there are service providers in these towns, they have tended to focus almost exclusively on the statutory side of the market. The facilitator's service provider, called CAI, wishes to franchise its ten financial consultancy products to existing service providers in these towns. In order to do this it needs to develop its products so that their quality standards can be assessed, train the franchisees, and assist the franchisees in a certain amount of promotion.

Because of its past and successful relationship with the facilitator, CAI approached the facilitator for assistance in making this franchise operation a reality. The pre-feasibility of CAI estimates a potential turnover of $95 000 in the first year of operation with an additional client load of about 2000 small enterprises. After discussions with the facilitator, a risk-reduction strategy is adopted of starting with a first phase in four towns to pilot the products and verify the offer. The facilitator and the promoter, CAI, agreed to split the development costs at this stage into 33 per cent for the facilitator and 67 per cent for the promoter. This amounts to about $450 for the facilitator and about $1300 for the service provider. The facilitator paid for the advertising and promotion to attract franchisees in four pilot towns and the franchiser paid for the logistics and the initial training of the potential franchisees.

A second intervention in this sector is related to demand stimulation and takes place in the capital, but is directed at microenterprises. The target sub-sectors within the microenterprise sector are selected, in the market area, and they make up more than 3000 enterprises. The chosen intervention is 'social marketing', or marketing of a general nature to promote the expanded consumption of financial consultancy services among the target group selected. The same market research, as for the previous intervention, is used to assess constraints to purchase among the target group. These include: the fact that many are not aware of the service and its benefits, that the services seem too expensive, that the services can be done in-house, that they do not see accounts, financial and taxation services as being a problem for their firm. Conversely, the factors that are driving purchases among those that do buy are: that some of these services are required by the government, they cannot cover the work in-house, they need the specialized skills to cope with the growing complexity of the business, and that it is less expensive than doing this in-house. As previously mentioned, the market research indicates the level of spending in these services at about $44 per annum. The objective of the intervention is to use the social marketing campaign to stimulate demand to increase purchases of this service well above the $44 level, based again on the logic that increased voluntary purchases will have an impact on business performance. The critical elements of the campaign included: hiring a sector specialist to ensure that the most frequently asked questions about accountancy, financial and taxation services are addressed in the advertising campaign, hiring an advertising agency to frame the campaign and to produce the public relations materials needed to publicize the campaign, identifying distribution points for the PR materials, determining the 'calls to action', defining the indicators to use in the monitoring of the campaign, capacity building of the service providers to ensure they can meet the additional demand, organizing a trade fair to link service providers with customers in the target group, and organizing sponsorships within the private sector.

The impact indicators are: the number of responses to the 'calls to action', the number of brochures distributed, additional contacts of service providers, the number of visitors to the trade fair and, eventually, measuring the increase in the level of purchase by the target market of the selected accountancy and financial services beyond the base line of $44 per business. Because this is fundamentally a public benefit intervention, the costs allocated to the facilitator are greater than the private partners: $51 000 from the facilitator, $10 000 from private partners and $10 000 from other donors interested in the intervention.

Case 2 Promoting the carpet sector

The second case study involves promoting the carpet sector in Nepal. This sector employs about 80 000 people, which represents about 10 per cent of the country's manufacturing employment. It is a major export commodity with about 65 per cent of all its carpets going to Germany. Germany is the most significant market for hand-knotted carpets in the European Union, accounting for 46 per cent of the market. Nepal has about 13 per cent of the market in Germany, but the world market for floor coverings has declined by 38 per cent in the past few years, and as a result the market has become much more price sensitive. As prices decline, the country faces stiff competition, particularly at the lower end, from other competitors, such as India.

The facilitator, together with key informants from the carpet sector, looked for areas to cut costs without sacrificing quality. In its investigation of costs, it became clear that there was an unnecessary transaction cost associated with government regulation. Many years ago, when the carpet sector was booming and foreign currency restrictions were more regulated, a floor price or minimum export price was established by the government to ensure that it could recover sufficient foreign currency to pay for the importation of the New Zealand wool needed to make the carpets. In the meantime, the average per metre export price of Nepali carpets has fallen from $48 to about $32. The government regulation, however, has not changed in ten years. The effects of this regulation are the following: (1) for an exporter who is selling at $32, and needs to follow the government regulations, foreign currency must be bought on the grey market in Nepal, routed to a bank in Hong Kong and then sent back to his or her bank so that the difference between $48 and $32 can be made up; (2) the exporter has to over-invoice the buyer in Germany, presenting the buyer with a tax and accounting problem that takes time and energy to explain to their revenue collectors; and (3) since the exporter has over-invoiced for the carpets (meaning he has received less income than reported) he has to pay taxes on income that he has not received. All of this represents significant additional direct expenses and unnecessary transaction costs for the exporter and the importer.

The facilitator, together with the local business membership organization, the Nepal Carpet Exporters Association (NCEA), devised a plan to lobby the government to address this problem. The plan involved sponsoring the Minister for Industry to go to the most important international trade fair for carpets, which takes place each year in Germany. In a public event organized by NCEA at this fair, the minister met several German importers all of whom explained the irrelevance of the regulation and the urgency for the government to address this issue so that the Nepali carpet can maintain its competitiveness. The event had the desired effect, and on his return the minister reduced the floor price to $32, with a promise of its eventual elimination. In this intervention, the carpet exporters put up $20 000 for their airfares and accommodation to accompany the minister, while the facilitator prepared an 'executive brief' for the minister and paid for his air ticket. This amounted to 10 per cent of the cost of intervention. This is a good example of how a facilitator can work with a BMO on policy-level changes, thereby developing advocacy as a viable and more sustainable service for the BMO.

Case 3 Tea growers

The last case study comes from the 'orthodox tea' sector and relates to the influence a facilitator can also have on the market for financial services. Orthodox tea, such as Darjeeling, is black tea that is grown at a high altitude. Nepal produces about 750 tons of this tea (dwarfed by India) and has about 30 000 farmers employed producing green leaf. There are 11 newly established factories that are working at about 50 per cent of their installed capacity. Orthodox tea is a good cash crop for small farmers in the middle hills of the country, where income-generating possibilities are few. The production potential is good, and if farmers replaced some of their existing subsistence crops with tea their incomes would increase and production of the green leaf needed for the factories could easily double in the next five years. Tea is a crop that requires at least four years before it yields an income, after which the tea bush can produce all year round for about 80 years. Because of the four-year gap between changing from subsistence to a cash crop, most farmers need some form of credit.

The facilitator discussed this problem with the local BMO that represents all of the tea producers, the Himalayan Orthodox Tea Producers' Association, HOTPA. It turned out that one of the local development banks (ADB/N) used to finance tea, but it ran out of refinancing sources. The demand for credit was strong from the farmers because they had seen many of their neighbours do well from tea, and at the same time the demand for green leaf was strong from the tea factories that were operating well below their installed capacity. The facilitator organized several meetings with the key stakeholders and the trail led to the central bank of Nepal (the Rastra Bank), the most likely source of refinancing for the ADB/N. A meeting was arranged at the central bank with HOTPA, ADB/N and the facilitator. The economic case for the expansion of green leaf production was made. The president of the central bank was convinced, provided that disbursements were indeed made to small farmers. He agreed to provide a refinancing facility for the ADB/N worth $1.3 million for the next fiscal year, and the facilitator agreed to support the establishment of 25 additional savings co-operatives (this model of financing already exists with excellent repayments) in the tea-growing area. This will cost the facilitator $15 000 in local technical assistance over the next two years.

Most enterprises join BMOs for collective advocacy, yet their membership fees hardly cover more than about 30 per cent of their expenses. They expect their BMOs to advocate for their benefit but hardly ever see the connection between advocacy and membership fees. To make advocacy a more sustainable service, members need to see a more direct connection between successful advocacy and a sustainable BMO secretariat based on membership fees. This last case is an example of how a facilitator can influence, again with the right BMO, the financial services or credit market for the selected target group without getting directly involved with the provision of the service itself, and in the process create more value added for the members of the BMO involved, thereby making advocacy a more viable service.

Conclusion

The objective of this chapter has been to show how a facilitator can become engaged in small enterprise promotion with a range of private and public service providers by using market intelligence, good common sense and small grants. The market development approach takes us beyond the widely misunderstood narrow definition of the service provider in much of the BDS literature, as being private. Rather it incorporates both BMOs and government as legitimate providers of public benefit services such as country or sector promotion and regulatory support. By adding these two types of business service providers to the list of the facilitator's potential partners, a broader range of support activities immediately falls within the scope of the donor's non-financial enterprise promotion project. Having said this, however, the facilitator needs to adopt a discretionary posture that is consistent with all three sets of partners. This consistency is achieved through respect for market development principles and the recognition that each one of these service provider types has a distinct role in enterprise promotion: private service providers are best at private benefit services, BMOs are best at advocacy and area or sector promotion, and governments are best at arbitration and establishing a supportive business environment.

About the author

Jim Tomecko has worked for the past 30 years with GTZ, UNIDO, ILO, World Bank and others in enterprise development, mainly in Asia and Africa. He is the co-ordinator for GTZ's knowledge management network of professionals in Asia in the field of economic and employment promotion and is currently Team Leader for GTZ's Private Sector Promotion Project and the director of a GTZ International Services project for a donor consortium in Bangladesh.

17 Gender and the growth of microenterprises

JEANNE DOWNING

This paper was first published in March 1991.

This chapter explores the issue of gender-differentiated patterns of growth; do female and male entrepreneurs have different interests in their business strategies and display different patterns of growth? If they do, what factors explain these differences? This chapter provides evidence supporting the hypothesis that women more often than men use available resources to increase the diversity of their enterprise portfolios rather than the size of a single firm. These tendencies toward 'occupational multiplicity' (Massiah, 1988), it is argued, have important implications for research and intervention design. They suggest that research which measures growth solely in terms of firm size underestimates the earnings of women's enterprises. Additionally, interventions aimed at promoting the growth of firm size may fail in assisting female entrepreneurs, who focus on different goals.

THERE HAS BEEN CONSIDERABLE DEBATE in recent years over the trade-offs between economic growth and the poverty-alleviation approaches to microenterprise development. Much of the Women in Development literature warns of the dangers of growth-oriented strategies, given the concentration of women in low-growth, low-return microenterprises. Growth-oriented strategies for microenterprise development threaten to neglect the large numbers of female entrepreneurs at the survival level, ignoring the importance of their earnings, however small, to human capital investment.

Proponents of growth-oriented strategies (Liedholm and Mead, 1987), on the other hand, argue that given the meagre resources of most governments and the inability of many countries to generate growth of any kind during recent years of recession and structural adjustment, it is imperative to target the available resources towards dynamic sub-sectors which have the greatest potential for contributing to economic growth.

Tinker (1987) adds yet another dimension to the debate. She asserts that the growth of firm size may not be a relevant basis upon which to judge the success of female entrepreneurs since they have different goals and employ different business strategies to men. The goal of women, more than men, is to feed and educate their children. To achieve this goal, women seek means to secure their income in diverse ways. Men, free of much of the burden of the family, are able to pursue individual interests and to take business risks in search of profits. The consequence of gender-differentiated business goals and strategies, according to Tinker, is that women and men display different patterns of growth.

Gender-differentiated patterns of enterprise growth

Gender-differentiated growth patterns, according to Tinker (1987), derive from gender differences in management and investment strategies. While men tend to be drawn into the world of individual pursuit, women operate more commonly in 'human economies', based on family and other mutual support networks. After feeding their children, women tend to devote their income to kinship networks, for example, to enterprises for their sisters, brothers, or mothers. Male entrepreneurs, on the other hand, invest their profits in the growth of their enterprises. The consequences of these investment strategies is that men's enterprises more often grow in size while women's expand in an 'amoeba-like' fashion, increasing in number rather than size. Tinker asserts that women have fewer interests in growth than men; they have economic priorities over and above profits. Moreover, she contends, they have little time or inclination to assume the management and other headaches associated with larger enterprises.

The contention that women have little interest in growth ignores intervening variables that explain women's enterprise strategies. The model in Figure 17.1 is meant to be a framework for exploring variables influencing entrepreneurial behaviour and gender-differentiated patterns of growth.

This model of entrepreneurial behaviour is partly based on the research of Grown and Sebstad (1989), who hypothesize that entrepreneurs adopt different strategies for increasing or stabilizing their income. The poorest, they argue, are primarily agricul-turalists, and although within agriculture they grow a diversity of crops on dispersed lots, they have limited non-farm investments. These survival-oriented entrepreneurs, with their meagre resources, attempt to diversify their agricultural activities to spread the risks of commodity price fluctuations and the environmental hazards that result in crop loss. Once survival is secure and sufficient income is generated, these primarily farm-oriented entrepreneurs attempt to diversify into non-farm activities. As their secu-rity base expands, they continue to increase the diversity of the portfolios. Entrepreneurs at yet a higher and more stable level of income, at some point and in some environments, are willing to specialize in fewer, or even single activities.

Grown and Sebstad suggest that men much more than women are able and willing to assume a growth orientation. Women's greater security orientation is attributed to the meagre resources to which they have access, primary responsibility for feeding the fam-ily, and the threat of abandonment and divorce. This threat, they argue, motivates women to invest their income and profits in the security offered by family networks. Men, on the other hand, not only have access to larger amounts of capital, but also have more latitude in terms of how and where they invest – partly because of their wives' security orienta-tion. Moreover, there is evidence that where men make more risky investments, women

| Survival oriented   → | Security oriented   → | Growth oriented |
→	Diversification →	Specialization
Includes both women and men who are very poor, mostly involved in agriculture, with limited non-farm diversification.	This group includes women and men, though men from the previous group will move into this category first by means of non-farm investments. This group diversifies activities to spread risks. Individuals may farm as well as have more than one enterprise.	Men will move into this category faster than women, who tend to spread the risks of men's enterprises with their diversified portfolios and who assume responsibility for the children. Growth-oriented enterprises are larger and more specialized, use more hired labour and external sources of capital.

Figure 17.1 *Model of the dynamic of entrepreneurial behaviour.*

tend to invest in safer ventures in order to spread the risks of their husbands' investment.

Within the model, diversification refers most generally to Tinker's lateral growth pattern in which investment capital is used to finance new enterprises. However, diversification could also involve the addition of a new product line to a retail outlet or manufacturing firm, or the addition of a new function, for example, a retail outlet to what was formerly only a production unit. Specialization, on the other hand, is associated with a growth orientation, and is defined here as investment in a single enterprise to expand its size and productivity. It typically involves the transformation of raw materials into finished products and increasing the number of steps and participants, each specializing in a smaller part of the total process.

A key question is whether women's business activities more than men's expand through diversification rather than specialization. Men, with greater access to capital, fewer constraints on their mobility, and a stronger connection to the market economy, are more able to take advantage of high growth activities and to amass capital for productivity-enhancing investments. With relatively less time, mobility, and capital resources, women may find lateral growth in the high-risk environments in which they operate a more effective income strategy.

While distinguishing between growth patterns that lead to greater specialization and those that do not is analytically useful, it can also be simplistic. *Diversified strategies may indirectly lead to economic growth and development.* They may represent a means of increasing and stabilizing income levels to allow greater risk taking and specialization in other segments of the economy. For instance, Schmink (1984) notes that households tend to engage simultaneously in survival and income-mobility strategies on a gender basis; women generally assume survival strategies and men mobility or growth-oriented strategies. Women's low but steady income, she contends, allows men to seek greater absolute returns at heightened risks.

The prevalence of diversification

How prevalent is Tinker's amoeba-like growth pattern, across regions, social groups, and among female-headed households? Evidence from Kenya, Nigeria, the Sudan, and Burkina Faso attests to the importance of non-farm diversification as an income strategy among rural farm households (Liedholm and Mead, 1986; Bendavid-Val, 1989). Intra-household analyses, however, reveal that women have their own diversified portfolios, the income from which they control. For example, female marketers in the Kutus region of Kenya stated that beyond the time they devoted to their 'full-time' marketing enterprises, they spent an additional 50 per cent of their working time farming (Downing and Santer, 1989). Vegetable vendors in rural Liberia earn income from selling vegetables and swamp rice, both of which they grow on their own plots; in addition, they farm family plots (Downing, 1990a). Although Liedholm and Mead (1986) assert that diversified income strategies are more prevalent in rural than urban areas, Gorton's work in Maseru, Lesotho, revealed urban female entrepreneurs with anything from two to four businesses (Gorton, 1990).

Research in the eastern Caribbean by Massiah (1988) found that over 50 per cent of the participants of a sample of several hundred were involved in more than one income-generating activity. Some combined formal employment with part-time self-employment, while others had interests in multiple enterprises. Other data collected in the region on 72 female entrepreneurs revealed similar findings (Downing, 1990b). Over 55 per cent of female entrepreneurs owned more than one business and 20 per cent owned three or more businesses.

Life histories revealed a common strategy for entering self-employment. A woman typically began her career as an employee, using the secure basis of a job to experiment on a part-time basis with self-employment, such as selling part-time 'out of the back of her car'. If and when her business was successful, she would eventually leave her job for full-time self-employment. As her business grew, she would invest profits in another enterprise and, over time, another and perhaps another. A particularly successful businesswoman on the island of Montserrat began as a hairdresser. When she was interviewed, she owned five businesses, including a car rental business, a floral boutique, and an apartment management firm, and rental property. Her husband had his own separate business.

These Caribbean entrepreneurs were also asked about their future business plans. Those who claimed to be interested in further business expansion were asked whether they were interested in increasing the size of an existing business or investing in a 'new business in addition to an existing one'. Almost one-third stated that if they had funds they would start a new business (Downing, 1990b). Similarly, in Lesotho, Cobbe (1985) found that Basotho women, rather than being income generating, were 'enterprise generating'. Although Cobbe's sample was small, under 50, her in-depth analysis revealed important evidence concerning women's motivations for their 'enterprise generating' behaviour, which will be discussed in the next section. Nevertheless, 85 per cent of her sample had more than one income-generating activity. Cobbe writes that Mapetso, a Basotho entrepreneur:

> had at least seven active enterprises and three or four 'in the works' at the time I was doing my field work. She sewed clothing, sold it, operated two cafes, rented flats, stored and transported goods, and sold eggs and vegetables. She was in the final stages of establishing a bottle store, restaurant, butchery, and poultry selling business.

In Huarez, Peru, Babb (1985) discovered that diversification was more family- than individually based. 'The need to diversify means that it is common to find families that engage in all three forms of production ... subsistence farming and household labour, petty production and commerce, and capitalist wage labour.' Babb also noted the smaller size of business of female sellers as compared to their male counterparts, who were often able to draw on resources generated from other forms of employment, travel greater distances to purchase goods, and sell a larger volume at a lower price than females.

These gender-based differences in business size suggest that although families in Huarez engaged in diversified income strategies, women did not receive equal access to ¦family money to invest in their enterprises.

Although Tinker's (1987) evidence from Indonesia and the Philippines points to an amoeba-like growth pattern of women's enterprise portfolio, Hackenberg's and Barth's research of female-owned 'sari-sari' stores in the Philippines showed that those business owners with greater resources, who could afford electricity and refrigerators, invested profits into expanding the volume of their inventory and diversifying their product lines (Hackenberg and Barth, 1984).

Factors contributing to entrepreneurial diversification

Under what conditions do female and male entrepreneurs diversify rather than specialize? How do these conditions differentially affect female and male entrepreneurs?

Acheson and Wilson (1990) assert that the prevalence of 'small, unspecialized operations run by one or two kinsmen with a minimum of capital equipment' can be explained by thin markets and high internal transaction costs which exceed high external transaction costs. The thin and fragmented markets common in so many rural areas in developing countries limit the quantity of any single product an entrepreneur is able to sell. To survive, entrepreneurs must diversify their portfolios or their product lines in order to fill market niches when and where they arise.

Gender differences in terms of access to resources, geographical mobility, and market entry, however, make women especially vulnerable to shallow markets. While male marketers have the freedom to travel considerable distances to a number of markets to purchase inputs and sell products, women's mobility in many regions is circumscribed by their domestic responsibilities and their need to be close to home. Gender-specific roles tend to limit the number of product markets that women are able or willing to enter and to further diminish the scope and size of the markets to which women have access. As a result, female more than male entrepreneurs suffer from atomistic competition, and their enterprises are small and unspecialized (Watts, 1984). Female entrepreneurs try, to the extent possible, to find diverse pockets of demand that they can meet without facing such extreme competition.

Evidence from the eastern Caribbean supports the hypothesis that entrepreneurs operating in thin markets tend to have multiple enterprises. Research in Montserrat, Dominica, St. Lucia, and Grenada revealed a higher incidence of multiple enterprises on the smaller as compared to the larger islands (Downing, 1990b). Female entrepreneurs in Montserrat, with a population of 12 000, were the most extreme both in terms of the percentage with multiple enterprises and the number of enterprises within a portfolio. And while Cobbe (1985) argues that multiple enterprises in rural Lesotho were most common among those at the lower income levels, in Montserrat women at all levels of income had multiple enterprises. When asked why they had multiple activities, all pointed to the small market for their goods and services on the tiny island of Montserrat.

In Kingston, Jamaica, Bolles' (1985) and LeFranc's (1989) research showed female entrepreneurs employing a diversified strategy as a means of achieving a more growth-oriented portfolio. Female entrepreneurs in Kingston utilized capital from their full-time wage job to start a home-based 'buy and sell' business (Bolles, 1985). These 'buy and sell' enterprises were often initiated on a seasonal basis, for example to sell a particular item during the Christmas season. Successful entrepreneurs could then use their seasonal profits to enter higher-return and less seasonal product markets and become what LeFranc referred to as 'informal commercial importers'. These importers travelled periodically to Miami or New York to buy specialized products to sell in Kingston, amassing considerable amounts of capital, which they in turn reinvested to increase further their enterprise profits.

Kingston's low-income female entrepreneurs, on the other hand, were considerably less fortunate than these importers. Without access to capital, they produced or sold low-return products next to male vendors selling higher-priced items. While their male counterparts reinvested their profits into their businesses, these low-income female entrepreneurs were forced to devote their earnings first to feeding their children, and only then to maintaining or increasing their inventory. Their primary responsibility for feeding their family put them at a severe disadvantage to their male counterparts. According to Bolles (1985), these low-income female entrepreneurs had little concept of 'profit'; their goal tended to be survival rather than strategic enterprise investment.

Bolles' (1985) and LeFranc's (1989) research suggests that, where female entrepreneurs have the security of a steady income, for example from wage employment, investment capital from their earnings, and access to a strong market, they are willing to adopt a growth orientation and to take risks. However, those with very meagre capital resources tend to stagnate in low-return product markets and to adopt a survival orientation.

According to Acheson and Wilson (1990), high internal and external transaction costs limit the size and specialization of enterprises. Internal transaction costs are incurred 'in hiring, organizing, and training employees' and are heightened by opportunism, illiteracy, a lack of accounting and business skills, and a lack of effective communication. External transaction costs, on the other hand, accrue from the expense of acquiring inputs and marketing outputs. Poor communication, a lack of co-ordination between supply and demand, irregular supplies of goods, and unpredictable changes in prices elevate these costs.

To lower internal transaction costs, women entrepreneurs tend to limit the hiring of employees to a small number of trusted relatives or close friends. In Jamaica, for example, female informal commercial importers, despite their strong growth orientation, relied almost completely on real or fictional kin to assist them in their businesses (LeFranc, 1989). In Ghana, Asante female traders in all commodities were deterred from hiring employees because of the fear of having to take responsibility for employee debts (Clark, 1989). Almost half of these female traders studied by Clark in Kumasi, Ghana worked alone, and an additional 35 per cent had only one helper. These helpers were largely daughters, but another large percentage was made up of 'equivalent' or fictional kin. These examples illustrate the effect of internal transaction costs – in particular the ability to trust in both the honesty and capability of employees – on enterprise size. Clearly, where employee hiring is limited to a small cadre of trusted kin, enterprises will remain small.

Women's more widespread illiteracy and their more limited access to lucrative markets lead to higher external transaction costs and to greater vulnerability to opportunism than men face. Women, like men, attempt to establish exchange relationships with long-term ties, kin, or gender-based affiliations to diminish external transaction costs. However, women's geographical immobility and the dominance of men in the market place and the transport sector can force women to sell wherever they are able, even at very low prices.

Women's greater illiteracy, innumeracy, lack of business skills (in many developing countries) and limited access to extension services and other sources of information put them at a disadvantage in comparison to men in managing their enterprises. Additionally, women's dual productive and reproductive responsibilities and the resultant time constraints can leave them with little time or inclination to expand the size of their firms. This hypothesis is supported by data from the ADEMI project in the

Dominican Republic, which indicate that, despite the greater efficiency (output to labour ratio) of women's small-sized firms in the textile industry, males entered into a 'growth' mode, by hiring employees, at a faster rate than females.

The type of enterprise may also be a causal factor in women's greater involvement than men in multiple enterprises. Manufacturing firms are able to increase their profitability through specialization, that is through increasing the steps in the production process and the number of employees, each specializing in a smaller pan of the total process. Service and retail firms, on the other hand, increase their profitability by selling to larger numbers of consumers and thereby reducing the overhead costs per unit sold. Retail and service firms operating in thin domestic markets, however, have limited access to customers. Given women's higher participation level in retail and service as compared to manufacturing firms, they are more likely than men to start multiple enterprises in order to increase sales and reduce risks.

Cobbe (1985) further suggests that multiple enterprise portfolios can be a strategy for amassing start-up and working capital. In her study of female entrepreneurs in Lesotho, Cobbe (1985) writes of one woman, engaged in seven enterprises, who used her different businesses as a means of accumulating working capital. After starting a cafe, this Basotho entrepreneur often found herself without income to replenish her stock – so she started making and selling 'fat cakes'. In other words, she initiated an 'auxiliary' commercial activity in order to finance the start-up costs and early development of her 'core' enterprise.

Implications of diversified strategies for economic growth

Bendavid-Val (1989) and Collier (1990) concur that diversification can be a means towards increasing income. Their evidence shows incremental increases in income as the diversity of earnings increases. Nevertheless, there are some caveats with regard to a diversification income strategy. While it has the advantage of spreading risks, evening out an entrepreneur's income stream, and allowing capital to be shifted from one activity to another depending on return rates and financing needs, there are also numerous disadvantages that have implications for economic growth.

A diversified portfolio of economic activities can stretch too thinly a woman's limited time, and managerial and financial resources, thereby hampering the profitability of all enterprises in the portfolio. Additionally, many microentrepreneurs, especially women, are unable to move beyond a diversified portfolio of small, unremunerative enterprises to more specialized and productive activities (Collier, 1990; Babb, 1985). In other words, out of desperation they get trapped in a diversification strategy with limited income, from which they are unable to escape.

Even more importantly, diversification impedes specialization, so fundamental to economic growth and development. Specialization is the means for attaining economies and thereby increased productivity and profitability. To the extent that diversification precludes the realization of scale economies and the greater division of labour, it probably hampers economic growth processes.

As proposed earlier, however, diversified strategies may indirectly lead to economic growth and development. They may represent a means of increasing and stabilizing income levels and thereby attaining a certain level of security, so critical to women.

This security may then become the basis for an eventual increase in specialization. On the other hand, women's greater diversification than men's may represent the most efficient adaptation to an environment of shallow markets, limited access to financing, and an undeveloped legal system. For the large numbers of women involved in retail and service enterprises who cannot realize the same economies as manufacturing firms, diversification may be the most efficient means for them to increase their incomes.

Implications of diversified strategies for research and intervention design

The implications for research of women's involvement in multiple enterprises are particularly striking. Research that focuses on the firm as the unit of analysis and uses the changes in size and profits of a single firm as indicators of growth will fail to measure the growth and dynamics of women as entrepreneurs. Unless the definitions of microenterprise research are expanded beyond the classical economic focus on the firm, women's microenterprise earnings are likely to be grossly underestimated, the utility and rationale of their business strategies misunderstood, and perhaps the extent to which they contribute to economic growth undervalued.

Interventions need to be based on an understanding of women's present business strategies and growth patterns. If diversification is indeed a strategy for moving towards a growth orientation and greater specialization, then it should be promoted. If, on the other hand, women get stuck with diversified portfolios of low-return, low-potential enterprises, then interventions are needed to facilitate their sub-sectoral mobility (see Collier, 1990).

Multiple enterprise portfolios also have important implications for sub-sector-based interventions since selected sub-sectors may represent only a small slice of the activity important to women producers. On the other hand, sub-sectoral investments, if they lead to an increase in profitability, might later foster greater specialization and productivity.

References

Acheson, J. and Wilson, J. (1990) 'Modernization and the Generation of Firm: a transactional approach', Orono, University of Maine, unpublished monograph.

Babb, F. (1985) 'Producers and Reproducers: Andean marketwomen in the economy', in *Women and Change in Latin America*, ed. J. Nash and H. Safa, South Hadley, Mass., Bergin and Garvey.

Bendavid-Val, A. (1989) 'Rural-urban linkages: Farming and farm households in regional and town economies', unpublished manuscript.

Bolles, A. Lynn (1985) 'Economic crisis and female-headed households in urban Jamaica', in *Women and Change in Latin America*, ed. J Nash and H. Safa, South Hadley, Mass., Bergin and Garvey.

Clark, G. (1989) 'Separation between trading and home for Asante women in Kumasi Central Market, Ghana', unpublished monograph.

Cobbe, L.B. (1985) 'Women's income generation and informal learning in Lesotho: a policy-related ethnography', dissertation submitted to the Florida State University.

Collier, P. (1990) 'Gender aspects in labour allocation during structural adjustment', Unit for Study of African Economies, University of Oxford.

Downing, J. (1990a) 'Opportunities for exporting specialty crops in Liberia: Women's constraints and incentives', prepared for the Office of Market Development and Investment. Africa Bureau, USAID, Washington, DC.

Downing, J. (1990b) 'Women in small and microenterprises in the eastern Caribbean', prepared for USAID's Regional Office for the Caribbean and the Office of Women in Development, Bureau for Program and Policy Coordination, USAID, Washington, DC.

Downing, J. and Santer, J. (1989) 'Women in rural-urban exchange: Implications for Research and Intervention Identification', SARSA research report for the USAID, Clark University, Worcester, MA.

Gorton, M. (1990) 'Nontraditional income generation by women in Lesotho', prepared for USAID/Lesotho and the Office of Women in Development, USAID under CID/WID Cooperative Agreement.

Grown, C and Sebstad, J. (1989) 'Introduction: Toward a wider perspective on women's employment', *World Development*, Vol.17, No.7. July 1989.

Hackenberg, G. and Barth, J. (1984) *Women in the Urban and Industrial Workforce*, Canberra, Australian National University.

LeFranc, E. (1989) 'Petty trading and labour mobility: Higglers in the Kingston Metropolitan Area', in *Women and the Sexual Division of Labor in the Caribbean*, ed. K. Hart, Kingston, Consortium Graduate School of Social Sciences.

Liedholm, C. and Mead, D. (1987) *Small-scale industries in developing countries: Empirical evidence and policy implications*, MSU International Development Paper No.9, East Lansing MI, Michigan State University.

Liedholm, C. and .Mead, D. (1986) 'Small-scale industries in Africa: An overview', in *Strategies for African Development*, ed. R.J. Berg and J.S. Whitaker, Berkeley, CA, Berkeley University Press.

Massiah, J. (1988) 'Researching women's work: 1985 and beyond', in *Gender in Caribbean Development*, ed. P. Mohammed and C. Shepherd, Cave Hill, Barbados.

Schmink, M. (1984) 'Household economic strategies: A review and research agenda', *Latin American Research Review*, Vol.19, No.3.

Tinker, I. (1987) 'The human economy of microentrepreneurs', paper presented at the International Seminar on Women in Micro- and Small-Scale Enterprise Development, Ottawa, October 26, 1987.

Watts, S. (1984) 'Rural women as food processors and traders: Eko making in the Ilorin area of Nigeria', *The Journal of Developing Areas*, No.9, October.

About the author

Jeanne Downing is the Senior Business Service Development Advisor at USAID's Division for Microenterprise Development. This chapter was written in the early 1990s with the assistance of Tulin Pulley, who at that time worked for USAID's Office of Women in Development. Others contributors to the paper were Marguerite Berger, Carl Liedholm, Don Mead, Jennifer Santer, and Elizabeth Rhyne. The chapter was written as part of the Growth and Equity through Microenterprise Investments and Institutions (GEMINI) Project and with funding from USAID's Office of Women in Development. While these contributors provided invaluable assistance in the writing of the original paper from which this chapter is taken, the views expressed here do not necessarily reflect those of the GEMINI Project.

18 Measuring informal sector incomes in Tanzania: some constraints to cost–benefit analysis

DANIEL KOBB

This paper was first published in December 1997.

Roughly 600 informal sector entrepreneurs in Dar es Salaam, Tanzania, were surveyed in order to compare incomes of project beneficiaries with those of a suitable control group. The aim was to carry out a cost–benefit analysis and ultimately to gauge whether the project intervention could be justified in terms of increased incomes. However, the act of measurement significantly affected the results. It strongly mattered who asked the questions and how the questions were actually worded. Furthermore, project participation should not be considered a truly exogenous variable. In all probability it is systematically correlated with stated income and with the degree of truthfulness in the interviewee's response. In the light of these problems, a variation on willingness to pay is suggested as a more appropriate monitoring and evaluation indicator.

FROM 1988 TO 1993 the donor community channelled roughly US$5.8 billion of development assistance to Tanzania. Averaging $974 million per year, this aid forms the backbone of the nation's economy. For example, in 1993 aid totalled 44 per cent of GDP and 195.8 per cent of the country's exports. On a per capita basis, aid was equivalent to $43 per year (UNDP, 1994). This chapter investigates one project's attempt to answer whether it would have been better to provide this assistance in the form of a single cash payment. That is, would it have been better to drop this aid from a hypothetical aeroplane on a windy day, or to provide it in the form of in-kind project benefits, as of course was ultimately done. I describe how a cost–benefit analysis was actually performed, on the ground, and in the context of training and small enterprise promotion.

SIDO-GTZ's Crafts and Small Enterprise Promotion Programme (CSEPP) assists self-help organizations in Dar es Salaam, the capital of Tanzania, by providing group training and organizational assistance. (SIDO is the Small Industries Development Organization, a parastatal under the Tanzanian Ministry of Trade and Industries; and GTZ, the German Agency for Technical Co-operation, is a major implementer of German bilateral aid projects. For a more complete description of the project see Schulz (1994).) The project focus is the group, not the individual entrepreneur.

SIDO-GTZ aims to strengthen group leadership, to encourage transparency, accountability and democratic decision-making, and to assist groups in the provision of shared infrastructure (for example, water, roofing, and security). Self-help organizations form voluntarily and range in size from 25 to over 100 members. Amongst other activities, they sell fruit and vegetables at markets and along the roadside, they repair cars in vacant lots, they cook meals for the city's workers, they produce furniture, they make wood carvings, they unload trains, and they recycle metal. Since its inception in 1991, the project has supported 176 self-help organizations and roughly 14 000 entrepreneurs.

Including the salaries of expatriate personnel and the purchase of capital equipment, project expenditures averaged $420 per beneficiary. Was this investment in human and organizational capital worthwhile? Did the project's intervention increase individual incomes sufficiently to justify this financial outlay? An M&E (monitoring and evaluation) mission suggested a cross-sectional study in which incomes would be compared between project beneficiaries and a suitable control group. It was feared that a time-series study comparing income before the project intervention with income after the project intervention would fail to separate income differences due to project participation from income differences resulting from macroeconomic changes or government policy towards the informal sector. The exact indicator, as it appears in the project's planning matrix, is whether 60% of all project-assisted entrepreneurs had incomes 20% higher than non-assisted entrepreneurs (Balzer, 1995).

A brief look at the results

In 1995 daily incomes were estimated for 224 project group members and 112 control group members. Despite the methodological problems outlined below, the 1995 results were considered 'interesting' and the exercise was repeated in 1996. The second time around, 195 project group members and 106 control group members were interviewed. Descriptive statistics are provided in Table 18.1.

Incomes were skewed and highly variable. Several high-income earners significantly influenced mean incomes. For example, if the five highest earners in 1995 are removed from the 'project' sub-sample, mean incomes drop a full 18.1%. These entrepreneurs comprise only 2.2% of the sample. As is common with cost–benefit analysis, a side constraint dealing with distributional issues or justice may be appended. It was decided that median rather than mean incomes would be used as the relevant benchmark. Using medians, daily incomes of project beneficiaries were $0.47 higher than their control group counterparts in 1995 and $0.16 higher in 1996. These differences are amenable to standard cost–benefit analysis. If 1995 figures are used, the payback period turns out to be 2.4 years; if 1996 figures are used the payback period can be calculated to be 7.2 years. Assuming entrepreneurs operate for only 10 years, the average internal rate of return upon the per capita project investment of $420 is 39% using the 1995 data on medians, and 6% using the 1996 data on medians. These figures are interesting to compare with World Bank (1995) internal rates of return to schooling in sub-Saharan Africa (41% for primary education, 27% secondary education).

Table 18.1   A comparison between the incomes of project-assisted entrepreneurs and a control group

Statistics	1995		1996	
	Control group	Project	Control group	Project
Interviewees	112	224	106	195
Mean daily income ($)	5.95	7.93	6.40	7.27
Median daily income ($)	4.53	5.00	4.59	4.75
Standard deviation of income ($)	4.46	12.29	5.87	8.94

As is typical, the standard deviation of incomes was rather high. For example, a 95% confidence interval for 1996 daily incomes would stretch from Tsh3609 to Tsh5115, for the project sub-sample and from Tsh3167 to Tsh4507 for the control group (there are roughly 600 Tanzania shillings to 1 US dollar). There is obviously a large degree of overlap. In fact, only at slightly less than a 70% confidence interval can the null hypothesis (H_0) that the SIDO income was less than or equal to the control group income be rejected. Sampling error can be reduced by increasing the number of interviews; using 1996 data, a sample of roughly 550 project and 550 control group interviewees would be necessary to conclude with a 95% confidence interval that the project income is higher than that of the control group.

Before rushing out worldwide to duplicate the project's methodology, both the validity of these figures and the types of inferences drawn from them demand closer scrutiny. This I attempt to do in the following four sections. The next section describes two of the methodological problems encountered in this study; arriving at a definition of income, and coping with the importance of interviewer personality. The following section questions the logic of drawing conclusions from cross-sectional income data. Next a rough statistical framework to review the problems encountered in this evaluation is provided. Finally, some alternative measures are suggested.

Methodological overview: accuracy

This study attempted to measure entrepreneurs' daily income for the previous day. This was done by performing revenue and expenditure calculations. This methodology arose from the loose language used when interviewees were asked directly about their incomes ('how much profit do you make?'). Upon direct questioning, respondents typically replied: 'about 2000 shillings', 'between 2000 and 3000 shillings', 'up to 3000 shillings', 'at least 2000 shillings', '3000 shillings on a good day', '2000 shillings' and 'it depends'. All of these responses are probably 'correct'. With median incomes in the vicinity of 3000 shillings, the project's indicator is concerned with a band of approximately 600 shillings (20%), a figure I suspect is covered by 'about', 'between', 'up to' and 'at least'. We used 'the previous day', rather than the more general 'how much profit do you usually make?' in order to minimize the loose language and rough approximations. (Daily figures are more appropriate when comparing income across two groups in a relatively short time frame. Throughout the year, there is a good deal of seasonality.) While testing the questionnaire, we tried out the standard idea of gauging income by totalling expenditures. This proved even more untenable. Given the constancy of most urban informal businesses, interviewees were less sure about expenditure than they were about their daily incomes.

Revenue and expenditure calculations are bound to contain numerous errors, simplifications and omissions. They are in fact guesses, nothing more, nothing less. Informal sector businesses are not as simple as they may first appear. A non-exhaustive list of problems would include: the difficulty of accounting for spoilage and stock accumulation, the omission of rare events, and the padding of income by over-purchases (and subsequent sales) of inputs pre-paid by customers. Records are rarely kept, and in some instances entrepreneurs sold a wide variety of products. In Tanzania there is a lot of deal-making, in essence the capitalization of informational differences.

Table 18.2   A comparison of calculated income with statements of income made by the entrepreneurs

Case	N*	Mean	Median
Both calculations and direct income statements made	203	35% difference	43% difference
Daily income by calculations ($)		7.21	4.75
Daily income by direct statement ($)		5.33	3.33
Both calculations and income ranges given	58	24% difference	45% difference
Daily income by calculations ($)		5.22	4.54
Daily income = midpoint of stated range ($)		4.21	3.13

* N = number of observations

To show the importance of wording and methodology we compared the results of income caculations (made by the interviewer as expenditures minus costs), with both exact statements of income ('I made 3000 shillings yesterday') and vague ranges of income ('I made between 2000 and 2500 shillings'). Table 18.2 highlights the 1996 data.

Looking solely at medians, there were 203 cases in which interviewees provided both a direct statement of their incomes ('I made 2000 shillings profit yesterday') and where interviewers were able to calculate their profits through a description of quantities, prices, inputs and outputs. The median 'calculated' income was $4.75 (second row, last column), while the median 'stated' income was $3.33 (third row, last column). This difference may arise either from interviewees systematically under-declaring direct income or from interviewers failing to account for several of the entrepreneur's costs. Regardless of its source, the definitional differences of income shown in the table above dwarf the project's indicator of success (a 20% income increase, or roughly $1.00). This very strongly undermines the confidence of the survey's results.

A second major methodological problem concerns the drawing of a control group sample. The project covers a large majority of self-help groups across the city. In 1995, the first year of the survey, all groups that were eligible for support and that had requested support, successfully entered into a co-operative agreement with the project. what remained as 'control' groups were organizations which either failed to meet the project's conditions or organizations that were uninterested in project support. In essence: the dregs. By 1996 things had somewhat changed and the project had several eligible groups on their waiting list. These were interviewed. The inclusion of a more comparable control group in 1996 may explain the decrease in income differences between 1995 and 1996.

Although both project and control groups were randomly selected in 1996, individual interviewees were not. Many organizations, especially control groups, did not have recent lists of their groups' membership. In other cases, membership lists were held by chairmen and secretaries, many of whom were not at the group's site on the day of interviewing. Enumerators were therefore forced to use their discretion in selecting 'representative' interviewees. In one instance a young male enumerator interviewed an inordinate number of young female entrepreneurs. (The importance of supervising enumerators should not be underestimated: corruption in Tanzania is significant and the tendency of enumerators is to fill a quota, even if at times this entails fabricating interviewees.) In other cases, when the interviewer forgets a question or two he or she merely extrapolates from previous interviews. In this study, enumerators worked in teams of three (where some collusion might be necessary to fictionalize a day). In 1996 we re-interviewed a subset of the 1995 interviewees, and the personal characteristics of the interviewee remained quite constant. Sampling is not the only way in which characteristics of the interviewer (not the interviewee) can conceivably drive the results. Technique is crucial. Income (and expenditure) figures are quite personal and the interviewer needs to establish trust and rapport in a very short period of time. In both 1995 and 1996 daily incomes varied enormously by enumerator. Some of this variation is undoubtedly due to luck: enumerators were placed in groups of three and then interviewed roughly 10 groups per year. Some groups had higher incomes than did others. Not surprisingly there was some correlation of mean incomes within teams of interviewers (see Table 18.3). To give a flavour of the variation of 'measured income', by personality, average income by interviewer is sorted from lowest to highest in both 1995 and 1996. For example, in 1995 'interviewer 14' reported an average daily income 3.8 times higher than 'interviewer 1'. In 1996, 'interviewer 13' interviewed individuals having incomes 3.1 times higher than 'interviewer 1'.

Measurement, screening and inferences: does 'A' really imply 'B'?

Incomes were provided orally, were taken on face value, and were not substantiated using secondary sources. Interviewees are likely to provide strategic rather than truthful answers. To say it in the most blunt terms, many lied. For example, interviewees may understate income due to a fear of taxation or fears that the disclosure of information may encourage free-loading or loan requests from relatives, friends and neighbouring entrepreneurs. Generally speaking, Tanzanians are sure to hide their wealth whenever and wherever possible. Conversely, it is conceivable that interviewees could overstate their income in order to impress the interviewer.

More significantly, honesty-related factors may be correlated with project inclusion.

Table 18.3 How the mean income of entrepreneurs measured by a particular enumerator varied

Interviewer	1995		1996	
	Interviews	Mean income ($)	Interviews	Mean income ($)
1	7	3.96	20	3.61
2	20	4.28	27	4.53
3	31	4.96	22	4.78
4	24	5.19	26	4.98
5	23	5.77	30	5.01
6	25	5.93	23	5.06
7	34	5.99	20	6.11
8	11	6.17	25	6.21
9	27	6.80	23	6.18
10	26	7.66	6	8.71
11	19	7.77	23	9.60
12	29	8.28	25	10.13
13	29	8.91	28	11.21
14	31	15.15	3	24.66
Entire sample	336	7.27	301	6.96

Although enumerants were not project personnel, they were in fact perceived to be 'agents' of the project (regardless of the introduction provided). Since many groups had been interviewed in the past, project members probably had more confidence in the interviewer than would control group members. they may therefore have not understated income to the degree their control group counterparts did. This in itself would cause a higher income for the project sub-sample.

Even more damaging: co-operating with a project is a voluntary choice. This choice mechanism may itself screen low-income from high-income groups. Even if we were statistically confident that a quantitative difference existed, it becomes difficult to attribute this difference to the 'project'. For example, suppose income depends on entrepreneurship (creativity, risk taking and organizational capacity) and, furthermore, that groups do differ with regard to incomes. Better organized, more entrepreneurial and therefore higher income groups may be more attracted to projects. To review, groups take the first step in initiating contact with the project.

The problem of screening can be further generalized within the M&E framework; the underlying data may be correct but the inferences and conclusions drawn from them may not be. The standard reasoning is: project members have higher incomes than control group members. Increased income resulted from the project's intervention. This is an enormous leap of faith. An equally plausible explanation is that project groups had higher incomes than control groups even before they became 'project groups'. The counterfactual is even more interesting. Suppose project incomes are lower than control group incomes. Outside evaluators could as easily conclude: 'the project successfully targeted low-income earners in Dar es Salaam'.

The 1996 results provide even more room for speculation. This survey took roughly 10 days to complete. After six days of data collection median project incomes were actually lower than control group incomes. Suppose the survey had stopped there. If one believes in consistency the logical conclusion is: 'the project had a negative impact on incomes'. This conflicts with other pieces of information: for example, groups paid for project services and presumably groups would not pay for something which would decrease their incomes. (Similarly, 170 out of 186 groups requested, at cost, a second sub-project.) Again, imposing consistency: what is one to make of the smaller differences in income from 1995 to 1996? That the quality of project services has diminished across years?

Regression: a statistical formalization

In this section, I outline a rough, hypothetical regression analysis. It formalizes the main problems discussed above. If income is endogenous, what 'causes' it? For simplicity, suppose income is linear in several broad characteristics. A simplified regression equation might be:

$Income_t = \beta_1$ Measurable personal characteristics$_t$ +
β_2 Project inclusion$_t$ +
β_3 Entrepreneurship$_t$ +
β_4 Measurable macro effects$_t$ +
estimation errors

The object of the evaluation exercise was to estimate the regression coefficient β_2, the effect of project participation on income, with all else held constant. (Project inclusion is taken to be a dummy variable, zero or one.) If β_3 and β_4 were both equal to zero (or did not exist) and if there were no problems with the error specification, then a cross-sectional comparison of incomes across project and control group members would indeed capture the project's effect. 'Measurable personal characteristics' could include age, experience, capital accumulation (itself endogenous), activity (a proxy for risk), gender and countless other variables.

The problem of screening is modelled by the inclusion of an 'entrepreneurship' variable. By definition, this variable is invisible and unmeasured by the researcher. Ignoring entrepreneurship statistically biases β_2 to the extent that entrepreneurship is correlated with project participation.

The problem of 'strategic answers' can be modelled by breaking the estimation error into two parts. The income on the left-hand side of the equation is the entrepreneur's orally stated income. Suppose in most cases this is an understatement; in other words, suppose the error term is comprised of a 'lying premium', and the typical error term hypothesized by statisticians (identically and independently distributed). Under this scenario β_2 is biased to the extent that the lying premium is correlated with group inclusion (in other words, whether the size of the lie depends on whether the interviewee is in a project group or not).

Finally, this simple framework can be used to highlight the difference between cross-sectional and time series analysis. If the equation above is written for the previous year (time$_{t-1}$) and then subtracted from the above equation, the resulting regression is:

Change in income$_t$ = β_1 Change in measurable personal characteristics$_t$ +
β_2 Change in project inclusion$_t$ +
β_3 Change in entrepreneurship$_t$ +
β_4 Change in measurable macro effects$_t$ +
Change in lying premium +
statistical estimation errors

In general, entrepreneurs' 'measurable personal characteristics' will change little; they will generally subtract out. The variable 'project inclusion' changes only if an entrepreneur was not associated with the project in year one, but was associated with the project in year two. Presumably entrepreneurship (innate business acumen) and the lying premium are fairly constant, and many of the earlier problems will also conveniently subtract out. An exception is the macro effects, the original problem that a change in individual income may be driven by economy-wide factors, not project inputs. These macroeconomic effects may be smoothed out over the longer term, or it may be assumed that any increase above and beyond the average country-wide growth rate is attributable to project interventions.

Some alternative measures

Participatory data collection relies upon case studies and qualitative measures. One advantage of this methodology is its reliance upon verifiable, observable indicators. In this vein, a longer run tracer study could form the centrepiece of an 'enterprise development PRA' (participatory rural appraisal). Many groups form in order to secure land tenure. This would be captured in a locational mapping of informal sector groups throughout Dar es Salaam. Over the years, a group's movement and existence would be charted. Because moving is costly, stronger groups will be more successful in capturing a location. Similarly, membership within a group could also be mapped.

Contrary to most PRA techniques, mapping is not 'quick and dirty'. It is therefore best undertaken as an internal project indicator. Second, although mapping indicators might imply positive project benefits, they are not capable of answering quantitative cost–benefit questions.

The 'lying' and 'screening' problems could be combated simultaneously by interviewing only those entrepreneurs who keep internal records. Two key assumptions need to be made: first that record keepers in the project and control groups come from the same entrepreneurial class, and second that records to oneself are in fact accurate. In our 1996 survey, only 3% of those interviewed claimed to keep records. All refused to show us these documents, typically claiming 'the books are at home'. A second conceivable solution to the 'screening' problem would be to test for entrepreneurship. For example, a series of ten true–false business questions could be designed. Control and project groups could then be stratified according to the number of questions they answered correctly. Conceivably, such a test might screen for business acumen, which is not captured by age, education and experience.

The best solution is to use indicators which are based upon observed action rather than interview responses. The best of this class is probably willingness to pay. The most common method of measuring a beneficiary's valuation of project services is to force them to pay for them. Without invoking 'capital market imperfections' this method is prone to circular reasoning. If the benefits of training indeed justified its costs, a private sector supplier would long ago have provided it (as they do in Dar es Salaam in the case of computer training). This is clearly not the case.

Most human capital investments are recouped over long periods of time and most entrepreneurs cannot afford to pay for these services up front and in cash. Loans are generally not feasible in Tanzania because of the high costs of contract enforcement, loan monitoring and loan recovery. Under these circumstances cash payments will comprise only a fraction of the service's true cost. A way around this dilemma would be to offer the entrepreneur a willingness-to-pay choice: would the entrepreneur prefer free training or a cash payment? This method is applicable only once the project service has been extensively supplied, so entrepreneurs can make informed decisions as to the service's expected benefits.

Summary

Measuring project impact through income changes takes cost–benefit analysis to its clear and logical conclusion. In theory it is a desirable exercise. In aid-dependent economies it is highly relevant to know whether welfare transfers, the opportunity cost of projects, are more beneficial than in-kind project services. From the classroom, what first appears to be a clear impassioned case of crunching the numbers is in fact an exercise plagued by value judgements. From the field, the problems are obvious. They result naturally when measurement tools are crude and the impact, for example with human capital investments, is likely to be small but sustained over time. In this survey the act of measurement (asking the question) significantly influenced the results; it strongly mattered who asked the question and how the question was worded. This problem is far-reaching. National income measures in Tanzania are calculated by asking farmers about the quantities they produce and the prices they are paid. Typically this 'data' is supplemented by rules of thumb assumptions as to the size of 'their income', or in other instances the contribution of whole sectors, such as manufacturing. When most of the economy is informal and self-sufficient, income can only be measured as a rough ball-park figure.

This implies the World Bank type policy evaluation exercises, where incomes are compared 'before' and 'after', are highly tenuous. In terms of monitoring and evaluation, project participation is not a truly exogenous variable. In all probability it is highly correlated with incomes and the degree of truth in the interviewee's response. In the light of these problems, I have suggested willingness to pay as a viable alternative. This I do in the spirit of M&E, not cost recovery. Because of capital market imperfections, many project beneficiaries will not be able to pay up front, and thus cover discounted project benefits. Instead, a sample of informed beneficiaries should be offered a choice between project participation and a cash payment.

References

Balzer, G. (1995) 'Support to the revision of the project planning matrix and the formulation of an internal M&E system', GTZ, Dar es Salaam.

Schulz, M. (1994) 'The informal sector and structural adjustment: strengthening collective coping mechanisms in Tanzania', *Small Enterprise Development*, Vol.16, No.1, pp.4–14.

UNDP (1994) 'Development co-operation report: Tanzania', Dar es Salaam.

World Bank (1995) 'Tanzania: social sector review executive summary', Washington DC.

About the author

Daniel Kobb is a consultant economist living in Tanzania.

INDEX